Believing in Jesus

A Popular Overview of the Catholic Faith
by Leonard Foley, O.F.M.

Revised edition.

Nihil Obstat:
    Rev. Hilarion Kistner, O.F.M.
    Rev. John J. Jennings

Imprimi Potest:
    Rev. Jeremy Harrington, O.F.M.
    Provincial

Imprimatur:
    + Daniel E. Pilarczyk
    Archdiocese of Cincinnati
    June 28, 1985

The *Nihil Obstat* and *Imprimatur* are a declaration that a book or pamphlet is considered to be free from doctrinal or moral error. It is not implied that those who have granted the *Nihil Obstat* and *Imprimatur* agree with the contents, opinions or statements expressed.

Cover, book design and illustrations by Julie Lonneman.

SBN 0-86716-079-2

Foreword

This book is unabashedly idealistic. It tries at the same time to be down-to-earth. Whether or not it succeeds, the attempted union has good precedent: In Jesus Christ, the infinite God joined himself to everyday human nature.

The Good News of this God-man is the message of Catholicism. The message is both unchanged by the passage of centuries and in constant need of freshening for each new generation and era. (This second edition of *Believing in Jesus* itself represents an attempt to "freshen" the message.) Our own time has seen a profound concern for a more meaningful expression of Catholic belief and public prayer. In the wake of Vatican II, many "born Catholics" are struggling with questions they never had to ask before and searching for a deeper experience of faith.

As a speaker at adult education programs, I have entered into discussions—some pleasant, some painful—with many of these people. I sense in them a curious mixture of anxiety about the changes in the Church and a serene confidence in God. I have acquired a deep respect for the wisdom of their faith, which cannot be sidetracked from the essentials no matter how strange and threatening the new horizons they face.

This book is for them, the wonderful people I have met. I hope it will both inform and inspire them. I hope that "born Catholics" will find here some deeper understanding of the beliefs and practices they have held all their lives.

But I want it to be helpful also to those who approach the Catholic Church for the first time. To this end, the book includes an essay describing how it can be integrated into the Rite of Christian Initiation of Adults (p. 185), as well as a chapter-by-chapter study guide (p. 191).

Catechumens deepening their acquaintance with the Church will still need a lot of help from their sponsors. Countless details of Catholic life are not included here: missalettes and Mass stipends, days of fast and abstinence, holy water and the Stations of the Cross, St. Anthony's bread and the St. Blase blessing, monsignors, worship commissions and the future of bingo.

I am not one who thinks that nothing happened before 1965. (How could I, when 50 years of my life passed before then!) Indeed, one title suggested for this book was *Almost Everything Sister Said Was True*. But since then, Catholics have grown in wisdom and grace because of—and in spite of—the cultural explosion of the last few decades. I think we are now a more mature Church, even though scarred and possibly still a little scared. I hope this book will help some scared and scarred people and challenge some others.

Speaking of scars, I must extend immense gratitude to Carol Luebering and Karen Hurley of St. Anthony Messenger Press, who patiently deciphered, organized, streamlined, sanitized and biblicized the hieroglyphics that came from my typewriter. May their eyesight be restored.

Leonard Foley, O.F.M.

Contents

Part I:
Getting to Know the Bible

1.

Jesus' Bible:
The Old Testament

If you can get through this first chapter, the rest of the book may be comparatively easy going. If we are to understand as much as possible about Jesus, we
have to be acquainted with his roots in Jewish history, and with the only Bible
he had—the "Old" Testament.

We may be tempted to say, "Why bother with all that ancient history? Is
it really important for today—Moses and the Red Sea, Jonah and the whale,
Adam and Eve and the snake? We have the Ten Commandments, and that's
enough."

Well, suppose you wanted to understand the life of Abraham Lincoln.
Could you ignore everything before 1809, the year he was born? Could you
know what his aims and values and sorrows were without some knowledge of
slave ships from Africa and the development of a "North" and a "South"?
Shouldn't you also know about the precarious new world of 13 colonies, the
cold and fear of Valley Forge, the long debate over the Constitution?

In a somewhat parallel way, we cannot begin to know Jesus as he really is
unless we have at least a glimmering of what was *in his consciousness* as he
heard the story of his people read in the synagogue all his life, or took the
scrolls into his own hands for study. He pondered the love of his Father, the
glory of his people and their sin. He heard the fierce denunciations of the
prophets and their consoling assurances that *someone* would come to free his
people from misery. He must have seen himself, and his future, in each column
of the unrolling parchment and accepted his vocation.

The life of the Chosen People was a journey towards Jesus. We will try to
enter into that life. In many respects, perhaps more than we realize, their story
is our story even now. It is not really an "old" testament; it is the perennial
story of humanity with and without God, and the story of the determination
of that loving God to save us in spite of ourselves.

The Bible is not merely a record of events, but it is also an *interpretation*
of those events. It is the sad-wise account of the ups and downs of the Chosen
People's relationship with God and of the *meaning* of God's acts in their history.

The Chosen People gradually built up a collection of narratives, songs,
prayers, meditations, prophetic utterances and "underground" writings all
centering around their God Yahweh. Much of this tradition was transmitted
by word of mouth from generation to generation. It was sung around camp-
fires and commemorated in liturgical feasts like Passover. Finally, over a period

of centuries beginning about the year 1000 B.C., this tradition was written down.

For a people not allowed to have images of God, the Chosen People had a daring way of describing their "Yahweh." God has a face, eyes and ears and nostrils, a strong arm. He speaks and laughs, whistles and hisses; he is delighted and disgusted; he loves and hates with a passion; he regrets; he pities. He is *alive*.

Israel is his child, even his spouse. God holds his people like an infant to his cheek, while Israel vacillates between being a tender lover, a spoiled child and an adulteress. God gives and demands total surrender; but he is faithful and endlessly forgiving.

The Bible cannot, therefore, be read as merely a list of dusty dates and battles long ago. It must be experienced by someone who has outgrown that childhood fallacy that the world started when he or she was born—and who now puts an adult meaning to the question, "Where do I come from?"

This question found a thrilling answer in the consciousness of Jesus, and we can all share his experience by making the story of the Bible our own story.

The contents page of your Bible will reveal that there are three kinds of writing in the Old Testament: *historical* books, tracing God's relationship with his people; *prophetic* books, recording the prophets' warnings in the face of the people's sin, as well as their consoling assurances; the *wisdom* books, prayerful meditations on human life.

In this chapter we try to combine a basic consideration of the main *events* of Israel's history in chronological order with the *books* in which these events (and their meaning) are recorded.

Historical Books

The first five books of the Bible are called the Pentateuch ("five books") or the Torah ("the Law"), which Tevye in *Fiddler on the Roof* longed to contemplate in retirement. The first of these, Genesis, deals with the origin of the human race and, more importantly, of the Chosen People.

Genesis. For our present purpose, let us summarize the first 11 chapters of Genesis as follows: God creates man and woman and gives them his friendship along with a world in which to enjoy it. But Adam and Eve choose to be little gods themselves; they abandon God's friendship and their innocence and honesty. Untruth and unlove seep through the world like poison, until people are so absorbed in their own selfishness that no one can understand or communicate with others. Everyone seems to speak his or her own "foreign" language. Men and women plunge from Paradise to Babel.

This is not merely an earthly setback or tragedy; it is the total collapse of life itself—physical and spiritual. "The moment you eat from it [the forbidden tree] you are surely doomed to die" (Gn 2:17). Mankind embraced sin and begot death.

Abraham, Our Father in Faith. Now God intervenes in a special way.

About 1,900 years before Christ, he chooses a man, Abraham, who lived in what is now Iraq, to be the father of a new people. Through this man and his household, God enters human history in a new way and begins a special revelation of himself. Abraham is the seed of the savior to come, as God begins to unveil (in Paul's words) "that mystery hidden from ages and generations past" (Col 1:26).

It may sound odd to us that God "intervenes" in our history by his special relationship with Abraham and his people, Israel. After all, God has the whole world in his hands and is "here" already, supporting every atom and spirit in existence. Nevertheless it is true to say that God now begins to unfold an eternal plan that will be fulfilled by definite historical events beginning with Abraham and "ending" with Jesus.

God's purpose is to prepare (and at the same time save from sin) a people "acceptable" to himself. He must free human beings without forcing them to love. Ultimately he does this by his own free act of love in Jesus' death.

God's basic purpose is liberation. We are by inheritance and choice enslaved to our own pride and passion. He must continually throw light on both real beauty and real ugliness; he must let us suffer the logic of sin—called punishment—and bring us, painfully, to what should be a commonsense decision—to choose to live.

Israel, symbol of mankind, has a monotonous history of being loved, of responding with sin, of being punished, of repenting, of being forgiven, of being unfaithful again, etc. God has a refreshing history of being himself: one who loves faithfully.

Exodus. The book of Exodus ("a way out") is the story of Israel's liberation from physical and spiritual slavery in Egypt—the model of our ultimate liberation in Jesus. We join his "exodus" through death to life.

God strikes the Egyptians, but *passes over* the homes of the Israelites who have put the blood of a lamb on the doorposts of their homes and partaken of a meal of its flesh. Now, under the leadership of Moses (foreshadowing Jesus), they go (perhaps as a straggling mass of refugees) through the water of the Red Sea to freedom.

The Exodus, together with the covenant that followed at Sinai, is the central event of Israel's history.

We cannot exaggerate the importance of these events for the Jews and, ultimately, for us. What the death and resurrection of Jesus is to us, the exodus-covenant was to the Chosen People. It foreshadows our own exodus, in Jesus, from slavery to freedom, from death to life, again in the blood of the Lamb. It foretells the family meal of the Eucharist and the "drowning" and "rising" in the water of Baptism.

The Exodus is not a simple affair. The Israelites wandered in the Sinai desert for 40 years—sometimes faithful, sometimes grumbling. God gave them signs of his presence and his protection. As always, he was a hidden God who could be seen only by faith.

In the desert, Israel was alone with God. There was no place to run and hide. The desert is the symbol of death and of human loneliness. There we must each decide either to die or to survive in the only way possible: by total surrender to God.

The Ten Commandments. At the mountain of Sinai, God makes his covenant with the Israelites. Through Moses, God says, "You have seen for yourselves how I treated the Egyptians and how I bore you up on eagle wings and brought you here to myself. Therefore, if you hearken to my voice and keep my covenant, you shall be my special possession, dearer to me than all other people. . . . You shall be to me a kingdom of priests, a holy nation. . ." (Ex 19: 4-6). The people all answered together, "We will do everything that the LORD has told us" (Ex 24:3).

The Covenant. God gave his people the Ten Commandments not as a burden, but as a way of keeping the Sinai Covenant. They were, when not unfaithful, happy to have this guide on how to be God's people. In the book of Exodus, the list of the commandments is followed by several chapters of guidance and specific details on observing God's way.

The Blood. It is important to realize what blood meant to the Israelites: Blood is life. So, at the dramatic liturgy ratifying the covenant, Moses took the blood of an animal and poured half of it on the stone altar—representing God—and threw the other half on the assembled people, saying the words Jesus would fulfill: "This is the blood of the covenant which the LORD has made with you" (Ex 24:8).

It is *one blood,* on the altar and on the people. God and his people are united. The blood of the covenant is the symbol of the marriage of God and his chosen ones, of their union, their oneness. "I will be your God, and you will be my people" (Lv 26:12).

Covenant Love. In the generations after Moses, the covenant remained a focus of Israel's life. Beneath all the customs and ceremonies that gradually developed and in spite of continuing unfaithfulness, the Israelites, like spoiled children, could always be sure of one thing: They might sin and wander, but God is faithful. They used a special word for this love: *hesed.* It is a love that cannot be worn down, the love of kinship that is simply faithful.

This love goes beyond all expectation, all just dues. It pours itself out in generosity. Best of all, it is unstoppable, unquenchable. The more his children sin, the more God pursues them with mercy. He is faithful to the spouse who is continually adulterous.

Passover. It is extremely important to understand three things Jesus did: he lived the covenant perfectly; he celebrated the Passover; and he transformed the "old" covenant into a new and eternal one. His death and resurrection was his own passover-exodus, and it became the exodus for all mankind.

Why did Jesus celebrate the Passover? First, because he was an observant Jew. The Jews had always said, down the centuries, that God's covenant is remade with each new generation. With their usual children-of-the-house boldness, they said, "Not with our fathers did he make this covenant, but with us, all of us who are alive here this day" (Dt 5:3).

Every year at Passover each household procured a lamb, one year old and without blemish. They ate it with loins girt, sandals on their feet and staff in hand—like those who are in flight (see Ex 12:11).

Our Passover is Jesus, in whose blood the new and eternal covenant is made. His blood is "upon us," and in us, symbolizing a true union between God and us. We eat his flesh, as those who are in flight from slavery. We drink his blood, sealing the covenant.

The Law: Powerless to Save. The Torah—the Law—cannot save. As St. Paul keeps on saying, it is merely our teacher. It is powerless, except to reveal all the obstacles of sin between us and God.

Our reverence for the Ten Commandments should never deceive us into thinking that we can save ourselves by observing them. St. Paul spent most of his Christian life insisting on this. We have the Law, but we cannot observe it by ourselves. We are not *self*-righteous (though that is the word we use for people who think they are). God leads us, his people, through glory and misery, sin and faith, to a growing consciousness that we need him absolutely.

Leviticus. The third book of the Bible gets its name from Levi, head of the priestly tribe. The book gives many directives for sacrifice and ritual. The central theme is this: "Be holy, for I, the LORD, your God, am holy" (Lv 19:2; see also 11:44; 20:26).

Numbers. The book of Numbers (so called because it records two censuses of the Hebrew people) continues the story of the journey begun in Exodus. It describes the life of the Israelites for 38 years in the desert, from their coming to Sinai to their arrival at the border of the Promised Land.

For their murmuring, God prolongs his people's stay in the desert while simultaneously deepening their relationship with him and preparing them to be a missionary nation.

Deuteronomy. The name means "Second Law." It is not really a *new* Law, but a repeating and completing of the Law given on Mt. Sinai. Moses, in a series of discourses (similar to those of Jesus in John's Gospel), presents the theme of covenant renewal, of living religion. He exhorts and threatens his people, reminding them of the special claim the Lord has on them.

The events described in this book took place between the end of the desert journey and the crossing of the Jordan and entry into the Promised Land under Joshua. The book was written after the Israelites had lived in the Promised Land for centuries and is presented as a kind of testament of Moses.

Joshua. This book shows God's faithfulness in giving the Israelites the inheritance of land he had promised. God acts through Joshua, and the Chosen People cross the Jordan and begin the gradual capture of the Promised Land. At this point Israel renews the covenant with Yahweh.

The history of the conquest of Canaan is a foretelling of the spiritual conquest of the world under the leadership of Jesus (*Joshua* is an earlier form of the name *Jesus*). Under Jesus, the New Moses, there will be a new covenant,

a new Mount Sinai, a new Passover, a new Passover Lamb, a new commandment.

The book of Joshua may be summed up by these words, "In the future,
when the children among you ask their fathers what these stones mean [12
stones from the Jordan], you shall inform them, 'Israel crossed the Jordan
here on dry ground.' For the LORD, your God, dried up the waters of the Jordan in front of you until you crossed over, just as the LORD, your God, had
done at the Red Sea. . . ; in order that all the peoples of the earth may learn
that the hand of the LORD is mighty, and that you may fear the LORD, your
God, forever" (Jos 4:21-24).

Judges. This book takes its name from the "judges," 12 military heroes sent by
God to lead his people in the interval between the death of Joshua and the
institution of the monarchy. The book shows that Israel's fortunes go up and
down according to whether or not they obey God's Law. When they rebel, they
are overcome by pagan nations; when they repent, God raises up new leaders
to liberate them.

It is the same cycle again: from faithfulness to unfaithfulness, to punishment, to repentance, to forgiveness and deliverance.

Kingship—Under or Instead of God? Eventually Israel decides it wants
earthly kings instead of being a theocracy, a people ruled directly by God.
Three pairs of books (each once a single scroll) describe the period: 1 and 2
Samuel; 1 and 2 Kings; 1 and 2 Chronicles.

1 and 2 Samuel. The books of Samuel span the history of a century (about
1100-1000 B.C.) and relate a series of episodes centering around the persons
of Samuel, Saul and David. Central to our interest is the oracle of Nathan
(2 Sm 7) which promises David an eternal dynasty. This is the basis for the
development of the idea of an earthly Messiah.

1 and 2 Kings. The two books of Kings cover similar ground, but also extend
to the most tragic happening in Israel's history: the exile in 587 B.C., on which
more will follow in a moment.

A central figure of the Old Testament is King David, who foreshadows
the King to come. He succeeds in forming the confederation of 12 tribes into
a united kingdom and setting up a new capital, Jerusalem. God renews his eternal covenant with this king. (David sins, as movies have emphatically pointed
out, but did penance with equal vigor.)

The kings were, as was to be expected, a poor substitute for the rule of
God. Consequently the prophets (on whom more will follow) spend a large
part of their careers denouncing both moral and religious aberrations. A later
biblical writer looks back over history and says sadly, "David, Hezekiah,
Josiah—these three kings only were exempt from the guilt of their line" (Sir
49:4).

In 930 B.C. David's united kingdom is split into two: in the north, the 10
tribes of Israel; in the south, Judah (whose people come to be called "Jews"),

consisting of the two tribes of Judah and Benjamin—the tiny remnant that will eventually fulfill God's promises.

In 721 B.C. Assyrian invaders conquered the northern kingdom of Israel, deporting its citizens and recolonizing the land with foreigners. Thus the expression: the "lost tribes of Israel." It is important to note that the sacred writer says, "The king of Assyria then deported the Israelites. . . .This came about because they had not heeded the warning of the LORD, their God, but violated his covenant, not heeding and not fulfilling the commandments of Moses, the servant of the LORD" (2 Kgs 18:11-12).

The terrors of exile also came to the southern kingdom (587 B.C.) under the armies of Babylon. Again the sacred writer sees the meaning: "Early and often did the LORD, the God of their fathers, send his messengers to them, for he had compassion on his people and his dwelling place. But they mocked the messengers of God, despised his warnings, and scoffed at his prophets, until the anger of the LORD against his people was so inflamed that there was no remedy. Then he brought against them the king of the Chaldeans, who slew their young men in their own sanctuary building. . . .They burnt the house of God, tore down the walls of Jerusalem, set all its palaces afire. . . .Those who escaped the sword he carried captive to Babylon. . . .All this was to fulfill the word of the LORD. . ." (2 Chr 36:15-17, 19, 20, 21).

1 and 2 Chronicles. The two books of Chronicles treat the same period as the two pairs of books just described, but from a different viewpoint. They cover the period from Samuel to the return from exile in 538 B.C.

Solomon is presented as an ideal king, second only to David. His great achievement is building the Temple and promoting a magnificent liturgy of sacrifice, prayer and praise. The ideal of one people united in the worship of the true God in Jerusalem is achieved.

But at the end, in the return from the agony of exile (a second Exodus) the *remnant* knows the political greatness of Israel is past. They have had a national "holocaust." They will now be a people under God or they will be nothing. The past will show the way to the future: There will be emphasis on David's blessed line, on Jerusalem as the divinely established place of worship.

But the way into the future is not easy. When the remnant returns they find the "people of the land"—descendants of those who had escaped being carried into exile—have mixed with foreigners and developed a new religion, hence, tension.

Prophetic Books

The word *prophet* means "one who speaks for" ("in the place of" or "on behalf of"). Prophets communicate with God in prayer, visions, dreams and, by God's grace, understand the meaning of God's self-revealing and the horror of the sin that repudiates it. They stand up courageously against sin and injustice, whether in king or slave. They warn of God's punishment and, when it befalls, bring God's consolation. They demand faithfulness and promise deliverance.

8

They attack all violation of the covenant, sexual immorality, social injustice, human degradation. They are the conscience of Israel.

Moses may be considered a prophet, and also Elijah, the "troubler of Israel." Some prophets, like Nathan, are written about in the historical books. Other prophets, or their followers, recorded their own vision and message.

The 18 prophetic books are the work of the so-called "classical," or writing, prophets. They cover a period from Amos' denunciation of the sins of Israel in the north around 750 B.C. to the hopeful book of Daniel in the second century before Christ.

Amos. Let us spend a few moments with Amos, a shepherd from the southern kingdom who was sent north sometime between 780 and 740 B.C. The people of Israel are not even aware how deeply their conduct offends a holy God, who must therefore say,

> I hate, I spurn your feasts,
> I take no pleasure in your solemnities. . . .
> Away with your noisy songs! (Am 5:21, 23)

Like the prophets after him, Amos speaks of the "remnant" that God will save—though it will be like a shepherd rescuing from the mouth of the lion "a pair of legs or the tip of an ear of his sheep" (Am 3:12).

He gives a new meaning to an expression that runs throughout the Bible: "the day of the Lord." To a suffering people, it meant the day God would judge the enemies of Israel and vindicate his people. But now Amos reminds the Chosen People that it will also be a day of gloom for them—not just their enemies. For those who are sinners, unfaithful, it will be a day of judgment when God destroys their pride.

Hosea. Like Amos, Hosea thunders in the north, and at about the same time (during the later years of the reign of Jeroboam II—786-746 B.C.). Yet he is one of the most touching examples of God's mercy. His own marriage to the prostitute Gomer becomes a symbol of God's marriage relationship with Israel. After three children, Gomer reverts to being a prostitute. But Hosea seeks her out and takes her back—as no Jewish husband could or would do—as an example of the way God pursues and welcomes back his unfaithful people.

Isaiah. The writings of several prophets appear in the one book we now call Isaiah. Only the first segment (Chapters 1-39)—and not all of that—is the work of the actual person Isaiah who prophesied between the years 742-687 B.C. Chapters 40-55, sometimes called Second Isaiah, are generally attributed to an anonymous poet at the end of the Babylonian exile (around 538 B.C.). Chapters 56-66 were written at a still later period by followers of Isaiah.

Excerpts from the book of Isaiah are read 57 times in the three-year cycle of Sunday readings, an indication of the importance these prophets still hold for us.

First Isaiah. Isaiah is the greatest of the prophets. He lives at a crucial time in salvation history, his career covering the years 742 to 687 B.C. After the north is destroyed, Judah in the south has its turn on center stage. It is to Judah that Isaiah preaches.

His great vision is of the holiness of God—and the horror of human sinfulness in contrast. The frightful abyss between God's holiness and human sin overwhelms Isaiah. He denounces both north and south for seeking security in military alliances; he summons Judah to faith in God as her only hope.

But again, in the tradition of Amos, Isaiah foresees that only a remnant will be saved to see the desert bloom, and the splendor of our God:

> Here is your God,
>   he comes with vindication,
> With divine recompense
>   he comes to save you. (Is 35:4)

Second Isaiah. Chapters 40-55 are called "The Book of Consolation" and were written toward the end of the Babylonian exile. The anonymous author sees that the Chosen People will be liberated, the captives will return. The prophet rebuilds their shattered morale and paints a vision of a glorious future:

> It is I, I, who wipe out,
>   for my own sake, your offenses;
>   your sins I remember no more. (Is 43:25)

> Can a mother forget her infant,
>   be without tenderness for the child of her womb?
> Even should she forget,
>   I will never forget you. (Is 49:15)

Very prominent in Second Isaiah is the promise to the remnant. There will be the small number of humble and faithful people who will be God's new Israel, with whom he will make a new covenant. They are purified by the sorrows of exile. They are the "poor" and the "poor in spirit" whom Jesus praised. From our perspective we can see Mary, the flower of Israel's faith, standing at their head.

The four "Songs of the Suffering Servant" are an important feature of Second Isaiah (42:1-4; 49:1-7; 50:4-11; 52:13—53:12). The Servant is, first, the motley remnant of the poor who listen faithfully to the prophet's words; and, second, he is also an individual figure who will save the people from their sins. Chapter 53 reads like a description of the passion of Jesus.

Still, when the return from exile is complete, the ideal Israel is not fully restored. God must still create a new heaven and a new earth. Someone will come who will be the true Servant.

The Messiah. Much of the teaching of Isaiah, as well as the other prophets, converges on the messiah who is to come. The figure takes form slowly, very slowly, over the centuries.

The word *messiah* means "anointed," that is, commissioned like a king, priest or prophet. The messiah will fulfill Israel's destiny, save his people, protect them. He will lead his people to delight in the fear of the Lord. He will judge—that is, vindicate—the poor and "with the breath of his lips he shall slay the wicked" (Is 11:4).

Coming in the line of King David, he will create a holy nation, which will be "a kingdom of priests, a holy nation" (Ex 19:6; cf 1 Pt 2 9) The inner core of his work is to eliminate sin and restore mankind to intimacy with God. Isaiah sees his work as centered in the Temple. All nations will come there, as to the center of the earth. He heartens his fellow Jews with a vision:

> The people who walked in darkness
> have seen a great light. (Is 9:1)

> A child is born to us. . . .
> His dominion is vast
> and forever peaceful. (Is 9:5a, 6)

Jeremiah. Jeremiah was called to be God's prophet about 627 B.C. For 40 years—through the reigns of Judah's last five kings he warned of coming disaster and begged king and people to turn back to God. He was ignored, abused, arrested and publicly disgraced. In 587 the Babylonian army destroyed Jerusalem and took the people into exile. Jeremiah stayed behind with the remnant in Judah, but later fled to Egypt and presumably died there.

Speaking for the Lord, Jeremiah says,

> Two evils have my people done:
> they have forsaken me, the source of living waters,
> They have dug for themselves cisterns,
> broken cisterns, that hold no water. (Jer 2 13)

But Jeremiah has words of hope of the eventual victory of God: "The days are coming, says the LORD, when I will make a new covenant with the house of Israel and the house of Judah. . . .I will place my law within them, and write it on their hearts; I will be their God, and they shall be my people" (Jer 31:31, 33).

His influence was greater after his death than before. The exiles read and meditated on his lessons, and his influence can be seen in Ezekiel and Second Isaiah.

Ezekiel. Ezekiel becomes a prophet while he suffers among the deportees in Babylon (c. 587 B.C.). He is often called the "prophet of the exile." He helps the exiles accept the destruction of Jerusalem, pointing out, like his fellow prophets, that the people's past and present sins are wreaking their necessary fulfillment. Perhaps the saddest words in the Bible are those of Chapter 10:18:

11

'Then the glory of the Lord left the threshold of the temple. . . ."

But, finally, Ezekiel offers a sure hope. He begins to announce God's promise of a new covenant and describes a new and ideal Israel rising from the graveyard of Babylon (the dry bones come together in Chapter 37). But salvation will be the work of God, not man. God will create a new heart and a new spirit in his people (see Ez 36:26). The Temple will be purified, and God will be present among his people (see Ez 43:1-7).

After the Exile Until the Time of Christ. Just as the people had been liberated from Egypt in the Exodus, so eventually the small remnant is delivered from captivity in Babylon in 538 B.C. They are a chastened people. They discover the Torah anew and become more convinced than ever that they are God's chosen ones.

The exile has made them a people with an unshakable faith in the one God. They no longer have earthly kings, only God, whose representative is the high priest.

The Jews are never again a nation of power. But after the exile they are benevolently treated by Cyrus the Persian. A magnificent Temple is built by 515 B.C.

The Persians retain control until the time of Alexander the Great. With him begins a "Greek period" whose influence continues into New Testament times, even though the land was under the Ptolemies of Egypt in the third century B.C. and the Seleucids of Syria until the time of the Maccabees.

Jonah. This much debated book was written some time between 400 and 200 B.C. It is not historical narrative, but didactic fiction, a story designed to teach a lesson. The lesson is this: God loves all people, not just the Jews. When Jonah is sent to prophesy to the pagan Ninevites, they turn to God; but the Chosen People sometimes refuse. It is a parable of mercy aimed against narrowness and self-righteousness.

Ezra and Nehemiah. The transformation of the Jewish people after the exile is important for our understanding of Jesus. This is the period of the Restoration. The two men most responsible for this reorganization of Jewish life are Ezra and Nehemiah. (The books attributed to these men fall into the category of historical books, but are treated here for the sake of chronology.)

Ezra provides spiritual unity. Without his firmness, Judaism has no chance of resisting absorption by Greek culture. He sets the tone of the post-exilic community characterized by fidelity to the Torah.

Nehemiah, like Ezra, helps Judaism maintain its identity during difficult days in the post-exilic restoration.

Daniel. This book represents a special kind of biblical writing called "apocalyptic." It looks to a direct intervention of God as the only way the world will be transformed. The writing abounds in symbols, often difficult to understand— parts of the body, animals, colors, numbers. Apocalyptic writers foresee a cataclysm: The heavens will open and the future will crash into the present.

In the New Testament, the book of Revelation (the Apocalypse) is written in this style. Jesus uses this form in his description of the Day of the Lord (see Mark 13).

The book of Daniel is born during the persecution of the Jews in the second century before Jesus. It firmly asserts that God is the Lord of history. Deliverance and glory is coming; God's people should stay strong in temptation and suffering.

In the seventh chapter, the author speaks of

One like a son of man coming
   on the clouds of heaven. . . .
His dominion is an everlasting dominion
   that shall not be taken away,
     his kingship shall not be destroyed. (Dn 7:13-14)

1 and 2 Maccabees. Again, for the sake of chronology, we insert a book classified as part of the historical writings.

Judas Maccabee (and later his brothers) led a Jewish revolt against the Seleucid kings who were persecuting the Jews. It was a courageous reaction to the attempt to suppress Judaism in Palestine in the second century before Christ. For a time the Jews again have religious and political independence. Again it is hoped that the salvation of the Jews will involve the creation of a Jewish state with political autonomy from foreign conquerers.

The Roman power enters Palestine in 63 B.C. Herod the Great, a Jew favored by the Romans, is declared "King of Judea," reigning from 37 to 4 B.C. Herod's son, called Herod Antipas, rules Galilee until 39 A.D., but Roman governors, called procurators, hold the real power.

One of them is named Pontius Pilate.

Wisdom Books

A third type of literature in the Old Testament comprises wisdom books. These are meditations on human experience and the problems of life: good and evil, death and life, happiness and suffering. They are concerned with moral information—that is, how to live in God's presence. There are seven of them, comprising about one-fourth of the Old Testament.

Psalms. The psalms are the prayers of Israel and continue to be the prayers of the Catholic Church today. They are a collection of 150 religious poems, about half of them attributed to King David. Some were undoubtedly written during the exile or even later, until about 300 B.C.

These are the prayers Jesus said, with all his family and friends. They are an intimate part of the Church's prayer today, and should receive our special attention.

Proverbs. This is an anthology of didactic poetry aimed at helping the young and inexperienced along the road to wisdom; consideration is also given those who desire advanced training. Solomon is the author of at least part of the collection.

Job. The book of Job, written somewhere between the seventh and fifth centuries B.C., is a drama in poetic form which treats the problem of the suffering of the innocent.

Why do the good suffer? There is no answer, if one wants to know why God did not create a world free of suffering. God wants humble and trustful acceptance of his providence and deep faith in his steadfast covenant love.

The Song of Songs. Written after the exile, this is a portrayal of ideal love between man and woman. This love is a symbol of the love between the Lord and his people.

Ecclestiastes. The author, writing about 300 B.C., considers such human ambitions and aspirations as the pursuit of wealth, pleasure, luxury, knowledge, wisdom, bravery. Are they good or bad? He concludes: "Vanity of vanities! All things are vanity!" (Eccl 1:2). The meaning: These values are not deserving of a wise person's full time and energy, because the human spirit cannot be fulfilled by any earthly values—human, social or material.

Sirach. This catechism of good conduct, cast in the traditional categories of sin and virtue, was written about 200-175 B.C. How can one be wise for God? The author treats of humility, giving alms, filial piety, sincerity, friendship, pride and presumption, prudence and temperance.

Wisdom. This exhortation addressed to Jews scattered in lands far away from Palestine urges them to be faithful and warns them not to be taken in by the pagan immorality of their surroundings. It is the last-written book of the Old Testament (about 100 B.C.).

Summing Up

Over a period of 2,000 years, God forms a people. He chooses a missionary group, liberates them from slavery in the great Exodus from Egypt, makes a covenant with them at Sinai. They waver between faithfulness and sin, between majestic worship in the Temple and adulterous running after idols.

They go through the cycle of friendship, rebellion, punishment and reconciliation over and over again—a paradigm of the life of the Church. They—or at least a faithful remnant—are purified in the fires of oppression and exile. Reduced to human helplessness, they long for the messianic age. Some look for a new time of prosperity, others for the great king who will rival the glory and power of David and lead them to freedom, reestablishing the kingdom.

Among the poor of God who wait is a girl of Nazareth, the virgin womb of Israel, prepared for by prophet, priest and king. She, the flower of the "poor of Yahweh," the remnant, sums up all her people's longings and the love of those who have kept faith. She learns of the Passover Lamb, the covenant, the Promise.

And we can imagine her praying these words of Isaiah, not knowing the full depth of the words which had come down to her:

> I rejoice heartily in the LORD,
>   in my God is the joy of my soul;
> For he has clothed me with a robe of salvation,
>   and wrapped me in a mantle of justice,
> Like a bridegroom adorned with a diadem,
>   like a bride bedecked with her jewels.
> As the earth brings forth its plants,
>   and a garden makes it growth spring up,
> So will the Lord GOD make justice and praise
>   spring up before all the nations. (Is 61:10-11)

2.

Jesus in Inspired Human Words: The New Testament

Drop a stone into water, and the ripples run in circles to the edge of the pond. Explode the resurrection of Jesus at the center of human history, and its power ripples to the very edges of time—past and future—and is merged in the mystery of eternity.

What began in the darkness of a Jewish "Monday morning" became a light and fire ignited first in the hearts and minds of a few men and women, and then in concentric circles of Christians down the centuries.

Twelve men, transformed by a vision, went out to proclaim boldly the simple, unbelievable fact: *Jesus is alive!* He has conquered the evil that strangles the world and has risen to a mysterious new vibrant life, in accordance with all the Jewish Scriptures had promised. All that Israel had believed and hoped for in its blessed-tragic history is now fulfilled—though still awaiting full completion when Jesus "comes again." He is not "somebody back there," but one present among us, in us and with us.

The apostles did not "preach"; they "proclaimed"—that is, gladly declared, as a fact, the Good News of Jesus. They were heralds, hurrying into cities and towns to announce the fact that the slaves are freed. The Good News may be summarized like this:

The prophecies are fulfilled, the new age has dawned.
The Messiah, of the House of David, has come.
He is Jesus of Nazareth, who
was baptized by John,
did mighty works by the power of God,
suffered and died for us,
rose from the dead,
was exalted at God's right hand,
will come again in judgment.
Repent and be baptized for the forgiveness of sin.

(Summary by Patrick Fannon in *The Four Gospels;* see examples of the apostolic proclamation in Acts 2:22-24, 32-33; 3:12-26; 10:36-43.)

New Testament Writings

The 27 "books" of the New Testament include:
- Four Gospels: Mark, Matthew, Luke, John
- The Acts of the Apostles
- 13 Letters of St. Paul
- Seven "Catholic" Letters of John, Peter, James, Jude
- The Letter to the Hebrews
- The Apocalypse, or Book of Revelation.

As in the Old Testament, we have here a "library" of diverse styles and purposes: the clear simplicity of the Synoptics (Matthew, Mark and Luke); the mystical depth of John; the ardent personal witness of Paul; the excitement of a growing Church in Acts; the practicality of apostles' advice given in letters; the quiet contemplation of our Priest; and the serenity of a people faithful in persecution.

The Gospels. Like the books of the Old Testament, the New Testament writings are equally concerned with facts *and faith*. The Gospels are not cold, impartial history (supposing there is such a thing), but the announcement of salvation through Jesus. The writers make no bones about stressing the importance of Jesus. And they are more concerned about the *meaning* of his life than with a tape-recorded account.

They want to inform us, but they are more concerned to inspire us. They want to shout out their own faith and arouse it in us. It doesn't really matter to them whether "scientific" history, archeology, etc. give us evidence that Jesus actually had a home in Nazareth, or was crucified on a hill outside the walls of Jerusalem, or left the imprint of his body on a shroud. Faith does not ultimately rest on any "proofs."

We may compare the Gospels to a memoir. Suppose you and your brothers and sisters want a special remembrance of your mother. One of you has the gift of writing, and you tell him or her to "put your mother on paper." This writer now combines events with meaning: combining, for instance, many glowing family dinners into one typical one, making up a song or poem that expresses your mother's endless cheerfulness with words gathered from a hundred or a thousand days; expressing the writer's own feelings through hers at the time of your father's death; making a scenario of their courtship through the letters left behind.

This would not be a dull list of things she did and said, but a record of her spirit, her soul, her meaning. And you would all say, "That's our Mom."

So the New Testament writers let faith color all their narratives. Their concern is to show the working of God in history. They are not concerned with "proving" anything to outsiders; they are writing for the family.

The Gospel According to Mark (65-70 A.D.). The earliest Gospel was put together by John Mark. He is called "the interpreter of Peter" by one of the earliest Church writers and is described in Acts as working with both Peter and Paul. We may presume that this Gospel gives at least the flavor of Peter's emphasis.

Mark never lets us forget that Jesus is a suffering, crucified savior, but one who proclaims both penance and good news. In Mark, Jesus' "teaching" is the gradual unfolding—mostly in action—of the mystery of Jesus as embodying and revealing the Kingdom. Sadly running through the Gospel is the strain of the disciples' obtuseness and lack of understanding.

The Gospel According to Matthew (70-85 A.D.). Matthew is thoroughly Jewish, exploring the Hebrew Scriptures for the Messianic signs now fulfilled. Jesus is the new Moses, giving us a new covenant on a new Mount Sinai. He is the son of David the king, the Messiah the Jews could recognize. Jesus brings the Law to perfect fulfillment, and is superior to it. He is Lord over it, but he does not annul it any more than adulthood annuls childhood. The Law can now be reduced to one commandment: love.

Matthew is a gold mine for quotations from Jesus, who is never so much the "Teacher" as here. Matthew records five "sermons" of Jesus: on the Mount (5:1—7:29), about his missionaries (9:35—11:1), the Kingdom (13:1-52), the Church (18:1-35) and the last things (24:1—25:46).

A central theme in Matthew is the Kingdom, the rule of God in the hearts and minds of his people. This Kingdom comes in Jesus, whom he shows to be the Messiah—not the king Messiah ruling over a Jewish world empire but a humble suffering Messiah who offers the Kingdom to those who will submit freely to the will of God.

The Gospel According to Luke (70-85 A.D.). Luke wrote a two-volume work, a Gospel and the Acts of the Apostles. Some identify him with Luke the physician, friend of St. Paul. He was a Gentile—hence always feels the need to explain Jewish customs to his readers. As a Gentile, he understandably stresses the universal nature of salvation. He shows Jesus as friend to sinners, outcasts, the suffering and, particularly, women, then in a despised social condition.

17

His is a sensitive and cultured mind. Some of the optimism and joy of the early Church breaks through his writing. The Church is beginning to realize that the "day of the Lord" is not necessarily imminent; the coming of the Holy Spirit, for whatever length of time, is the all-important "substitute."

The Jesus of St. Luke is very human, sympathetic, merciful, but Luke is perhaps sterner than the others in presenting the demand to carry one's cross every day.

The rich variety of the Gospel can be seen in the various titles it has been given: "The Gospel of the Great Pardons," "The Gospel of Universal Salvation," "The Gospel of the Poor," "The Gospel of Absolute Renouncement" and "The Gospel of Prayer and the Holy Spirit."

Luke's Acts of the Apostles (80-85 A.D.). This book concentrates on the "acts" (that is, the work) of only two apostles, Peter and Paul, from the events of the Ascension and Pentecost to the end of Paul's captivity in Rome (63 A.D.) when the gospel has been preached to the ends of the known world. Luke's purpose is to show how the Christian community grew under the guidance and control of the Holy Spirit. In the pages of Acts, Christians separate from Judaism, welcome Gentiles, and spread the Good News to the world.

The Gospel According to John (90-100 A.D.). We immediately recognize this as a different kind of Gospel. It is written "from scratch," as it were, rather than being a combination of polished beads on a string, as the other Gospels are.

John has the deepest theology as well as the longest and most dramatic accounts. His is the most symbolic of the Gospels, moving through the familiar-mysterious world of water, wine, blood, bread, life and light. His emphasis is on the "already now" rather than the "not yet" in the history of Jesus' saving work.

More forcefully than in the other Gospels, the mature faith of the Church in the *divine* Jesus shines through. In John, Jesus speaks with the majesty and assurance of one already raised to the right hand of the Father—from the beginning of his public life. The world does not pursue and crush him; *he* is in command. The world is on trial, not he.

"More symbolism is found in John than in the other Gospels," points out Raymond Brown in *The Jerome Biblical Commentary.* "More attention is called to the spiritual significance of apparently routine happenings and to the fuller meaning of words and events. The 'beloved disciple,' the man born blind, Lazarus represent at times not only historical personages but all Christians. Mary, the Mother of Jesus, is the Church itself. Such symbolism is extended to other events and persons and makes it necessary for us to read John with close attention lest his full meaning escape us."

The Letters of St. Paul (50-64 A.D.). We will be devoting a later chapter to a short course on St. Paul (Chapter 9). Suffice it to say here that 13 letters are attributed to him (though he may not personally have written the Pastorals—1 and 2 Timothy, Titus—and even Ephesians and Colossians). The letters are written over a period extending from about the year 50 (at least 17 years after

18

the resurrection) to the year of his death in 64 A.D. These are the earliest writings of the New Testament, antedating all the Gospels.

Paul usually wrote to deal with a particular problem or occasion in one of the Churches, but his fiery spirit always rises above that situation to shout the Good News of Jesus. Jesus is central, the beginning and the end. There is no salvation in human effort; the initiative is God's. The Jews are privileged, but they are not the whole of God's people; God's love in Jesus is seen eagerly reaching out for every human being on earth, Jew and Gentile alike.

The Seven 'Catholic' Letters. These letters are so-called because their authors (James, Peter, John and Jude) address the universal Church rather than believers in a particular city.

James, a salty, practical man, writes in the spirit of Old Testament wisdom literature. This letter is famous for having been rejected by Luther ("a straw epistle") because of its insistence on the need for good works.

The First Letter of Peter is addressed to Gentile Christians, the new People of God. Some scholars think it is taken substantially from an early Christian baptismal liturgy because of the many references to that sacrament.

The most important of the letters of John is the first, written to certain Christian communities where some members were advocating false doctrines. As in his Gospel, John's emphasis is on the great commandment of love.

The Letter to the Hebrews (80-90 A.D.). This letter, of a high literary style, is often attributed to St. Paul, but it was not written by him. It is notable for its treatment of the priesthood of Jesus. He is the great high priest who expiated our sin in loving faithfulness to the Father. His is an everlasting priesthood which fulfills the promise of the Old Testament and its sacrifices. We have a high priest with the Father, one who understands our life, praying for us.

The Apocalypse, or Book of Revelation (81-96 A.D.) This most difficult of the New Testament books was written in a time of crisis to assure Christians that Jesus is always with his people. It is "resistance" literature, sustaining those who suffer persecution. It stresses the fact that, although ultimate salvation and victory will take place only when Jesus appears in glory, the victory has already been won. It is a prophetic book, reminding the Church that she is being purified in suffering for her wedding with "the Lamb that has been slain" (see Rv 5:6).

The difficulty arises from the literary style, called "apocalyptic" (see Chapter 1, p. 12). One must realize the symbolic meaning of numbers, animals, colors, clothing, etc. Without the help of biblical scholars, the reader may be led into fanciful conclusions.

The Formation of the New Testament

The New Testament grew over a period of time. The original basic proclamation was enlarged to include first a detailed account of the passion and death of Jesus, then a gathering of many little units of narrative and teaching. These had been passed around orally and become well-worn and polished over the years by constant repetition. Unimportant details fell away and the result was a collection of "beads" which the writers could then "string" as they chose.

In 1964, the Pontifical Biblical Commission approved the conclusion of scholars concerning three stages of tradition by which the life and teaching of Jesus have come down to us in the Gospels.

1) First, there is what Jesus actually did and taught. In his words, Jesus followed the ways of reasoning and explaining that were in vogue at the time.

2) As the apostles proclaimed the death and resurrection of Jesus and the whole meaning of his coming, they took into consideration the circumstances of their listeners. As the Church prayed about and lived the Christ-life, its understanding deepened. The apostles "interpreted his [Jesus'] words and deeds according to the needs of their listeners. They used catechesis, stories, testimonies, hymns, doxologies, prayers and other literary forms" (Biblical Commission, 1954).

3) When the actual Gospel writers took up their task, each one used "a method suited to the peculiar purpose which each author set for himself. They selected the things which were suited to the situation of the faithful and adapted their narrative to that same situation" *(ibid.)*. They explained the words and deeds of our Savior now in one context and now in another, depending on their usefulness to the readers.

Therefore, Pius XII said, the interpreter of Scripture must examine the particular literary genre (style, form) used by the writer to see how this contributes to a true and genuine interpretation.

The book of Revelation, for example, is a literary form quite different from the straightforward narrative of Mark. Paul's Letter to the Romans is really addressed to the whole Church, whereas the Letter to Philemon is very personal. Matthew's is a "teaching" Gospel; John, writing after the other three, shows a greatly advanced stage of theological reflection in the Church.

Different but equally authentic interpretations of the parables are offered. In Mark, for instance, a time of persecution is in the background of the parable of the seed: "Pressure or persecution overtakes them" (Mk 4:14). Luke applies the parable to the trials of everyday life: "They believe for a while, but fall away in time of temptation" (Lk 8:1).

Content and emphasis are determined by purpose. As the Church's faith fastened on Jesus, there were two choices. One was to concentrate on the earthly life of Jesus, his words and actions up to his ascension. This is the way of the synoptic Gospels.

The other way was to concentrate on the risen Jesus, established in power and glory, lifted to the right hand of the Father and present with and in his friends on earth. This is the emphasis of St. Paul and, in a way, St. John.

Key Concepts for Understanding the Bible

We conclude with a brief discussion of terms that recur in connection with the writing and reading of the Bible.

Inspiration. The Bible is a unique book. It is, literally, *God's Word in human words.* To say that the Bible is inspired is to say that God had more to do with this book than with any other writing in history, even the most lofty flights of mysticism or the most ardent outpourings of the saints.

This does not mean that God "dictated" words or thoughts to the minds of the writers. They remain themselves—with their own literary style, their particular purpose, their opinions, temperament and background—and it all comes through.

What does it mean to say, then, that God is the "principal author"? It means, first, that God comes to his people through many avenues of revelation: through the events of his relationship to them from Abraham through the life, death, and resurrection of Jesus through all the experiences of the Church. The people of God are aware of God's presence, but they can't put all the facts and ideas and feelings into words very well. Among them and of them is the poet/ prophet, one of those who in any culture speaks what the heart knows. This speaker-for-God comes to a more explicit understanding of the meaning of all God is doing and saying, especially in Jesus. Under the guidance of the Spirit, the whole Church and this prophet finally get the truth into words.

The words have such power that the meaning keeps on unfolding for generation after generation. Gradually such writings were recognized as wonderfully fitting expressions of what the faith was all about. Gradually they were "canonized" by the Church as inspired. They are not inspired because the Church says they are; they are called inspired because the Church's faith *recognizes* them as such.

There were many spiritually uplifting documents current in the early Church, even other "Gospels." Why did the Church not include them in the sacred list? In some of them the instinct of faith saw error or a false direction; others made no claim to being part of the original proclamation. It may be a surprise to some to know that the "canon," or official list of books of the Bible, was not explicitly defined by the Church until the 16th century though there was a clear listing as early as the fourth century.

Revelation. As was said above, revelation is not concerned only with truth, but with a personal self-giving of God. God gives a message, indeed; but more importantly he gives himself to his people. We have a knowledge of his acts and purposes, but we also have God himself given to us, out of infinite love for his children. The raw material of revelation is the everyday life of his chosen people, beginning with the first of his children and developing in the children of Abraham. Prophets understood God's actions and helped us realize and accept not just a meaning but also a person.

Finally, God gave himself perfectly in his son Jesus. He is the full revelation of God—truth, indeed, but also eternal life within us.

Tradition. In *Fiddler on the Roof,* Tevye's song should be written with a small

21

"t": *tradition.* Small-"t" traditions are customs that may be a century old, even more, but are transitory. There is a tradition of jostling jollity in Times Square on New Year's, but this is hardly something essential to the spirit of the United States. But the celebration of the Fourth of July is something we will never cease doing. It is imbedded in our history.

In the Church, there are many traditions. To mention a non-controversial few: It is small-"t" tradition to have pews in church, for bishops to wear special headgear called "miters," to use white smoke to indicate that a pope has been elected, or to sing Gregorian chant at Mass.

It is big-"T" Tradition, on the other hand, that Jesus is truly God and man, that his passion, death and resurrection are made present to us in the Eucharist, that he gathered a visible people around him and appointed Peter and the other apostles to guide and sanctify them. Sacraments, prayer, mission—the list is long.

Tradition literally means "handing on"; it also refers to what is handed on. In the words of Vatican II describing Tradition: "Now what was handed on by the apostles includes everything which contributes to the holiness of life, and the increase in faith of the People of God; and so the Church, in her teaching, life and worship perpetuates and hands on to all generations all that she herself is, all that she believes" (*Constitution on Divine Revelation,* # 8).

Tradition is expressed in (and grows from) the Church's creeds, the records of the Church's liturgy, the writings of the great teachers, the decrees of popes and councils, the prayer and faith of the people.

In the polemics of the Reformation, now softening, Protestants rejected what they thought was an undue Catholic emphasis on Tradition, and relied on Scripture alone. Catholics asserted all the more firmly that, although Tradition is under the judgment of the inspired Word, it nevertheless existed before the New Testament: the words and acts of Jesus were not mechanically transmitted by tape recorder and movie camera. Tradition is the way the *essentials* of Christianity are lived by the Church throughout the centuries.

Tradition develops in the sense that the Church probes more deeply into the meaning of all that has been handed on. The Holy Spirit guides its growth and explanation. Each age must express the age-old Tradition of the Church in the forms of its day. The essentials remain, the application and form may change.

The Church is a living organism; in each generation, it must respond to God through the language, culture, problems and opportunities of its own day. The Church *remembers its experience* and *listens to the living Word of Jesus in the Bible* and is thus led by the Spirit to show Christ to the world.

Part II:
Jesus' Journey to Death and Life

3.

The Missionary Jesus: 'He Went About Doing Good'

Imagine Jesus, after his long slow trip down the Jordan valley from Galilee, as he stands watching the prologue of his life's drama. A spiritual revival is taking place on the banks of the Jordan, just above the Dead Sea. Everyday people are flocking to hear the rugged desert prophet, John the Baptist. He is announcing tremendous news: The Messiah is finally coming, and he will baptize his people with the fire of the Spirit. In preparation, John baptizes them in the waters of the Jordan as a sign of their repentance.

Jesus sees the new people of God being formed, and he loves them. He walks into the water to be one with them. John at first refuses to baptize him—apparently because of long acquaintance with his cousin's holiness. But Jesus insists. He is an observant Jew eager to share all the practices of good Jewish life.

As Jesus comes up out of the water, he sees the sky "rent in two" in fulfillment of Isaiah's prayer that God rend the heavens and come down (see Is 63:19–64:3). Jesus sees the Spirit, in the form of a dove, come and rest on him. The dove, which referred to the Israel of old, is the sign of the new Israel, the new people of God coming up out of the water in a new Exodus as they once came through the Red Sea to freedom.

A voice from heaven thunders the fulfillment of the prophecy of Isaiah about the Suffering Servant to come: "You are my beloved Son. On you my favor rests" (see Mk 1:9-11). God had said, in Isaiah:

Here is my servant whom I uphold,
    my chosen one with whom I am pleased,
Upon whom I have put my spirit;
    he shall bring forth justice to the nations. (Is 42:1)

Then the Spirit *drives* (Mk 1:12) Jesus into the hot and barren Judean desert. Alone with the wild beasts, he faces the Devil. What kind of Messiah will he be? Why not a powerful one, Satan urges. Just a practical little beginning would do—like, say, turning stone into bread to still his hunger.

Not that? Well, Scripture says that the Messiah shall not even stumble on a stone. What is to prevent a spectacular leap off the pinnacle of the Temple? *That* would bring followers!

The final practical way to go, of course, is political. The Devil offers Jesus the world, his kingdom, for a simple price: a Faust-like selling of his soul.

Unlike the old Israel that was unfaithful in its 40-year sojourn in the desert, Jesus stands unmoved. He is totally given to his Father.

The Good News. Now one career ends, and another begins. John the Baptist is suddenly silenced in prison by a vengeful Herod, and will soon be put to death. Jesus now steps into the public eye, knowing he faces the same dangers as John. Mark says, very simply, "Jesus appeared in Galilee proclaiming the good news of God" (1:14).

What was—and is—the Good News? It was that God was making his long-promised "move." Now he would *decisively* defeat the powers of evil in the world and *definitely*, once and for all, establish his Kingdom.

This may sound very warlike and political. It took Jesus a long time to convince people (relatively few people) that victory would come through defeat, and life through death; and that the Kingdom was not a place, or even a people, but exclusively God's powerful, divine saving and loving action— his *reign*.

Jesus therefore says, in so many words, "This is it. The time God set is here. All promises will be fulfilled. God will rule! He will destroy evil and fill you with his life, his love and his power. Believe this Good News! Change your whole way of thinking and acting!"

Remember that Mark, like all the Gospel writers, is looking backward from the time after the resurrection of Jesus. By then it had become obvious that *Jesus himself was the Good News.* He was God fulfilling an eternal plan. He was the Promise fulfilled, the Gift of God. He *was* God.

Jesus' Two Great Activities: Healing and Proclaiming the Good News. The simplest way to describe Jesus' life is to use St. Peter's words: "He went about doing good works and healing all who were in the grip of the devil" (Acts 10: 38). There is danger that in trying to summarize Jesus' teaching, miracles and proved mastery over the Devil, we may end with another "butterfly-on-a-pin," a list of events as dead as a newspaper index. But let us try.

The picture of Jesus in Mark's Gospel is that of a man *totally available,* totally generous, almost always in the middle of a pressing crowd. Almost the first thing told of him is that he went out into the street to help people in need. Mark spends little space on what Jesus said. He is concerned to show Jesus immediately curing a man possessed, healing Peter's mother-in-law and welcoming "all who were ill, and those possessed by demons" (Mk 1:32).

He is doing much more than being sorry for people. But Mark will never let us forget that he was sorry for them, pitied them, suffered with them. Jesus is moved at the sight of a leper and cures him. (1:41). Then the fuller secret begins to appear when he heals both soul and body of a paralytic (2:1-12).

Then a new element (3:1-5): Dare he cure on the Sabbath? No question. A good deed does not violate the Sabbath.

He goes over into pagan territory and releases a wild man from the Devil's power—a graphic short story (5:1-20); he comes back across the sea of Galilee and raises a little girl back to life, adding the touching instruction that they take care to give her something to eat.

A trembling woman is cured just by touching his garment, and he gives her his peace. He looks around at the crowd following him and pities them, "for they were like sheep without a shepherd" (Mk 6:34). Mark begins to be overwhelmed by his task, so he simply says, "Wherever he put in an appearance, in villages, in towns, or at crossroads, they laid the sick in the market places and begged him to let them touch just the tassel of his cloak. All who touched him got well" (6:56).

And always the great crowds—from Galilee in the north to Judea in the south.

Except for one chapter of parables, there is hardly a line of teaching in the first half of Mark's Gospel. That section ends with the climactic declaration of Peter that Jesus is the Messiah (Mk 8:29). The first explicit teaching, which immediately follows, is the doctrine of the cross (8:34-38).

This is not to say that the teaching of Jesus is unimportant, but to emphasize that Jesus put first things first: He first showed his love, unmistakably, in concrete actions, and then taught people its source, the infinite love of the Father.

His greatest act was to restore peace to hearts miserable in sin—the adulteress, Zacchaeus, Levi, Peter—but he was also concerned about empty stomachs and sightless eyes, leprous sores and crippled legs.

The Meaning of Jesus' 'Signs.' Jesus once reproached some people for "seeking signs and wonders." Yet he himself performed many "signs." He told those who wanted a razzle-dazzle Messiah that they would not believe even if someone were to rise from the dead. Yet he rose from the dead as the greatest "sign" of our hope.

Evidently, then, there are signs and there are signs. The danger seems to be that we expect *extraordinary* signs, miracles "coming through" from God, and we sometimes forget that love alone can see the real miracles.

Science has enriched our lives, no doubt. But it has taken away our childlike excitement at everyday wonders. We know the chemical composition of violets and how a sunset looks on radar. Jack Frost depends on isobars and sunspots, and we can write "music" with computers.

Not so boringly over-informed was the biblical person. If it rained, God sent the rain; thank God. If we lost the war, we were being punished. God told the sun, every morning, to get up and do it again.

So the "miracles" of the Bible are not much more marvelous to the Hebrew than sunrise over the desert or the birth of a deer. It would never have occurred to a contemporary of Jesus to worry about whether he should call a cure "natural" or "supernatural," or if the man possessed were merely epileptic.

God's greatest "sign" is Jesus. Not just certain things Jesus did, but simply Jesus—whatever he did, or said, or was—then and now.

Jesus is, above all, *the* "sign" or "sacrament" of God. As Jesus himself said, "Whoever sees me sees the Father." (See page 101.)

He is the Word made flesh. He is, in fact, God's last word. In Jesus God expressed and continues to express himself as perfectly as he can in human form, word and action. So Jesus' "signs"—whether the extraordinary ones we call miracles or the "ordinary" ones like putting the infinite love of God into a simple "good morning"—are the openings through which human love sees God and receives his life.

Many people saw Jesus' signs—raising a widow's son from the dead and asking a Samaritan woman for a drink of water—but the signs did not register. I don't know why. Maybe they were looking for entertainment. Maybe they wanted God to prove something. Maybe they wanted someone who could smash the Roman army.

But those who let the Father create a disposition to receive, to be healed, to be liberated—they read the signs.

They saw God assuring them of his love, and definitively breaking the power of evil, sin, suffering, death and the Devil. They saw signs of love and signs of power. They accepted the reality behind the signs—God's own life and love—and they were saved.

Jesus' Power Over the Devil and All Evil Spirits. In the Bible, evil and good spirits are simply taken for granted. In the New Testament the devils form a kingdom opposed to the Kingdom of God and manifested in the enslavement of human beings. The Church teaches that God created Satan and other devils to be good by nature, but that they chose evil by their own free will. The Bible sees these evil spirits as *personal.*

If we are to be moved to faith by Jesus' power over the Devil, we had better ask whether we really believe there is such a thing. Some, after seeing "cute" devils like David Wayne in *The Devil and Daniel Webster* and being persuaded to buy lighter fluid by red-suited creatures with "devilishly" attractive mustaches, have relegated the Devil to a sideshow in Disneyland. This temptation not to take the Devil seriously is a phenomenon explored with deadly perception by C. S. Lewis in *The Screwtape Letters.*

St. Paul reminds us that our warfare is against "principalities and powers" (Eph 6:12). The *Good News Bible* translates this passage: "We are not fighting against human beings but against the wicked spiritual forces in the heavenly world, the rulers, authorities and cosmic powers of this dark age." These, according to the *Theological Dictionary* (p. 379), have been "vanquished in the cross and resurrection of Jesus Christ, but their impotence has not yet been laid bare; they still saturate the atmosphere of 'this world,' so that it exposes Christians to temptation and leads to their persecution."

One of the clearest "signs" of the Devil I have seen is the picture of grinning soldiers driving little sticks into Vietnamese children's eardrums. I believe it was the same group who shipped severed human ears back to their families.

Some references to "possession" in the Bible may refer to human illness such as epilepsy. This is probably the case, for instance, in Mark 9:14. But the New Testament writers often attribute disorders to the Devil. This comes from seeing the Devil, sin, death, suffering and all human ills as the miserable inheritance of sin. Jesus is God's final, definitive destruction of all evil, and those who let Jesus possess them will be liberated from all evil.

The Synoptics place Jesus' head-on confrontation with the Devil at the very beginning of his public life, immediately after his baptism. Mark almost immediately relates an incident which shows Jesus' power over the devils. In the synagogue at Capernaum, "a man with an unclean spirit shrieked, 'What do you want with us, Jesus of Nazareth? Have you come to destroy us? I know who you are—the Holy One of God!' Jesus rebuked him sharply: 'Be quiet. Come out of the man.' At that the unclean spirit convulsed the man violently and with a loud shriek came out of him. All who looked on were amazed. They began to ask one another: 'What does this mean? A completely new teaching in a spirit of authority! He gives orders to unclean spirits and they obey!' " (Mk 1:23-27). In Mark's "typical day's ministry" in Capernaum (1:21–3:5), Jesus' expelling demons is referred to twice in the first 13 verses.

In Luke's Gospel, the 72 disciples Jesus sent to cure the sick and proclaim the Kingdom exclaimed upon their return, "Master, even the demons are subject in your name!" Jesus replied, "I watched Satan fall from the sky like lightning" (10:18).

When Mark's Jesus sends the Twelve forth into the whole world after the resurrection, he says that one of the signs that will accompany *those who have professed their faith* is that "they will use my name to expel demons" (Mk 16: 15).

An essential part of Jesus' saving work in Matthew is the conquering of "the devil and his angels" for whom "an everlasting fire is prepared" (Mt 25:41). All who give Jesus their lives are safe. No evil can touch them, even though they die on crosses, as he did, or suffer the humiliation of hatred and misunderstanding.

But nothing is automatic. If a person's new cleanliness is merely external, if one does not let the power and love of God possess the soul as totally as any devil ever possessed the human heart, then "the unclean spirit will bring back with it this time seven spirits more evil than itself" and "the last state of that man becomes worse than the first" (Mt 12:45).

It is the height of irony—and of the diabolical—that Jesus himself is accused of being in league with the Devil. After Jesus frees a mute, the Pharisees say, "He casts out demons by the prince of demons" (Mt 9:34); and, later, "This man can expel demons only with the help of Beelzebul, the prince of demons" (Mt 12:24).

The Last Enemy: Death. We will reflect, in the next chapter, on the central tragedy of humanity—physical and moral death—and how God liberated us from its enslavement. The Gospels relate three incidents of Jesus' raising persons from the dead, but these events are not particularly emphasized by the Synoptics. The conclusion of the story of Jesus' raising Jairus' daughter from the dead (Mk 5:21-24, 35-43) is delayed to insert an account of his healing of the woman with a hemorrhage (Mk 5:25-34). Only Luke has the touching story of Jesus' raising the widow's son (7:11-17). Death, disease, devils, the forces of nature—all are equally subject to the liberating power within Jesus. To the loving heart, one sign is as good as another.

John's Gospel, however, places climactic emphasis on the raising of Lazarus. It is the last and the greatest of Jesus' special "signs." To quote *The Jerome Biblical Commentary*: "In the narration of this miracle John gives at one and the same time a supreme proof of the Lord's life-giving power and a visualization of the doctrine contained in the conversations of vv. 23-27" (p. 446).

That conversation goes like this:

"Your brother will rise again," Jesus assured her [Martha]. "I know he will rise again," Martha replied, "in the resurrection on the last day."
Jesus told her:
"I am the resurrection and the life:
whoever believes in me,
though he should die, will come to life;
and whoever is alive and believes in me
will never die." (Jn 11:25-26)

The miracle is "a sign, therefore, both of the final resurrection and of the rising from sin that takes place in the soul of the believer" *(ibid.)*

All the "signs" of Jesus' life lead to the central event of his life and ours: his saving death and resurrection.

4.

Jesus' Teaching-Stories:
The Parables

Jesus' whole life, every word and action, was his teaching. But a special part of his teaching was done in the form of *parables*. In these fictitious stories people could recognize situations of everyday life: housekeeping, fishing and farming; wedding celebrations, midnight visits and happy meals; crooked judges, beggars and playing children; planting seed, baking bread and making wine. Sometimes, no doubt, Jesus' story referred to a recent happening—a burglary, a discovery of treasure, a rich man's downfall.

The parable has something in common with all stories: We want to know how it comes out. But Jesus' parables often carry us along, conceding the truth of one step after another, until we find that we have been trapped by the truth. What we have so readily admitted forces us to a conclusion which surprises and challenges us.

The best example of this technique occurs in the "story" Nathan told King David after the latter had stolen Uriah's wife and then arranged to have him killed in battle. Once, Nathan said, there was a rich man and a poor man. The poor man had only one little ewe lamb which grew up with him and his children, sharing his food, sleeping in his bosom. The rich man had huge flocks. Now the rich man, to entertain a visitor, stole the ewe lamb to make a meal. David was furious and interrupted Nathan to say. "The man who has done this merits death!"

Then Nathan said to David, "You are the man!" David was thus brought to an unsuspected judgment on himself (see 2 Sm 12:1-13).

Many of Jesus' parables do this. They tease us, they lead us to suspect there is more here than meets the eye, something which applies to our own life and which we ought to face.

In the parable of the Prodigal Son, with whom do we identify? The erring son, or the elder brother, or the father? Am I a Pharisee bragging in the front of the Temple, or the contrite publican in the back? Am I the priest or the Levite passing by the needy, or am I—surprise ending—being loved most by those whom I despise—the "Samaritans" of my life?

Many parables explicitly refer to the Kingdom—"the kingdom of heaven/ the reign of God is like. . ." They reveal not so much what the Kingdom actually is, but the kind of dispositions one must have to enter it. We are drawn into a realization of the divineness that lies within what seems to be merely the "natural" in life.

The parables were no leisurely and patient explanation of a religious system by a famous rabbi. Rather, as events were quickly to prove, they were related to crisis—with Jesus in the center. They did not speak of some comfortably distant, terrible/beautiful "Day of the Lord." Rather, the time is *now*. *You* are the one. Jesus' whole public life is pressured by a crisis situation: This is God's last Word; we must decide *now*.

One of Mark's verses regarding the parables must be clarified. Jesus says to the Twelve: "To you the mystery of the reign of God has been confided. To the others outside, it is all presented in parables, so that they will look intently and not see, listen carefully and not understand, lest perhaps they repent and be forgiven" (4 11-12).

This harsh quotation is from Isaiah 6:9 and can only reflect the Hebrew mind which saw God as doing *everything*. If a man killed himself with drink, God did it. If wheat sprouted, or the rainbow filled the sky, they did not think of the laws of physics and botany; God did it. So when some people heard Jesus' message but did not understand, they saw this too as part of the divine plan. The results of humanity's own free decisions are said to be caused by God, because nothing happens outside his power.

We are not used to thinking this way, of course, and we must simply say: Jesus spoke his parables to everyone. It is true, however, that he did explain the parables to his disciples, not to the unbelievers.

Scholars have shown that some of Jesus' parables acquired new applications as the Church grew older. For example, the parable about the workers who got full pay for the last hour's work was first directed against those who murmured at the Good News of God's mercy. Later it was also seen as exemplifying an insistence that no "work" earns salvation; it is purely God's gift.

The great German scholar Joachim Jeremias has summarized the meaning of the parables in this way:

1) Salvation is here.
2) God is merciful.
3) God will certainly deliver you from the coming tribulation.
4) Catastrophe is imminent; the nation is rushing to its destruction.
5) It may be too late; take resolute action now.
6) The way will be the way of the cross.

Here is a most unpoetic capsule summary of what the parables tell us about the Kingdom.

What Jesus Says About the Kingdom. The Kingdom comes in Jesus, and this is as evident as the coming of spring in the green leaves (Mt 24:32-35). It starts very small, like a tiny seed, but it will grow into a large tree (Mk 4:30-32) because, in spite of all difficulties, God makes it grow (Mk 4:26-29). It will grow to an unbelievable harvest: 30, 60, even 100 times the planting (Mt 13:1-9). The Kingdom of God's power will work irresistibly through all humankind, like yeast through dough (Mt 13:33).

God calls everyone to the Kingdom, everyone on the highways and byways of life, even people we may consider unlikely (Lk 14:15-24). All are invited to the banquet (Mt 22:1-14). God gives the Kingdom for nothing: It is totally free; it is not merited or earned. God is like the vineyard owner who pays wages out of all proportion to the work done (Mt 20:1-16). So, even though it may seem that we work very hard for God and are deserving of great reward, we are really only servants. We are receivers, not givers. We do nothing for God; we only receive his power and love (Lk 17:7-10).

The Kingdom of God is the forgiveness of huge unpayable debts of sin out of God's mercy. Since this is so, obviously we must pay the comparatively small debts of forgiveness we owe others (Mt 18:23-35). God is like a merciful father who welcomes back his son to the table even though the son has deserted him and wasted his inheritance in sin. Other members of the Kingdom dare not resent this mercy of the Father (Lk 15:11-32).

God is happy over the return of a sinner, the way a woman cries with joy when she has found a valuable coin that was lost (Lk 15:8-10). God is the good shepherd who leaves the flock of 99 to seek the one sheep that is lost and carries it home on his shoulders (Lk 15:3-7). Even if we do not bear fruit at first, God will be merciful; but ultimately our tree will be cut down and thrown into the fire if we bear no fruit (Lk 13:6-9).

Some will reject the Kingdom, like tenants in a vineyard who would not give even some of the fruits to the rightful owner (Mt 21:33-46). They will be destroyed. Rejecters of the Kingdom are hypocrites: They complain both about too much strictness and too much leniency (Lk 7:29-35).

So the Kingdom will have good and bad in it, like a net that gathers all kinds of fish (Mt 13:47-50), or like a field where both wheat and weeds grow But they will be separated forever at the end (Mt 13:24-30).

The end will come suddenly. Watchfulness—that is, living constantly in God's love—is all-important. Then we are ready in gladness, not fear, for whenever God comes, even if suddenly (Lk 12:35-40).

The owner of the Kingdom may come to take it to himself at any time, like a man who has left his home in charge of servants (Mk 13:32-37). We are servants ready for God's coming at any time (Mt 24:45-51). We are ready for the marriage feast, even if the Bridegroom Jesus comes at midnight (Mt 25:1-10).

The Kingdom is important beyond anything else. It is like a treasure which a man finds, or a pearl. He gives up everything else as secondary in order to have the treasure, the pearl (Mt 13:47-50). Accepting the Kingdom is the greatest common sense, or prudence, such as worldly people use in business or war (Lk 14:25-35).

In the Kingdom it is those who turn to God and remain faithful to the end who will be saved (Mt 21:28-32). For, having received God's generosity, we must respond to his love and accept the invitation to the Kingdom feast (Mt 22:1-10). But having entered, we must wear the garment of grace God gives us (Mt 22:11-14). For if Jesus does not replace the Devil who is thrown out, the Devil will return and it will be worse than before (Mt 12:43-45).

If we want to be forgiven members of the Kingdom, we must humbly ask God's pardon like the sinful tax-collector, not brag before him like the Pharisee (Lk 18:9-14). We should settle our accounts while we are on our way, not wait until we are brought into court (Mt 5:25-26).

In the Kingdom, God wants us to pray to him unceasingly in order to realize our dependence on him, like people desperately knocking on a friend's door asking for bread at midnight (Lk 11:5-8); we should be so persistent that it seems God answers us just to get rid of us, like an unjust judge finally giving in to a widow (Lk 18:1-8).

In the Kingdom, everyone is our neighbor, not just those we like. It doesn't exclude those, like Samaritans, who are not "our own." Sometimes people we despise (Samaritans) are the real neighbors (Lk 10:25-37). Many sins are forgiven to those who love; and those who have been forgiven much love God very much (Lk 7:36-50).

The Kingdom is lost to those who put all their trust in the things of this world, like a rich man with full barns (Lk 12:13-21). We must use earthly things and money as a means to heaven, not obstacles (Lk 16:1-12).

Everyone in the Kingdom has a different gift. God expects us to do what we can with the gift he has given us (Mt 25:14-30).

Members of the Kingdom may seem to have a terribly painful life—like that of a beggar in the street—but they will be with God, while those who seem to be having a happy life may find themselves outside at the judgment (Lk 16:19-31). At the judgment it will be revealed that though many people talked a good game, Jesus did not know them, nor they Jesus (Lk 13:22-30).

Most important of all, at the judgment Jesus will reveal that what we did to others—or did not do—was done or refused to him (Mt 25:31-46).

5.
Jesus, a Danger to Church and State

Very few Israelites expected a Messiah like Jesus. Even his family thought he was a bit mad. Except for the few who saw in him the shadow of the Suffering Servant in the Old Testament, people felt that he simply turned human values upside down—which in fact he did—and were not prepared for such an anti-climax of history.

At the final showdown almost nobody was for him, and the might of both the religious and the secular establishment was against him. Like sunlight showing things exactly as they are, he had first frightened and then enraged the leaders of these two worlds who, with hands piously folded or swords hanging discreetly ready, had arranged a world with which God presumably agreed. In their world, external correctness was essential. Salvation was gained by mighty personal effort. Conformity to the letter of the law, rather than a free growth in responsibility, was of the essence. And "Roman peace" hung over all.

The little people heard Jesus gladly. He taught in the synagogue and "the people were spellbound by his teaching, because he taught with authority, not like the scribes" (Mk 1:22). Matthew uses the same word, *spellbound*, after the Sermon on the Mount.

After the curing of the paralytic, Mark records that "they were awestruck. All gave praise to God, saying, 'We have never seen anything like this!' " (Mk 2:12). He uses the word *amazement* for their reaction to the healing of both the Gerasene demoniac and the deaf-mute (5:20; 7:37).

In Mark, Jesus seems always surrounded by crowds, so that at times he could not even find time to eat (see Mk 3:20). After the multiplication of the loaves, they wanted to "carry him off and make him king" (Jn 6:15).

And at the climax, when he knew that death would soon remove any danger of an earthly enthronement, Jesus allowed the full adulation of the crowd. As he entered Jerusalem the week before Calvary,

> The huge crowd spread their cloaks on the road, while some began to cut branches from the trees and lay them along his path. The groups preceding him as well as those following kept crying out:
> "Hosanna to the Son of David!
> Blessed is he who comes in the name of the Lord!
> Hosanna in the highest!"
> As he entered Jerusalem the whole city was stirred to its depths. . . .
> (Mt 21:8-10)

But, in a sad commentary, John says, "While he was in Jerusalem during the Passover festival, many believed in his name, for they could see the signs he was performing. For his part, Jesus would not trust himself to them because he knew them all. He needed no one to give him testimony about human nature. He was well aware of what was in man's heart" (Jn 2:23-25).

And Jesus was forced to say to those who followed him after the multiplication of the loaves:

> "You are not looking for me because you have seen signs
> but because you have eaten your fill of the loaves.
> You should not be working for perishable food
> but for food that remains unto life eternal,
> food which the Son of Man will give you." (Jn 6:26-27)

Something had to happen before all the signs would merge into the one great sign of the cross. Enthusiasm, admiration, inspiration kindled by courageous and pure leadership—none of these were enough. The Kingdom could come only through the foolishness of the cross and the mystery of resurrection.
His enemies would make him victorious.

Jesus' Religious Opponents. It is one thing to be hated by those who put on no pious poses: gangsters, dope-pushers, communists, etc. But when the authorities of your own race and religion set out to kill you, you are either very good or very bad.

If ever there was a people whose religion influenced every facet of life, it was the Chosen People. They were the "People of the Book." The Torah—plus the endless commentaries made on it—regulated life down to the smallest detail. Several times a day the practicing Jew (like the Moslems we have seen on TV) stopped to pray. The Sabbath was an absolutely holy day set apart for God. Great feasts brought multitudes to Jerusalem; others were observed in the family and local community. Each village had its synagogue for prayer and meetings. And at the center of all was the magnificent Temple of Jerusalem (the third, built by Herod), undoubtedly one of the most majestic pieces of architecture to be seen at the time.

The Jews were a theocracy—that is, a nation ruled by God. His representatives were the high priest and the Sanhedrin, a kind of senate and supreme tribunal made up of members of the priestly class, the scribes and doctors of the Law, and the elders, outstanding laymen from the chief families.

An aristocracy of intellect and piety molded the thought of the nation. These were the "doctors" (i.e., teachers) of the Law. To the Western mind, the way in which they scrutinized the Bible was opposed to logic. Searching the minutest details, they found metaphorical meanings that went far beyond the writer's intended meaning. Their interpretations guided the people's life. Their purpose was to keep the people specifically Jewish—that is, real followers of Moses.

Like the doctors of the Law, the scribes were scholars and intellectuals who had *the* knowledge of the Law, the sum of wisdom, the only true learning. Though not necessarily of any sect or party, they were often Pharisees.

Pharisees and Sadduccees. All the people, from the highest to the lowest, thought of themselves as men and women of God; but there were two great divisions, corresponding to two reactions to paganism. One group held that there could be no dealing whatever with pagans. The good Jew must cast aside everything that was not purely Judaic. The true believer was to *separate* himself from paganism and all that smacked of it. This group became known as "the separated," in Hebrew the *perushim,* from which comes our word *Pharisees.*

On the other side, the Sadduccees believed in preserving the People of God by intelligence and diplomacy. The majority were truly religious, though some had no problem accommodating to the pagans. The Sadduccees drew their numbers chiefly from the well-to-do classes, higher officials, merchants, property owners, priests.

A second disagreement between the two had to do with the Law. The Sadduccees held only to the written Law of Moses and its 613 great principles. Where the Law was mute, they let reason decide. But the Pharisees insisted that the laws of religion must permeate the whole of human life. So the written Law had to be completed with the tradition or oral Law that the scribes (theologians) had been formulating since the return from exile. Most of the doctors of the Law were Pharisees.

In Jesus' time, the Pharisees could be compared to a powerful political party in modern terms. The real party members (the truly "separated") numbered between 5,000 and 10,000. But a large part of the Jewish people, especially the poorer classes, were sympathetic.

The Pharisees also felt they had a monopoly on the truth and had a deep contempt for those outside the Law. They no doubt had a deep and rigorous faith. They taught and practiced true charity. Paradoxically, they saw the oral tradition as constantly developing—under their interpretation. But once developed, their tradition became as sacred and rigorous as the Law itself.

The Talmud preserves a proverb which said, "There are seven kinds of Pharisee: the 'What do I get out of it?' Pharisee; the 'I look the part' Pharisee;

the 'Oh, my poor head' Pharisee who walks along the street with his head down so as not to see the women and who bangs into the wall; the 'pestle' Pharisee, who goes about so bent that he looks like a pestle in a mortar; the 'What is my duty so that I may do it?' Pharisee; the 'I do one good deed every day' Pharisee; and lastly the only real Pharisee, the one who is a Pharisee from fear of God and out of love for him."

The bitter opposition between Jesus and the Pharisees—the external explanation of why he was put to death—arose from the distorted view of religion of the first six classes just mentioned. Jesus accused them principally of *hypocrisy, pride* and *externalism,* thereby "neglecting weightier matters of the Law, justice and mercy and good faith" (Mt 23:23). It may come as a surprise to some how much of the Gospels is taken up with this controversy. But the result is no surprise at all.

Let us briefly trace the beginnings of opposition to Jesus from the scribes and Pharisees. It is part—but only part—of the explanation of why he "had" to die.

Conflict Over Sabbath Rigorism. A typical example of Pharisaic rigorism, if not hypocrisy, is found in the following incident. On their way to the synagogue on the Sabbath, Jesus' disciples pluck ears of wheat and rub the grains in their hands to make a rough meal. But this "preparation of food" was one of the 39 forms of work forbidden by the rigorist interpretation of the Sabbath rest.

When the Pharisees complain, Jesus gives both a rabbinical answer to show precedent in the Bible and then offers a humanitarian view of the Law: It is to be interpreted according to human needs and possibilities. "The sabbath was made for man, not man for the sabbath" (Mk 2:27).

On another occasion Jesus cured a man with a withered hand on the Sabbath. "The scribes and Pharisees were on the watch," Luke notes, "to see if he would perform a cure on the sabbath so that they could find a charge against him" (Lk 6:7). (There was a debate among rabbis as to when one could seek and accept medical aid on the Sabbath.) Jesus does not quibble. He simply says, "I ask you, is it lawful to do good on the Sabbath—or evil? To preserve life, or destroy it?" Luke says, "At this they became frenzied" (6:11), and Mark adds that the "Pharisees and Herodians"—strange bedfellows—"immediately began to plot how they might destroy him" (3:6).

On another occasion Jesus made mud paste and used it to cure a blind man. The Pharisees said, "This man cannot be from God because he does not keep the sabbath!" (Jn 9:16). One of the 39 works forbidden on the Sabbath (others included tying knots and walking more than 3,000 feet) was kneading, and Jesus had kneaded the clay with his spittle to make mud.

Rigorism Becomes Hypocrisy. The word Jesus used most often of the Pharisees was *hypocrites* or *frauds.* These words are used seven times in 17 verses of the terrible 23rd chapter of St. Matthew. Jesus says, "You have made a fine art of setting aside God's commandments in the interests of keeping your traditions!" (Mk 7:9). He gives as an example their not being "able" to support their parents because their money has been dedicated to God!

The charge of seeing the speck in another's eye and not the plank in one's own was aimed at the judgmentalism of the Pharisees. The teachings on prayer, fasting and alms in the Sermon on the Mount are put in the form of a contrast between the ostentatious piety of the Pharisees and the genuine piety which tries to conceal itself (Mt 6:1-18).

The 23rd chapter of Matthew alone would have doomed Jesus. He tells the people to follow the teaching of the Pharisees but not their practice, because their actions do not match their words. They interpret the Law severely, not humanely. Their religious garb is used to show off; they are greedy for public honors. They evade truthfulness by tricky formulas in taking oaths. They lay great stress on trivia and neglect the great commandments of justice, mercy and faithfulness.

In their fanaticism for externals they are "like white-washed tombs, beautiful to look at on the outside but inside full of filth and dead men's bones" (Mt 23:29). They are the true heirs of their ancestors who killed the prophets— and they will kill the one who is now continuing to speak with prophetic, fearless truthfulness.

Therefore, Jesus says, the people are to "be on guard against the yeast of the Pharisees, which is hypocrisy" (Lk 12:1).

The 'Scandal' of Jesus. In the eyes of the Pharisees, Jesus compounded the error of his ways by associating with disreputable people: tax-collectors (the hated quislings who "farmed" taxes for the Romans) and "those known as sinners"—that is, nonobservant Jews. When the Pharisees asked, "Why does he eat with such as these?" (Mk 2:16), Jesus' answer was framed in double-meaning words that were well understood: "People who are healthy do not need a doctor; sick people do. I have come to call sinners, not the self-righteous" (Mk 2:17).

Some Pharisees followed Jesus; for instance, Nicodemus, who came to see Jesus under cover of darkness. But for the great majority the cost was too great. It would have required as shattering a change of heart as occurred to that strictest of Pharisees, Saul of Tarsus. Jesus wrote his death warrant by an accusation that hurt their pride at its tenderest spot: He said their religion was spurious.

And this "free" man should be the Messiah? It was an insult to God that such a one should presume to reveal and mediate God's glory to Israel!

And so a "religious" coalition formed; scribes and Pharisees, chief priests and elders of the people. Jesus had to be destroyed. Some trick was needed to arrest and kill him. But "not during the festival, for fear of a riot among the people" (Mt 26:5).

Standing by were the Romans. Let there be found, then, some "Roman" reason to dispatch this dangerous man.

6.

 The Dying and Rising of Jesus:
The Heart of Christian Life

Many good men and women I've known don't think of themselves as "holy." There's nothing neurotic about it; they don't hate themselves; they just feel they could be more deeply "into" their religion than they are.

This used to bother me and I tried to tell them that St. Paul calls ordinary people *saints,* that it is God who makes us holy, not our own efforts.

But now I see there is something deeper here: *Ordinary Christians sense the depth of the mystery of Jesus, and are humble before it.* They realize that the life, death and resurrection of Jesus have a depth which is divine.

We can only feebly express or even experience what it means that God loves us so much. In love he bound a human body and soul to himself, lived our life in all its joy and pain, and entered freely into a degrading and apparently hopeless human death. Then, in a totally unexpected (though promised) and bewildering turnabout, Jesus is raised up newly alive—different, real and yet mysterious. He is seen only by those who believe. He is glorious, victorious, offering life, freedom, liberation, eternal happiness.

It is too much to grasp. It is frightening, because it offers more than we want to receive; yet it fulfills our deepest yearnings. It is also frightening because the price is absolutely high: We must do what Jesus did—die and rise. The dying is not just a one-time occurrence, but a daily happening. Deep down, we know that this is what it means to be a follower of Jesus: to die and to rise every hour. Or better, to let the power of Jesus put to death in us all selfishness and replace it with his Spirit.

We are reluctant to accept the offer. It is true, but it is too good. We know that in dealing with God it can only be a matter of 100 percent—not in terms of effort, but receiving, trusting, loving. And we—not instinctively, as the phrase goes, but in world-taught caution—hold back. Could it possibly be enough, we hope, to love God *almost* totally?

And so we say we are not "holy" meaning, I think, that we are not ready to let God give us all he wants to give.

The dying and rising of Jesus stands at the center of all history. Not merely in the center of time, as if there are to be as many years after as before, but in the center of *today.* Whether anyone knows it or not, accepts it or not, the dying and rising of Jesus is the central reality in every home, every factory, every school, every hospital, every theater, every prison, every supermarket.

With this feeble attempt to set the stage, we try now to understand two

38

things: 1) what happened, from a human viewpoint; 2) why it happened, from God's viewpoint.

The Events of Holy Week

St. Luke arranges his Gospel in a journey narrative. Jesus, at a certain point, begins his free and deliberate journey to Jerusalem from his native Galilee, fully aware that he will be put to death. The apostles realized what the trip meant. Thomas says bluntly and bravely that the rest of them might as well go along and be put to death too.

It is a literal "going up"—from below sea level in Galilee and from the depths of the Dead Sea up to the mountain of Jerusalem. John will continue the "lifting up" theme: Jesus is lifted up on the cross by human agents, lifted up out of death by his Father, and lifted up in glory to the throne of God from which he came.

On Palm Sunday Jesus finally allowed people to celebrate him as Messiah. There were only a few days left, hardly time for a revolution to form. He rode down from the Mount of Olives on a donkey, and then up through the Golden Gate, while people spread palm branches and even their clothing in his path, crying out:

"Hosanna to the Son of David:
Blessed is he who comes in the name of the Lord!
Hosanna in the highest!" (Mt 21:9)

"The whole city was stirred to its depths," St. Matthew adds (21:10), but one group was stirred by a special passion. The four Gospel writers variously identify them as chief priests, elders, scribes, Pharisees, high priests. They began to look for some way to "dispose" of him, St. Luke says.

"Then Satan took possession of Judas, the one called Iscariot, a member of the Twelve. He went off to confer with the chief priests and officers about a way to hand him over to them. They were delighted, and agreed to give him money. He accepted, then kept looking for an opportunity to hand him over without creating a disturbance" (Lk 22:3-6).*

The night before he was crucified, Jesus gathered his Jewish "family" of followers for a Passover meal. They did not realize it, but this was the fulfill-

---

*Let it be said again, in apology for the crimes Christians have committed against Jews down the centuries, that it is as unjust for Christians to blame "the" Jews for Jesus' death as it would be to say that "the" Americans killed Lincoln, or that "the" Arabs murdered a schoolhouse full of children in Israel. Nor is it correct to say that Pilate and other Romans represented us, "the" Gentiles.

On the other hand, the killing of Jesus is indeed the act of "the" human race, as we hope to understand in this chapter. If some Jews and some Romans were cold-bloodedly responsible for the death of Jesus, they are no more guilty than any human being who destroys the life of God in his or her own heart by cold-blooded sinfulness.

The Christian Church, it is well to remember, was for a while made up of *Jews alone.*

ment of all the Passovers since Moses and the beginning of a transformed Passover. His dying and rising a few days hence was "caught," real, living and all-powerful, in the Eucharist that began that night. In spite of all the human agony that would follow, he was ready. He was resolved to give himself for his friends. His victory, his liberating new life, were already present. His whole sacrificial love was embodied in this simple giving of Passover loaves and wine. They became *himself*, as the sign of his total self-giving and of the life-giving nourishment he would be for all who wished to live. (We will consider this more fully in Chapter 14.)

After the supper, down in Gethsemane in the deep valley below the Mount of Olives, Jesus felt the full human terror of death. Because his vision was so pure and his life so fully human, he realized, more than any of us can, the horror of human life being choked off. Perhaps the greatest consolation any suffering or dying person can have is to experience this Jesus in his naked helpless humanness, so transfixed with fear that "his sweat became like drops of blood" (Lk 22:42).

His enemies came, with their power, and he did not defend himself.

The Charges. It is difficult to interrelate the trial scenes in the four Gospels, probably because the Gospel writers, as usual, were writing not mere history but a record of faith. A generation or two later when the Gospels were written, the Church could see what was really happening, and it did not matter whether there was a trial or a pre-trial, whether it took place during the night or in the morning or both.

The real reason why Jesus was condemned to death by the Sanhedrin was that he claimed to be their king/Messiah and the prophet Daniel's mysterious "Son of Man."

After rejecting the title of Messiah all his public life, Jesus speaks clearly (in Mark) in answer to the high priest's question: "Are you the Messiah, the Son of the Blessed One?" Then Jesus answered: "I am" (Mk 14:61-66).

In the light of the resurrection, Christians down the centuries would hear echoes of Yahweh's only self-description: *"I AM."*

By the term "Son of the Blessed One" the Sanhedrin meant no more than the phrase signified in the Old Testament—the specially chosen one, especially the great Davidic king through whom God promises that the nation will reach fulfillment (See 2 Sm 7:14). *The Jerome Biblical Commentary* explains: "In the Sanhedrin's eyes, that Jesus should claim such a privilege insulted God: for this humiliated, rejected man to presume to reveal and mediate the Lord's glory to Israel was a supreme irreverence to God."

So they accused him of blasphemy. But by their own law, claiming to be Messiah could not merit such a charge!

They said he had threatened to destroy the Temple, choosing to take his words literally. What he actually said was, "Destroy this temple. . .and in three days I will raise it up." John adds, "Actually he was talking about the temple of his body" (Jn 2:19, 21). False witnesses chose to take his words literally (see Mk 14:58). Besides referring to the resurrection of his own body, Jesus no doubt often criticized the Temple and the cult for which it stood. The prophets had done that before him, most scorchingly Jeremiah, who stood at the entrance and said to the people entering: "Put not your trust in the deceitful words: 'This is the temple of the LORD! The temple of the LORD! The temple of the LORD!' Only if you thoroughly reform your ways and your deeds. . .will I remain with you in this place" (Jer 7:4-5, 7).

Even the false witnesses did not agree, but the Sanhedrin's mind was made up. "He deserves death!" (Mt 26:66).

The Death Sentence. Putting people to death was beyond the power of the Sanhedrin (see Jn 18:31), so the enemies of Jesus had to suffer the humiliation of approaching the hated Romans, the occupying power in a police state.

The Romans were totally uninterested in what they would have called the "religious squabbles" of their subjects. But they were wary of political activities. So now the charge becomes: "We found this man subverting our nation, opposing the payment of taxes to Caesar, and calling himself the Messiah, a king" (Lk 23:2).

Jesus assures Pilate that his Kingdom is not "of this world"—a statement, one authority has noted, which cannot be imagined in the mouth of the kind of Messiah popularly expected. The Jews expected a Messiah with a this-worldly kingdom—even if he were the more spiritual type of Messiah portrayed in the psalms.

In three of the Gospels, Pilate finally gives in simply because the mob keeps shouting, "Crucify him!" It is merely a cowardly act of political expediency. In John's Gospel, a deeper reason is clearly stated: Pilate wanted to release him, but the Jews insisted, "If you free this man you are no 'Friend of Caesar.' Anyone who makes himself a king becomes Caesar's rival" (Jn 19:12). This was the ultimate weapon: the threat of denouncing him to the emperor for having favored the emperor's enemies.

Pilate washes his hands, a pitiful charade of non-responsibility, and gives them their way. But he will have the last, cynical word: He orders an inscription placed on the cross which reads, *"Jesus the Nazorean, the King of the Jews."*

The Crucifixion. Jesus is scourged and made sport of by brutal Roman soldiers through the long night. Then the heavy crossbeam is placed on his shoulders and he is driven through the twisting, narrow streets of Jerusalem. Perhaps the hucksters did not even pay attention as he passed—just another poor wretch who had fallen afoul of the Romans.

They took him to a place of degradation outside the city walls and crucified him on a little hill that looked like a skull. It was the most humiliating of capital punishments.

As the *New Catholic Encyclopedia* explains, "The Romans considered crucifixion so shameful a penalty that it could not be inflicted on Roman citizens. Roman crucifixion was always preceded by a scourging of the victim at the place of judgment. Then the criminal, still naked after the scourging, was made to carry his own cross (that is, the crossbeam) to the place of execution, where he was exposed to public ridicule and death. On top of the upright stake was fastened a placard with the culprit's name and a statement of the crime for which he was being put to death. The full weight of a body hanging by the arms would prevent the correct functioning of the lungs and so cause death by asphyxiation after not too long a time. Therefore, to prolong the agony of the victim, support was given to his body by a kind of seat block and by binding or nailing his feet to the cross. Death could later be hastened by breaking the victim's legs, so that shock and asphyxiation soon ended his life. Sometimes, however, the side and heart would be pierced by a spear to cause immediate death. After death the body was left to rot on the cross as an additional sign of disgrace, and as a warning to the passers-by."

The Jews objected to a man's going about naked in public, so the Romans in Palestine allowed the condemned criminal to put his clothes on again after being scourged. When Jesus arrived at the place of execution, he was offered a drink of spiced wine to numb the pain, but he refused it. He was stripped of his garments and nailed to the cross, at least by his hands.

Jesus' Last Words. Jesus spoke seven statements, or "words," on the cross. Three are recorded by Luke, three by John, and a seventh by both Matthew and Mark.

1) *"Father, forgive them; they do not know what they are doing"* *(Lk 23:34).* The form of the verb Luke uses indicates that Jesus kept saying this over and over again. This is the great summation of his life: He came to bring God's forgiveness to all the world—to all sinners. It was only consistent that he show this depthless mercy of God at the moment of sinners' greatest cruelty to him.

2) *"I assure you: this day you will be with me in paradise" (Lk 23:43).* The words are spoken to the "good thief" who confesses his guilt and repeatedly begs to be remembered when Jesus enters into his royal glory. Jesus assures him that he will be with him *today* in his Kingdom. In contrast to those who should have known better, the criminal sees the truth and welcomes it.

3) *"Woman, there is your son. . . .There is your mother" (Jn 19:26, 27).* This is the loving concern of a son for his mother, but it is more than that. Mary is also the "woman" of Genesis 3:15 where God says to the serpent: "I will put enmity between you and the woman, and between your offspring and hers." Jesus' words show Mary as the New Eve, the true "mother of all the living" (Gn 3:20) through the death and resurrection of Jesus. She is the spiritual mother of the Church—that is, all Jesus' disciples as represented by John— as well as a symbol of the "mother" Church itself.

4) *"My God, my God, why have you forsaken me?" (Mt 27:46).* Jesus is praying the words of Psalm 22, not expressing any sense of despair or abandonment. Jesus was in pain, in emotional fear and agony, but his heart never was without the loving presence of his Father. The psalm is almost a description of the passion of Jesus, and its latter words should be noted. Jesus could have prayed them, too, as he remembered the psalm:

42

I will proclaim your name to my brethren;
in the midst of the assembly I will praise you. (Ps 22:23)

5) *"I thirst" (Jn 19:28).* Again, John intends more than one level of meaning. He sees the fulfillment of the messianic Psalm 69:

I looked for sympathy, but there was none;
for comforters, and I found none.
Rather they put gall in my food,
and in my thirst they gave me vinegar to drink. (Ps 69:21-22)

Father Raymond Brown in *The Gospel According to John* comments: "Perhaps the most plausible symbolism is to connect the episode with John 18:11: 'Am I not to drink the cup the Father has given me?' The cup was one of suffering and death; and now having finished his work, Jesus thirsts to drink that cup to the last drop, for only when he has tasted the bitter wine of death will his Father's will be fulfilled."

6) *"Now it is finished" (Jn 19:30).* Jesus has done what he came to do: the will of his Father, which was to save all his wandering, sinful children. He utters a cry of victory, of accomplishment. He has succeeded in a most unlikely way: by being defeated by the very sin he came to destroy. As always in John, it is Jesus who is in command. He has willingly been "lifted up" and the Father and he have achieved their purpose of salvation.

John adds, "He bowed his head, and delivered over his spirit" (19:30). Jesus was handed over by traitors, but now he hands himself over gladly to the Father.

7) *"Father, into your hands I commend my spirit" (Lk 23:46).* In Luke, the last words of Jesus are from Psalm 31:6 to which Luke adds the word *Father.* The words sum up Jesus' perfect disposition: Everything is in the Father's hands, and now he sums up his whole life by placing himself, body and soul, into those fatherly hands. He totally trusts his Father as he deliberately steps into the darkness of death. Humanly, it is a fearful moment: The darkness is the same as for anyone. But Jesus is the absolutely trusting child, the totally dependent creature, and his act replaces all the self-sufficiency and independence that have characterized human history. Jesus makes death the greatest act of love in his life.

Now the human actors must quickly finish their work. The Law must be observed scrupulously: A dead body could not be left hanging on the cross on the Sabbath. A lance is thrust into Jesus—assuring all that he is really dead— and blood and water pour out. The body is taken down and bound up "in wrappings of cloth with perfumed oils" (Jn 19:40). It is placed in a friend's new tomb nearby. A huge stone is rolled over the opening. It is officially sealed, and guards stand by.

The apostles sit numbed with fear and sadness behind locked doors. It is indeed "finished." As two disciples would say two days later, walking with Jesus and not knowing him, "We were hoping that he was the one who would

43

set Israel free" (Lk 24:21).

The women who had followed the body of Jesus to the tomb "observed the sabbath as a day of rest, in accordance with the law" (Lk 23:56). They did not know there was a new law.

Dying and Rising—From God's Viewpoint

We have considered the reasons why Jesus' enemies wanted to kill him—fear, envy, resentment. And it is easy to understand why he grated on some consciences. He contradicted the world in the name of simple, total love, truthfulness, humility before God. He suffered the fate of the pure person who, without uttering a word of condemnation, exposes the falsity and selfishness of others.

But these are human reasons, even if true. What did God have in mind, in what St. Paul calls the mystery hidden from all eternity (see Col 1:26)? What is the Father trying to do for us today in the dying and rising of Jesus?

We believe, first of all, that God let the world do its worst, and put his plan within the hateful actions that led to Jesus' death. He planted a seed amid hostile forces much as a farmer sows grain amid the benign forces of earth and water, sun and wind. God intervened through Jesus, but let himself be powerless before ignorance and hatred.

Why did Jesus die? Why did he consistently say, especially in the record of St. Luke, that he *must* die?

Let us obliterate as completely as possible one totally false reason: that God the Father "punished" Jesus for the sins of mankind. The idea of a "punishment of Christ" in place of sinners, says theologian Father Karl Rahner, *is rightly rejected.*

The fact is, God desired with infinite love to find a way to save the world from sin without destroying the gift of freedom. It was almost as if the Trinity had a meeting and decided it was best for the Son to enter the sinful world as a real man. St. Paul is clear on this: ". . .God, in Christ, was reconciling the world to himself. . ." (2 Cor 5:19).

What was it, then, that the God-man Jesus could do to reunite God's sinful children with their Father?

First, he himself is perfectly united to God. He is true man, and therefore humankind, at least in one human being, is united forever to God. Even should all the world rebel, God and humanity are now inseparable.

In this one man, there would be perfect *human* love and loyalty, trust and obedience. He would be the perfect opposite of sin, which is an attempt to be independent, to be self-sufficient, self-willed, self-powered. Jesus, the most mature human being who ever lived, was the perfect child before his Father.

The life and death of Jesus was not an "act," some "nice" gesture, but a reflection of reality. Reality *is* our total dependence on God's love and power and creation at every second of our lives. This does not involve any "putting down" of us by God; it is simply the way things are. Only God is God; all else is creation, dependent creation. "Even our desire to please you is itself your gift" (*Sacramentary*, Preface #40).

We must not inflict a mechanical holiness on Jesus. As a living, breathing, feeling human being, he allowed himself to be taken over completely by the love of God. He was simply wide open to all the goodness the Father wanted to give him, all the good that was to be done. He not only emptied himself, as St. Paul says, of the external glory due him as God; he also was empty and virginal as far as any self-will was concerned.

Again, let us remind ourselves, Jesus was not putting on an act, or doing something extra. He was merely acting as a creature should act. He was simply open to the ever-present gift of his Father's love. He let it enter and empower his every thought, feeling, word and action. It was what kept him alive: "Doing the will of him who sent me. . .is my food" (Jn 4:34).

But if Jesus is already the perfect loving child of the Father, why does he *have* to die?

Because giving up one's life is the *total* gift. Anything else would be less than perfect. There is nothing greater to give than life.

So Jesus had to give up his life because there was no greater way he could show his love of the Father. He had to give up his life because anything else would have been a lesser gift, and he wanted to do the perfect human thing.

But there is another reason why Jesus had to die. He came to a world lost in sin. How could he save that world? By showing it how God acts in the face of hatred. God refuses to be vindictive. He wants no pound of flesh. He wants only to forgive, to heal, to reconcile.

So Jesus enters into the world and all its misery, except that of sin. He is soaked through, as it were, with the misery of the human condition. And he maintains his perfect, never-swerving devotion to the Father.

In other words, he chose to be the totally loyal son. He would let his Father's love fill his life. If that aroused the hatred of evil—and it inevitably would—so be it. There was nothing the world could do to him that could deflect his childlike love one degree. He walked defenseless into an evil world.

It is sublime irony, as John points out, that because men "lifted up" Jesus on the cross, his Father was able to "lift him up" to new life and eternal glory. "Let his blood be on us and on our children" (Mt 27:25) were the truest words ever spoken.

Jesus had to reeducate his people as to the meaning of the Messiah. They would have to go back and read Isaiah 52. And at the moment when Peter makes his magnificent act of faith ("You are the Messiah!") Jesus must immediately set him straight: "He began to teach them that the Son of Man had to suffer much, be rejected by the elders, the chief priests, and the scribes, be put to death, and rise three days later" (see Mk 8:27-33).

Jesus was speaking of himself—not just of his followers—when he said that one must die to live, one must lose in order to win (see Mk 8:34-38).

This was the real Exodus. As the new Chosen People, Jesus would walk out of the imprisonment of humanity through the water of death, through the desert of perfect faith, to a new covenant on a new Mount Sinai.

From God's viewpoint, to use a heartless word, it was merely logical. To use the words of lovers, Jesus "had" to die because his love demanded that he give the greatest gift.

No wonder we shy away from the cross. Our problem is not that it is painful, but that it is too great a sign of love. *We* do not love that way, and we are embarrassed when God does.

Our life of faith, it would seem, is a gradual coming to accept the unbelievable tenderness of God. To be a member of Christ is to die every day, and rise every day.

Jesus' everyday dying was not like ours. He did not have to turn away from private deposits of self-will. But he did know the pain that total absorption with the Father can cost. We, on the other hand, must every day let the power of God's healing cut all the tendrils and vines and chains that want to tie us down in our own selfishness. That is our daily cross, and our greatest blessing.

For as we die, we rise. Salvation is letting Jesus bind us to himself. He is "safe," and so we are safe. He is God and with God; he is human and with us. If the power of his cross is in us, we are, with him, lifted to new life.

Part III:
The World Starts Over

7.

 The Rising of Jesus From the Dead

We could say the world started over when the Son of God was made flesh in the womb of the Virgin Mary. From that moment on, history was fundamentally changed. Or we could say the world started anew with the birth of Christ, when poor Jewish shepherds and inquiring Gentile astrologers represented the whole world before his crib.

But it is nearest the truth to say that the world started over with the death-resurrection of Jesus, for in that event God's saving plan was perfectly fulfilled. In the center of time and eternity, radiating power to the universe, is the risen Jesus, glorious in new and mysterious human life, divinity shining through humanity, inviting and empowering all the children of Adam to be joined to him in his victory and glory.

We must say "death-resurrection" for it is *both* these events or, perhaps better, this *combined* event that is crucial in all history. "Did not the Messiah have to undergo all this so as to enter into his glory?" (Lk 24:26). With typical Jewish parallelism Paul says, Jesus was "handed over to death for our sins and raised up for our justification" (Rom 4:25).

As we shall see through the rest of this book, this dying-rising of Jesus is the essence of Christian life. With him and in him we die every day and, in so doing, we rise every day.

What Happened? The Gospel accounts of the resurrection leave us with a feeling of mystery. Jesus is seen only by those who believe in him. He takes the initiative and comes to them, but obviously he must give them the power to *re*-cognize—to know again—him whom they had seen twisted in death on the cross. Magdalene, for instance, and the Emmaus disciples look at him without knowing who he is—until he opens the eyes of their faith.

We recall again that the Gospels are a family book—the record of the Church's experiences of faith and love centered in Jesus. Therefore we cannot use the New Testament to prove to atheists that Jesus really rose from the dead, that he is truly God, etc. But even an atheist would admit that Easter morning got off to a bad start as far as the faith of the Church was concerned. If there was a conspiracy to "make up" the story of the resurrection, it was very unconvincingly done.

Mark says that the women who found the tomb empty fled away "bewildered and trembling; and because of their great fear, they said nothing to anyone" (Mk 16:8). The only possibility Magdalene could think of was that the body of Jesus had been taken from the tomb (see John 20:2). Peter looked into the tomb, saw the wrappings that had clothed Jesus' body, and "went away full of amazement" (Lk 24:12). To the apostles "the story seemed like nonsense, and they refused to believe them [the women]" (Lk 24:11).

Jesus therefore had to *give* them vision, and the Gospel writers follow a pattern in narrating these "recognition" scenes: first, bewilderment on the part of people who are not expecting anything; then, the initiative of Jesus, enabling them to be aware of him; finally, their expression of faith.

So, for instance, Mary is weeping at the empty tomb. She sees Jesus and thinks he is the gardener. She suspects he is the one who may have taken the body (*note:* no concept of resurrection). Then Jesus says, "Mary!" and she "sees" who he is. She re-cognizes, knows again, the one who was Teacher. It is the same Jesus, now in new form (see Jn 20:11-18).

Another example of this is Luke's report of the experience of the two disciples on the road to Emmaus. They see Jesus as a fellow traveler and discuss with him, as with a stranger, the events of recent days. They stop to eat and invite him to join them. Then, "he took bread, pronounced the blessing, then broke the bread and began to distribute it to them. With that their eyes were opened and they recognized him; whereupon he vanished from their sight" (Lk 24:30-31).

A third recognition scene focuses on the doubting Thomas. He finally becomes a believer when Jesus gives him unmistakable proof of his reality—and praises the millions of Christians who would believe without seeing (Jn 20:24-29).

Besides the recognition appearances, the Gospel writers also record "mission" appearances in which Jesus sends his disciples into the world to be the witnesses of his death-resurrection to all people. For example, Matthew's Gospel ends with these words:

"Full authority has been given to me
both in heaven and on earth;
go, therefore, and make disciples of all the nations.
Baptize them in the name
'of the Father,
and of the Son,
and of the Holy Spirit.'
Teach them to carry out everything I have commanded you.
And know that I am with you always, until the end of the world!"

(Mt 28:16-20)

In John's Gospel Jesus commissions the Apostles in his first appearance on Easter evening:

"As the Father has sent me,
so I send you."

Then he breathed on them and said:

"Receive the Holy Spirit.
If you forgive men's sins,
they are forgiven them;
if you hold them bound,
they are held bound." (Jn 20:21-23)

Notice that John has Jesus breathing the Holy Spirit on the apostles in his first appearance, emphasizing the fact that in the new timeless life of Jesus everything happens at once, as it were. For John, the death of Jesus means his resurrection, which is his glorification at the right hand of the Father (that is, his ascension), which is the pouring out of his Spirit (Pentecost).

Luke, on the other hand, spreads Jesus' appearances over the 40 days before his ascension. During this time he records the "privileged" appearances of Jesus. There is a difference for Luke between these days and all following time. Even the appearance of Jesus to Paul (recorded four times!) he would put in a different category. In Luke's second volume (Acts), he describes Jesus' pouring out his Spirit in the thrilling experience of Pentecost. It is now the age of faith. The special appearances of Jesus are over.

The evangelists' approaches to the resurrection are different, but the meaning is the same. Something unbelievable has happened. The Jesus who was dead is alive in a new, mysterious life that can be seen only by faith. Despite human doubt and despair, Jesus fills the consciousness of his friends. Their reaction may be summed up in two sentences from the New Testament: The first is the reaction of the two men on the road to Emmaus who say, "Were not our hearts burning inside us as he talked to us on the road and explained the Scriptures to us?" (Lk 24:32). The second is the comment of bystanders at the conduct of the newly bold apostles after Pentecost: "They have had too much new wine!" (Acts 2:13).

What Kind of Body Does Jesus Have? The impossibility of recognizing Jesus without faith indicates that his risen body has different qualities than it had before his death. Obviously the resurrection of Jesus does not imply the resuscitation of a six-foot, 190-pound man. He did not "come back" like Lazarus. Jesus' risen body is a real body—material, yet now "spiritual."

What can this mean? Paul may help us, as he speaks of the kind of bodies we will have: " 'What kind of body will they have?' A nonsensical question! . . . When you sow, you do not sow the fullblown plant, but a kernel of wheat or some other grain. God gives body to it as he pleases—to each seed its own fruition. . . .What is sown in the earth is subject to decay, what rises is incorruptible. What is sown is ignoble, what rises is glorious. Weakness is sown, strength rises up. A natural body is put down and a spiritual body comes up (1 Cor 15: 35-38, 42-44).

Jesus no longer belongs to our space and time. There is now no hourglass in his life, and his power flows to the universe. He is simply "available" to anyone and everyone, any place and any time. He appears in special ways sacramentally, as we shall see.

The Inner Meaning of the Resurrection. Lest we miss the forest for the trees, we must ask ourselves what the resurrection of Jesus means for us today.

Starting at the end, we know that it means our bodies will rise as he did, and we will share his victory and glory and joy forever. But in a once-and-for-all sense, it means that the Father, as eternally planned, responds in this faithful way to the perfect childlike trust and obedience of Jesus. He raises him up, and with him all who wish to join him. Jesus *rose* by his own power, and he *was raised* by the Father (see Jn 10:18; Rom 6:4). It is all one—the merciful plan the Father, Son and Spirit formed from eternity.

Jesus is God's "Last Word." His death-resurrection-glorification-outpouring of Spirit are "all" that even the infinitely merciful God can do. Now there is nothing left to do—whether the world lasts a day or a million years—but to draw all who wish into the saving, enlivening life of Jesus. What Jesus is, all can be: free from death, sin, suffering, evil.

The union of God and human beings is sealed now, forever. It can never be broken because Jesus, the fully human one, has made the exodus through the waters of death to new life, which he shares with all who desire it. The dead heritage of sin is wiped out. God's life replaces death in the hearts of all who turn to him. The Kingdom has indeed come: It is Jesus and all his followers, living and deceased, allowing themselves to be fully possessed by the love of the Father.

The Christian life is the transformation of human beings by the power of Jesus' death and resurrection. We have seen this amazing change in those who at first stubbornly refused to believe. They bowed down and said, "My Lord and my God!" They recognized Jesus as the "LORD," one with Yahweh of creation.

So the death-resurrection of Jesus is indeed the world starting over. Jesus is the New Adam, lifted up out of the old Adam which was human life imprisoned in sin and death. The first Adam—and all of us—forfeited our gifts. The New Adam, truly human in the person of the Son, made the perfect at-one-ment (atonement). He fulfilled the purpose of all sacrifice: union with God.

The rest of this book—the Church, the sacraments, the Christian life—is simply about living out the death and resurrection of Jesus. We cannot have a once-and-for-all dying and rising and get it over with. We must (like the sun in biblical thought) get up every morning and do it all over again. Our baptismal dying and rising must be confirmed many times over.

The power of Jesus is with us always. It gives us the power to die—perhaps a hundred times a day—to selfishness and untruth and to rise—even though the taste of it may not be there—to a greater union with the risen Jesus.

8.

 Jesus, the Son of God: This Man

When we speak of the "mystery" of Jesus in St. Paul's sense, we are thinking of him as a sacrament—a "sign" that reveals as well as hides. He is the self-revealing of God through the sign of a human body.

He is a mystery in another way also, in that there is something beyond understanding in his makeup.

He is truly God.

He is truly man.

He is one person.

Jesus is not two persons cooperating in harmony. He is not God with a human facade, and he is not merely a human being with a very close relationship with God.

As a true human being, Jesus is psychologically a "person" in the way we understand that word today. But the doctrine of the Church sees only one Person in Jesus, that of the Son of God. After centuries of wrestling with the problem, the Church officially adopted the following way of talking about Jesus in the Council of Chalcedon (451 A.D.):

> We unanimously teach that the Son, our Lord Jesus Christ, is one and the same, the same perfect in divinity, the same perfect in humanity, true God and true man, consisting of a rational soul and body, consubstantial with the Father in divinity and consubstantial with us in humanity. . .in two natures unconfused, unchangeable, undivided and inseparable. The difference of natures will never be abolished by their being united, but rather the properties of each remain unimpaired, both coming together in one person and substance, not parted or divided among two persons, but in one and the same only begotten Son, the Divine Word, the Lord Jesus Christ.

We have to be a little philosophical for a moment.

1) *Two Natures in Christ.* "Nature" in this sense is the basic constitution of anyone or anything. When we ask, "*What* is that?" we are asking about its nature. "What is a pencil?" means "What makes a pencil a pencil and not something else?" "What is a human being?" means "What makes a certain class of being human?" We answer that to be human is to have a spiritual-physical way of being. We are neither angels nor animals, but "em-bodied spirits" or "spirit-

ualized bodies." When we say, "What makes Jesus Jesus?" we answer that he is a being who has the nature of being human and the nature of being divine, but is only one Person. He is absolutely unique.

2) *One Person in Christ.* When we say, *"Who* is that?" we are no longer asking *what* makes something to be what it is. Rather, we are now in the area of *persons.* We want to know the particular identity—the name—of some particular being. We can imagine ourselves saying, as we barely discern something lying in a field, *"What* is that?" But when we come closer and find that "it" is an unconscious human being, we say, "I wonder *who* this is?" We look for his name, his identity.

Now here is the mystery of Jesus. Every individual human nature we know of is a human person. Joe Smith is a human person, with a human nature. But Jesus is not two people more or less intimately tied together, God and man; he is one Person with a divine nature, who has assumed a human nature into his one Person. There is only one *who* in Jesus, but two *whats.* What he does is truly divine; it is also entirely human.

There is no "mixing" of natures, however. He is the wisdom and power of God, the eternal and infinite love of God; and he is this man with fully human emotions, making human decisions the way all his brothers and sisters make them, suffering the pains of human limitation and the joys of a full human life.

How do we put these two things together? We must simply say we don't know. We let the truths exist side by side, and we believe the mystery.

Jesus, True Man. In the course of history, just about every possible heresy has been advanced by somebody. Regarding Jesus, a heresy called Docetism (from the word for "seem") held that Christ only *seemed* human.

Sometimes, in our determination to preserve the divinity of Jesus, we verge toward Docetism. We downplay Jesus' humanity, as if it were somehow absorbed into his divinity. But it is just as incorrect to deny Jesus' full humanity as it is to deny his divinity.

As a four-year-old boy, Jesus did not have all future scientific and theological knowledge in his head. Like all human beings, he had to develop his body, his mind, his emotions, his character. St. Luke tells us, Jesus "progressed steadily in wisdom and age and grace before God and men" (2:52).

If Jesus were not truly man the Bible could not say: "For we do not have a high priest who is unable to sympathize with our weakness, but one who was tempted in every way that we are, yet never sinned" (Heb 4:15).

We can identify with Jesus, because he is one of us. He knew what it was to be hungry and thirsty, to be worn out physically with work or travel, to suffer the pain of heat or cold, of a splinter in his finger or the bite of an insect. The Gospels show him with all the human emotions: He enjoyed the company of friends, the innocence of children and the support of his followers. He could be fully angry, troubled, frustrated. He could be so humanly afraid and terrorized that "his sweat became like drops of blood" (Lk 22:44).

He had a human mind unspoiled by narrowness or selfishness, one which was simply open to all reality, especially to the Father's self-giving. He had a free human will to decide and strive and give. He loved as no one has ever loved, yet as everyone was made to love.

What was different about Jesus, of course, was that he had no sin, nor any of the heritage or "momentum" of sin that we have. He was not only a true man but a pure man. His humanity was not cramped or bent, but had only the normal limitations of space and time and finiteness.

Therefore he could enjoy the song of a bird, or the brilliance of a sunset, or the face of a human being more deeply than we who are distracted by our own selves. The truth was more thrilling to him. To love was more intense and whole-hearted.

Jesus' Human Knowledge. There are people who are shocked by some theologians' treatment of Jesus' human knowledge. They hold that since Jesus was God he knew everything.

The answer does not seem to be quite that simple. If Jesus was truly a human being, his mind had to work like a human mind. It had to grow from ignorance to knowledge, from known to unknown, from depth to greater depth of understanding.

Jesus was one person, but his divine consciousness was not his human consciousness. His divinity and humanity were not mixed together, like wine and water.

But why didn't his divine knowledge simply flood his human mind with all possible information? We must answer that he would not then have been truly human. To be human is to face reality, seek truth, choose what is good. This means looking for the facts, considering alternatives, weighing consequences, and then making decisions. That is how a human being takes responsibility for his or her life.

Jesus came among us to be fully human in every way except sin. He could not be characterized as human if as a four-year-old boy he was already aware of the intricacies of nuclear fission and the potency of penicillin.

The noted biblical scholar Father Raymond Brown, treating the knowledge of Jesus in an excellent book, *Jesus, God and Man*, speaks to the common objection raised to the view that Jesus had limited, human knowledge:

> But when all is said and done, the great objection that will be hurled
> again against any exegete (or theologian) who finds evidence that
> Jesus' knowledge was limited is the objection that in Jesus Christ
> there is only one person, a divine person. And so, even though the
> divine person acted through a completely human nature, any theory
> that Jesus had limited knowledge seems to imply a limitation of the
> divine person. Perhaps the best answer to this objection is to call
> upon Cyril of Alexandria, that Doctor of the Church to whom, more
> than to any other, we are indebted for the great truth of the oneness
> of the person of Christ. It was that ultra-orthodox archfoe of Nes-
> torianism (two persons or powers in Christ) who said of Christ,
> "We have admitted his goodness in that for love of us he has not

refused to descend to such a low position as to bear all that belongs to our nature, *included in which is ignorance.*"

Perhaps the clearest statement of the meaning of Jesus' true humanity is found in Hebrews:

"Surely he did not come to help angels, but the children of Abraham: *therefore he had to become like his brothers in every way,* that he might be a merciful and faithful high priest before God on their behalf, to expiate the sins of the people. *Since he was himself tested through what he suffered,* he is able to help those who are tempted" (Heb 2:16-18; emphasis added).

Jesus was not "tempted" as we are, by an itch or impulse towards evil. Yet to give his bread away meant that he was hungry; to work hard meant that he was tired; and to be faithful to his Father meant that he would be killed. It cost Jesus something to be the trusting child of the Father.

Jesus' Vocation. So Jesus' growth in knowledge was gradual, as well his growth in the love of God and his understanding of his own identity and mission. By prayer and meditation on the Scriptures, by the words and example of his parents, Jesus experienced the self-revealing love of his Father—similar to the revelation given to all human beings, but also unique: he is the Anointed One, the Messiah long promised.

How and when the Father revealed this to Jesus we do not know. What we must say is that Jesus accepted his vocation with full freedom and loving obedience. It was a responsible choice. He took his life and put it at the disposal of the Father. He let himself be totally possessed by the Father's love and power: "Doing the will of him who sent me and bringing his work to completion is my food" (Jn 4:34). He is the New Adam, not denying his fully human response to the Father's call, but opening himself completely.

His relationship with the Father is tender, intimate. His word of address is *Abba*—no doubt an imitation of the earliest sounds made by a baby to its parents. It is the word little Jewish children used for their father; on adult tongues it expressed warm affection. Our associations with the English word *Daddy* may be hard to transfer to God, but that is the closest translation we can have for *Abba.* "Abba!" was Jesus' life.

The purpose of discussing the humanity of Jesus and all it means is to keep Jesus from being "way up there," far above the pains and pleasures and worries of ordinary mortals. We have the absolute conviction and unquestioning faith that Jesus is true God, the eternal Son of the Father. But it is equally true that he is a real human being, like us in *everything* but sin. "Everything" must apply to knowledge, conscience, body, emotions, memory, imagination, conversation, sleep, meals—there is no area excluded except the sinful.

It is only by keeping the human Jesus along with the divine that we can really believe that he knows from experience what *our* experience is. We can then join his prayer in pain or joy, in failure or success, in frustration or anger or serenity and have his empathy and sympathy—and his power to be childlike before the Father.

Jesus, True God. Christians do not try to "prove" to anyone that Jesus is God. If Peter could not know Jesus was the Messiah unless the Father revealed it (see Mt 16:17), the gigantic step to belief in his divinity is infinitely less possible. We believe because we have the gift of believing. And again, we must say, if that seems to the world naive and unscientific, so much the worse for the world.

So we pray the Scriptures with joy and admiration rather than with questions and concern. And there is no better place to do this than the magnificent prologue of John's Gospel:

> In the beginning was the Word,
> And the Word was with God,
> and the Word was God.
> He was in the beginning with God;
> all things were made through him,
> and without him was not anything made that was made.
> In him was life,
> and the life was the light of men.
> The light shines in the darkness,
> and the darkness has not overcome it. . . .
> He was in the world,
> and the world was made through him,
> yet the world knew him not. . . .
> And the Word became flesh
> and dwelt among us,
> full of grace and truth;
> we have beheld his glory,
> glory as of the only Son from the Father. . . .
> No one has ever seen God;
> the only Son,
> who is in the bosom of the Father,
> he has made him known.
> (Jn 1:1-5, 10, 14, 18; RSV)

Passages like this are like prisms of eternity. Theology will do its best to explain, but in the end these simple and infinitely profound statements are the best way to express the mystery. The crux of the mystery is that the love of God appeared in Jesus. Not just that "God made his love known" but the *love* of God appeared. Jesus *is* the love of God, and the love of God made *visible*. He is "the reflection of the Father's glory, the exact representation of the Father's being, and he sustains all things by his powerful word" (Heb 1:3).

'The Father and I Are One.' John's Gospel shows the Church's 60 or 70 years of reflection on the mystery of Jesus and leads us to the mystery of the Trinity: Father, Son and Holy Spirit, one God. In St. John, Jesus' suffering humanity is not stressed as it is in Mark; his divinity shines through more clearly. He speaks as the God who has destroyed evil and saved his loved ones:

"If you really knew me, you would know my Father also.
From this point on you know him: you have seen him. . . .
Whoever has seen me has seen the Father." (Jn 14:7, 9)

Three times Jesus says, "I am in the Father, and the Father is in me. Believe me!" (see Jn 14:10, 11, 20).

The union of the Son and the Father is one of being—and of love. To this union of divine love Jesus brings a perfect, childlike human love: "The Father and I are one" (Jn 10:30).

What is the meaning and purpose behind all this? It is the final reason why God initiated his great plan of salvation. Just as there is a perfect union of the love in Father, Son and Spirit, so there is a perfect divine-human love between the Father and Jesus. *And this is the kind of love God in Jesus and his Spirit wants for us!* Jesus says, referring to his return to us in the resurrection:

"On that day you will know
that I am in my Father,
and you in me, and I in you." (Jn 14:20)

We who like to think of God as stern and remote should be humbled and chastened by these overwhelming words:

He who obeys the commandments he has from me
is the man who loves me;
and he who loves me will be loved by my Father.
I too will love him
and reveal myself to him. . . .
Anyone who loves me
will be true to my word,
and my Father will love him;
we will come to him
and make our dwelling place with him. (Jn 14:21, 23)

In a later chapter we will consider the fullness of this "indwelling of God" by exploring that of the Holy Spirit who, Jesus said, he has sent to be another Paraclete (defender and consoler) for us and who "will be within you" (Jn 14:17).

Jesus concludes his profound and touching discourse at the Last Supper with these words, addressed in prayer to the Father:

"To them I have revealed your name,
and I will continue to reveal it
so that your love for me may live in them
and I may live in them." (Jn 17:26)

So the final purpose of Jesus' coming is not just to give us knowledge of the Father, but to fill us with the Father's love and join us in a living union with Jesus and with the Father, through the presence of the Spirit. Jesus showed us what divinity is, and he showed us what true humanity is. He is God in a human way and man in a divine way. His human love is the embodiment of God's love for all of us to see and absorb.

9.

 Jesus Is Lord:
A Short Course
in St. Paul

About one-fourth of the New Testament is made up of the 13 letters of St. Paul. They offer a very powerful and unique vision of the mystery of Christ. Reading them, one senses a personality and approach quite different both from the writers of the first three Gospels and from another unique writer, St. John.

Paul's letters usually deal with concrete situations in the early Church, hence are independent of each other and not systematic. But Paul always manages to rise above the personal and the particular to thrill his readers with the outlines of the faith and to bring them to the practice of a more intense Christian life.

Intense seems a good word to describe Paul. He was a human dynamo, always 100 percent—whether as zealous Pharisee or lover of Christ. His constant emphasis was on the intimate connection between our salvation and the passion, death and resurrection of Jesus. Through these events Jesus has become a power producing a new life in us, beginning with dying and rising in Baptism and ending with our bodily resurrection to eternal glory in Christ.

One is tempted to say that no other Christian writer has influenced the Church as much as this "apostle to the Gentiles." Some of what he wrote is difficult to understand—even Peter has difficulty. But the majority of Paul's words are full of a passionate devotion to Christ that can illuminate our reading of the Gospels and be the power of deeper faith in us.

This chapter will attempt to let Paul himself speak—but in a systematic, 13-point way. This is the real St. Paul: the man on fire with love of Christ, the total convert, the fearless herald of the Good News. May we catch some of his spirit!

1) **Eternally, God Had a 'Family' in Mind, With Jesus at the Center.**

Even before the world was made,
God had already chosen us to be his through our union with Christ,
so that we would be holy and without fault before him.
(Eph 1:4; *Good News Bible*)

Those whom God had already chosen
he also set apart to become like his Son,
so that the Son would be the first among many brothers.
(Rom 8:29; *Good News Bible*)

2) **Jesus Is God and Man.** Paul simply lets these two facts stand side by side:

He is the image of the invisible God,
the firstborn of all creatures.
In him everything in heaven and on earth was created. (Col 1:15)

3) **The Son of God Became Man So We Might Share the Life of God.**

...When the designated time had come
God sent forth his Son born of a woman...
so that we might receive our status as adopted sons. (Gal 4:4, 5)

One of the magnificent passages in St. Paul sums up the story of Jesus:

Your attitude must be that of Christ:
Though he was in the form of God,
    he did not deem equality with God
    something to be grasped at.
Rather, he emptied himself
    and took the form of a slave,
    being born in the likeness of men.
He was known to be of human estate,
    and it was thus that he humbled himself,
    obediently accepting even death,
    death on cross!
Because of this,
    God highly exalted him
    and bestowed on him the name
    above every other name,
So that at Jesus' name
    every knee must bend
    in the heavens, on the earth,
    and under the earth,
    and every tongue proclaim

to the glory of God the Father:
JESUS CHRIST IS LORD! (Phil 2:6-11)

4) Jesus' Saving Death and Resurrection Are at the Heart of His Gospel. Jesus becomes the New Adam, fully human and experiencing the suffering of the first Adam. In a daring statement, Paul says God made Jesus to *be sin,* so that in him we might *become the holiness* of God. Sin and evil and death were able to "destroy" Jesus, but were themselves destroyed in the event by the power of God in Jesus' perfect love (see 2 Cor 5:21):

> . . .through one man sin entered the world
> and with sin death,
> death thus coming to all men inasmuch as
> all sinned. . . . (Rom 5:12)

But, Paul continues:

> . . .if by the offense of the one man all died,
> much more did the grace of God and the
> gracious gift of the one man, Jesus Christ,
> abound for all. (Rom 5:15)

> Just as through one man's disobedience all become sinners,
> so through one man's obedience all shall become just. (Rom 5:19)

> It was he who sacrificed himself for us,
> to redeem us from all unrighteousness
> and to cleanse for himself a people of his own,
> eager to do what is right. (Ti 2:14)

> He has robbed death of its power
> and has brought life and immortality
> into clear light through the gospel. (2 Tim 1:10b)

> I mean that God, in Christ, was reconciling the world to himself. . . .
> (2 Cor 5:19)

5) Jesus Joins His Brothers and Sisters to Himself in One Body, the Church.

> Each of you is a son of God
> because of your faith in Christ Jesus.
> All of you who have been baptized into Christ
> have clothed yourselves with him.
> There does not exist among you
> Jew or Greek, slave or freeman,
> male or female. (Gal 3:26-29)

It is he who is head of the body, the church:
he who is the beginning, the firstborn of the dead. (Col 1:18)

By the gift of God's grace, we are united to Jesus in his death and in his new life. This is the challenge of our life, and its hope.

Are you not aware
that we who were baptized into Christ Jesus
were baptized into his death?
Through baptism into his death
we were buried with him,
so that
just as Christ was raised from the dead
by the glory of the Father,
we too might live a new life.
If we have been united with him
through likeness to his death,
so shall we be through a like resurrection.
This we know: our old self was crucified with him
so that the sinful body might be destroyed
and we might be slaves to sin no longer. (Rom 6:3-11)

6) As Jesus Was Raised Up, So Are We, and So Shall We Be.

You can depend on this:
If we have died with him
we shall also live with him;
If we hold out to the end
we shall also reign with him.
But if we deny him he will deny us.
If we are unfaithful he will still remain faithful;
for he cannot deny himself. (2 Tm 2:11-13)

He will give a new form
to this lowly body of ours
and remake it according to the pattern
of his glorified body. (Phil 3:21)

Tell me,
if Christ is preached as raised from the dead,
how is it that some of you say
there is no resurrection of the dead?
. . .If the dead are not raised,
then Christ was not raised;
and if Christ was not raised,
your faith is worthless.

You are still in your sins,
and those who have fallen asleep in Christ
are the deadest of the dead.
If our hopes in Christ are limited
to this life only,
we are the most pitiable of men.
But as it is,
Christ has been raised from the dead,
the first fruits of those who have fallen asleep. (1 Cor 15:12, 16-20)

7) The Body of Christ Is the Church. It is one living organism filled with the
Spirit of Jesus. That essential unity of life and love must be maintained at all
costs. But within that unity there is a wonderful and beautiful variety.

Make every effort to preserve the unity
which has the Spirit as its origin
and peace as its binding force.
There is but one body and one Spirit,
just as there is but one hope
given all of you by your call.
There is one Lord, one faith, one baptism;
one God and Father of all, who is over all,
and works through all, and is in all. (Eph 4:3-6)

The body is one and has many members,
but all the members, many though they are,
are one body; and so it is with Christ.
It was in one Spirit that all of us,
whether Jew or Greek, slave or free,
were baptized into one body.
All of us have been given to drink
of the one Spirit. (1 Cor 12:12-13)

Now the body is not one member, it is many.
If the foot should say,
"Because I am not a hand I do not belong to the body,"
would it then no longer belong to the body?
If the ear should say,
"Because I am not an eye I do not belong to the body,"
would it then no longer belong to the body?
If the body were all eye,
what would happen to our hearing?
If it were all ear,
what would happen to our smelling?
As it is, God has set each member of the body
in the place he wanted it to be.

If all the members were alike,
where would the body be? (1 Cor 12:14-19)

There are, indeed, many different members,
but one body.
The eye cannot say to the hand,
"I do not need you,"
any more than the head can say to the feet,
"I do not need you." (1 Cor 12:20-21)

If one member suffers,
all the members suffer with it;
if one member is honored,
all the members share its joy. (1 Cor 12:26)

The great sin in the Body of Christ is to destroy its unity of faith and love by factions, false teaching, false standards:

Are you not aware
that you are the temple of God,
and that the Spirit of God dwells in you?
If anyone destroys God's temple,
God will destroy him.
For the temple of God is holy,
and you are that temple. (1 Cor 3:16-17)

8) The Holy Spirit Is the Life of the Church. This enlivening "soul" joins all together in oneness of love and faith. The Spirit is power and guidance. Because the Spirit lives in us, we have unshakable hope.

All who are led by the Spirit of God
are sons of God.
You did not receive a spirit of slavery
leading you back into fear,
but a spirit of adoption
through which we cry out "Abba!"
(that is, "Father").
The Spirit himself gives witness with our spirit
that we are children of God.
But if we are children,
we are heirs as well:
heirs of God, heirs with Christ,
if only we suffer with him
so as to be glorified with him. (Rom 8:14-17)

And this hope will not

leave us disappointed,
because the love of God
has been poured out in our hearts
through the Holy Spirit who has been given to us. (Rom 5:5)

. . .You were sealed with the Holy Spirit
who had been promised.
He is the pledge of our inheritance,
of a people God has made his own. . . . (Eph 1:13-14)

. . .It is [Christ] who anointed us and has sealed us,
thereby depositing the first payment,
the Spirit, in our hearts. (2 Cor 1:21)

The Spirit knows what and how we want to pray, and presents our prayer to the Father.

> The Spirit too helps us in our weakness,
> for we do not know how to pray as we ought;
> but the Spirit himself makes intercession for us
> with groanings which cannot be expressed in speech.
> He who searches hearts knows what the Spirit means,
> for the Spirit intercedes for the saints
> as God himself wills. (Rom 8:26-27)

> The proof that you are sons is the fact
> that God has sent forth into our hearts
> the spirit of his Son
> which cries out "Abba!" ("Father!"). (Gal 4:6)

9) No One Can Earn Salvation. It is entirely the gift of God. Once enlivened by God's life, we are able to cooperate with God's action in us. But, as the Christian community prays in the *Sacramentary,* "Even our desire to please you is itself your gift." This is one of the great emphases of Paul's teaching.

> . . .Your faith rests not on the wisdom of men
> but on the power of God. (1 Cor 2:5)

> It is not that we are entitled of ourselves
> to take credit for anything.
> Our sole credit is from God. (2 Cor 3:5)

> God has saved us and has called us to a holy life,
> not because of any merit of ours
> but according to his own design—
> the grace held out to us in Christ Jesus

before the world began
but now made manifest
through the appearance of our Savior. (2 Tm 1:9)

God is rich in mercy;
because of his great love for us
he brought us to life with Christ
when we were dead in sin.
By this favor you were saved.
Both with and in Christ Jesus
he raised us up and gave us a place in the heavens. . . . (Eph 2:4-6)

I repeat, it is owing to his favor
that salvation is yours through faith.
This is not your own doing, it is God's gift:
neither is it a reward
for anything you have accomplished,
so let no one pride himself on it.
We are truly his handiwork,
created in Christ Jesus. . . . (Eph 2:8-10)

10) We Are a New Creation. The world starts over in Jesus. Though we live in the midst of a sinful world and evil seems to dominate life, we are safe in eternal life. We must still experience the dying and rising of Jesus, but the victory has been won. Suffering, death, sin have no power to harm us against our will.

. . .If anyone is in Christ, he is a new creation.
The old order has passed away; now all is new!
All this has been done by God,
who has reconciled us to himself through Christ. . . . (2 Cor 5:17-19)

What you have done is put aside your old self
with its past deeds
and put on a new man,
one who grows in knowledge
as he is formed anew in the image of his Creator.
There is no Greek or Jew here,
circumcised or uncircumcised,
foreigner, Scythian, slave, or freeman.
Rather, Christ is everything in all of you. (Col 3:9b–11)

This is not just a "spiritual" re-creation. The created world itself, which we are learning to value and ceasing to abuse, is also in the redeeming love of God.

The creation waits in eager expectation
for the sons of God to be revealed.

For creation was subjected to frustration,
not by its own choice,
but by the will of the one who subjected it,
in hope that the creation itself
will be liberated from its bondage to decay
and brought into the glorious freedom
of the children of God.
We know that the whole creation has been groaning
as in the pains of childbirth
right up to the present time. (Rom 8:19-22; *New International Version*)

11) Since We Share the Dying of Christ, Our Life in Him Involves Suffering.
Jesus suffered because evil people felt the silent reproach of his pure life. While
never thinking of unfaithfulness, he nevertheless had to pay the price for being
faithful. We suffer, in Christ, the pain of dying to all that is not the love of
God: sin, selfishness, putting anyone or anything before the love of God. God's
creation is good; but the "world" is the spirit of malice and purposelessness,
says Vatican II.

Continually we carry about in our bodies
the dying of Jesus,
so that in our bodies
the life of Jesus may also be revealed.
While we live
we are constantly being delivered to death for Jesus' sake,
so that the life of Jesus
may be revealed in our mortal flesh. (2 Cor 4:10-11)

May I never boast of anything
but the cross of our Lord Jesus Christ!
Through it, the world has been crucified to me
and I to the world.
It means nothing whether one is circumcised or not.
All that matters is that one is created anew. (Gal 6:14-15)

Even now I find my joy
in the suffering I endure for you.
In my own flesh I fill up what is lacking
in the sufferings of Christ
for the sake of his body, the church. (Col 1:24)

I have been crucified with Christ,
and the life I live now is not my own;
Christ is living in me.
I still live my human life,
but it is a life of faith in the Son of God,

who loved me and gave himself for me. (Gal 2:19b-20)

12) What, Then, Is the Christian Life? It Is Love. As we have seen, God's love has been poured out in our hearts by the Holy Spirit. We are freely possessed by the presence of God. We are one with God in the love of Jesus. On this firm basis, we are able to love God as God loves us—and to show God's kind of loving toward our neighbor. Sin is a refusal to love, and a spoiling of the beautiful creation God has made.

The fact is that whether you eat or drink—
whatever you do—
you should do all for the glory of God.
Give no offense to Jew or Greek
or to the church of God,
just as I try to please all in any way I can
by seeking not my own advantage,
but that of the many, that they may be saved.
Imitate me as I imitate Christ. (1 Cor 10:31—11:1)

Owe no debt to anyone
except the debt that binds us to love one another.
He who loves his neighbor has fulfilled the law.
The commandments, "You shall not commit adultery;
you shall not murder;
you shall not steal;
you shall not covet,"
and any other commandment there may be
are all summed up in this,
"You shall love your neighbor as yourself."
Love never wrongs the neighbor,
hence love is the fulfillment of the law. (Rom 13:8-10)

Do nothing to sadden the Holy Spirit
with whom you were sealed
against the day of redemption.
Get rid of all bitterness, all passion and anger,
harsh words, slander, and malice of every kind.
In place of these, be kind to one another,
compassionate, and mutually forgiving,
just as God has forgiven you in Christ
Be imitators of God as his dear children.
Follow the way of love, even as Christ loved you.
He gave himself for us as an offering to God,
a gift of pleasing fragrance. (Eph 4:30-32)

Set your hearts on the greater gifts.

Now I will show you the way
which surpasses all the others.
If I speak with human tongues and angelic as well,
but do not have love,
I am a noisy gong, a clanging cymbal.
If I have the gift of prophecy
and, with full knowledge, comprehend all mysteries,
if I have faith great enough to move mountains,
but have not love, I am nothing.
If I give everything I have to feed the poor
and hand over my body to be burned,
but have not love, I gain nothing. (1 Cor 12:31–13:3)

Love is patient; love is kind.
Love is not jealous,
it does not put on airs, it is not snobbish.
Love is never rude, it is not self-seeking,
it is not prone to anger;
neither does it brood over injuries.
Love does not rejoice in what is wrong
but rejoices with the truth.
There is no limit to love's forbearance,
to its trust, its hope, its power to endure.
Love never fails. (1 Cor 13:4-8a)

There are in the end three things that last:
faith, hope, and love,
and the greatest of these is love. (1 Cor 13:13)

13) The Final Purpose of Life Is the Glory of God. Happiness is a by-product. We are made to love, and all love is ultimately love of God. We do not underestimate the value of human beings: They are infinitely precious to God. But our worth is a sharing in the infinite beauty of God, and we find our final satisfaction—what we were made for—in turning from ourselves to give God "glory," to praise him, to honor him. Turning from ourselves, we find ourselves, and our eternal happiness.

How deep are the riches
and the wisdom
and the knowledge of God!
How inscrutable his judgments,
how unsearchable his ways!
For "who has known the mind of the Lord?
Or who has been his counselor?
Who has given him anything so as to deserve return?"
For from him

and through him
and for him
all things are.
To him be glory forever.
Amen. (Rom 11:33-36)

To the King of ages,
the immortal, the invisible, the only God,
be honor and glory forever and ever!
Amen. (1 Tm 1:17)

10.
The Spirit Given Through Jesus

Luke wrote a two-volume work, and it is perhaps unfortunate that the pair became separated in the New Testament. His Gospel and the Acts of the Apostles were his presentation of the *one* full redeeming act of God. (I say "unfortunate" because the division may give the impression that Jesus goes back to heaven and rests in pleasant communion with the Father while the Holy Spirit now goes to work for the first time.)

The unity of God demands this: The *one* God never stops offering every single human being his life, his love, his healing and forgiveness, 24 hours a day, from the time he created the first people from the dust of the earth until the last persons are transformed from dust to eternal risen life. Even then, God's saving love does not stop. It supports his saved community forever.

Since we are human beings who can move only from moment to moment and space to space, God's saving action becomes concrete in certain historical events—primarily the earthly living, dying and victorious rising of Jesus. The full power of God's holiness, or Spirit, is unleashed—invisibly and visibly—by Jesus' death and resurrection. It is not as though God were somehow handcuffed until the moment of the resurrection. Otherwise the mere accident of being born, say in 1980 B.C., would have excluded a person from salvation.

Like the atmosphere, God's love has surrounded every human being at every moment of time. But human beings did indeed handcuff God. They refused to "let him in." (The doctrine of original sin means that the human race

69

itself turned away from God, cutting itself off *as a race* from the source of life, like a branch cutting itself off from the tree.)

So God "had" to resort to a plan that would bring about, *in human time, the whole world's reconciliation.* * This happened in Jesus' life, death and resurrection. Because of this visible, public, divine-human action, God's Spirit is now able to rush freely through the world.

An individual man or woman can still handcuff God, but every individual man and woman can, with absolutely certainty, receive God's Spirit in Jesus. (The crucial point here is that, since Jesus is no longer visible, he forms a visible body of followers to be the sacrament of the outpouring of his Spirit. We will talk more about this Body in later chapters.)

The Spirit in the Gospels. Acts has been called "The Gospel of the Holy Spirit," but the four regular Gospels also have a surprising number of references to the Spirit.

John the Baptist is filled with the Spirit in his mother's womb. So are his parents, Elizabeth and Zachary, filled with the Spirit. Mary is told that the Holy Spirit will overshadow her and, later, "she was found to be with child through the power of the Holy Spirit" (Mt 1:18).

Preparing for Jesus' coming, John promises that Jesus will baptize "in the Holy Spirit and fire" (Mt 3:11). When Jesus was baptized he saw "the Spirit of God descend like a dove and hover over him" (Mt 3:16). Jesus is then "driven" into the desert by the Spirit and returns after 40 days "full of the Holy Spirit" (Lk 4:1).

Jesus was filled with joy by the Holy Spirit. It was by the power of the Spirit, he said, that he cast out devils.

Again, at the Last Supper, Jesus continues to reveal the Spirit:

"I will ask the Father
and he will give you another Paraclete—
to be with you always. . . ." (Jn 14:16)

A paraclete is "someone called to my aid," an advocate. In court, it is my counsel or lawyer. An advocate is a helper, a comforter, defender, consoler. Jesus himself is a "paraclete" for us, but he promises to send *another:* "the Spirit of truth" who can be recognized because

---

*The Franciscan theologian John Duns Scotus (1266-1308) and his followers hold that the Incarnation was willed by God from all eternity independently of any foreknowledge of Adam's fall, simply as a manifestation of God's infinite love. In this opinion, the Son would not necessarily have come as one who was to suffer and redeem. The fact that Christ "had" to come as Redeemer was secondary in the mind of God. Scotus could not admit that the greatest good, the Incarnation, was occasioned by an inferior good, the redemption of humankind. In other words, the primary purpose of the Incarnation was to show God's love for all human beings. (Cf. *New Catholic Encyclopedia,* 4, pp. 1104-5.)

"he remains with you
and will be within you." (Jn 14:18)

The Spirit will instruct Jesus' followers in everything and remind them of all that he has told them.

But there is a condition. Jesus must "go":

"If I fail to go,
the Paraclete will never come to you,
whereas if I go,
I will send him to you." (Jn 16:7b)

Jesus must go all the way through death to resurrection, and then the floodgates are opened. Jesus will no longer be visible. The Paraclete is the presence of this apparently absent Jesus.

Finally the risen glorious Jesus breathes upon his disciples, like God breathing life into the first man, and says, "Receive the Holy Spirit" (Jn 20:21). This is not merely the life-force given to every human being at conception, this is the breathing into us of God's life. The apostles, and after them all who will, are re-created as new beings, children of God.

Pentecost. As we have seen, John has Jesus giving the Spirit on the first Easter. But Luke sets it apart as a separate event, 50 days after Easter, in the explosion of Pentecost. A miraculous transformation took place as the little Church, "gathered in one place," experienced the release of God's Holy Spirit through the power of the resurrection:

Suddenly from up in the sky there came a noise like a strong driving wind, which was heard all through the house where they were seated. Tongues as of fire appeared, which parted and came to rest on each of them. All were filled with the Holy Spirit. They began to express themselves in foreign tongues and make bold proclamation as the Spirit prompted them. (Acts 2:2-4)

When the crowd was amazed that each of the hearers could understand the apostles speaking in his own tongue, Peter tells them that this is the fulfillment of what Joel the prophet had promised:

"It shall come to pass in the last days, says God,
    that I will pour a portion of my spirit on all mankind:
Your sons and daughters shall prophesy,
    your young men shall see visions
    and your old men shall dream dreams. . . .
Then shall everyone be saved who calls on the name of the Lord."
(Acts 2:17, 21)

71

The fire of Pentecost is the fire of Sinai. God has completed the final and the greatest covenant with his people. Now the Spirit of Jesus, the Spirit of the Father, the Spirit of Love, is the spirit and life—we might say, the "soul"—of the Body called Church, the followers of Jesus. The Spirit keeps the Church alive and keeps individual Christians alive. In the words of St. Irenaeus, "Where the Church is, there also is the Spirit of God; and where the Spirit of God is, there is the Church."

'The Spirit of God Dwells in You.' What does this "giving of the Spirit" mean to us living today? Is it a magnificent spectacle that subsided like fireworks in the sky? A gift reserved for the apostles and the early Church? Or even something only for "special" people?

There has been great emphasis in recent years on certain gifts of the Holy Spirit, especially speaking in tongues, prophesying, interpretation. The charismatic movement was for a time almost identified with these things.

Now, no one tells God what to do. If the Spirit wishes to give these particular gifts to some of the faithful, the rest of us should be open to the good involved in them. These special gifts are not given for the sake of the recipients alone, but "to build up the body of Christ" (Eph 4:12). Some special gifts are obviously needed for the continuance of the Church: those given to apostles, prophets, evangelists, pastors and teachers. In a moving passage (1 Cor 12:1-11), Paul reminds us that there are many different gifts, but only one Spirit. All of us must use our unique gifts as best we can—and be happy for those who have different gifts.

But, as Paul says, we should "set our hearts on the greater gifts" (1 Cor 12:31) which are open to all and not overvalue the lesser gifts. The greatest gift is love, and he extols its excellence in 1 Corinthians 13.

We remember, then, that the primary gift of the Holy Spirit is to make each one of us *holy*. We do not achieve but rather *receive* holiness, and it is nothing to be embarrassed or falsely humble about. Holiness is the gift of God's Spirit who possesses us, silently and gently, at the slightest provocation.

First of all, our fundamental faith—not just the intellectual believing, but our personal self-giving and opening to God—is his gift: "No one can say: 'Jesus is Lord,' except in the Holy Spirit" (1 Cor 12:3).

Jesus described our life when he said,

> "If anyone thirsts, let him come to me;
> let him drink who believes in me.
> Scripture has it:
> 'From within him rivers of living water shall flow.' "
> (Here he was referring to the Spirit, whom those who came to believe in
> him were to receive. . . .) (Jn 7:38-39a)

The Spirit within us means the presence of *God* within us. St. Paul says it very simply and forcefully: "The love of God has been poured out in our hearts by the Holy Spirit who is given to us" (Rom 5:5). And the Spirit is given to us for the same reason it was given to Jesus: to make us holy.

We may be uncomfortable with being compared to Jesus. But we must always come back to the purpose of his life, death and resurrection: God emptied himself into human life so that our actual human lives may become divine. We are not called to do the same *things* Jesus did, but to do what we do with the same Spirit and spirit.

What happened to Jesus when he was baptized by John is the model of what must happen to us: We must let the Spirit lead us, "drive" us to a life of total devotion to the Father. The comfort and strength Jesus received from the Spirit in prayer is exactly the kind of comfort and strength the Spirit in us wants to give.

The full force of the Spirit—the *gift* of the Spirit, as the prayer of Confirmation says—is Jesus' final gift to us.

The Gifts of the Spirit. We must not try to "split up" the Spirit into various categories: the *particular* gifts, very special gifts for special purposes, versus *general* gifts to all Christians. The *one* God gives us divine life, presence, love, power, healing, glory. The Spirit of the one God possesses us.

Not forgetting this, we can speak of what might be called "general" gifts of the Spirit. They are not reserved for certain people—like, say, the gift of prophecy—but are open to all. Whether all are open to receive them, of course, is another matter.

Another name for these general gifts is the "seven gifts of the Holy Spirit." They are enumerated in Isaiah 11:2-3, but we should remember that the number seven in the Old Testament means completeness, fullness. This list is simply an attempt to show what the Spirit is trying to accomplish in us: wisdom, understanding, counsel, fortitude, knowledge, piety and fear of the Lord.

It is difficult to give precise definitions for these gifts: They are all expressions of the faith of our whole person, centered in our mind and will. They are "swift victory," as one book on the gifts was called, depending on the degree to which we let ourselves be "blown" by the wind of the Spirit.

All our good works are God's gift, of course, but the seven gifts might be compared to the sail of a boat. All we do is leave it hoisted; the wind does the rest. So, while even our cooperation, our "rowing," in good works is God's gift, in the case of the general gifts God simply gives us a certain ease in following the inspirations of the Spirit.

St. Paul speaks of the *fruits* of the Holy Spirit in contrast to the bitter fruits of our sin. The Spirit produces in us "love, joy, peace, patient endurance, kindness, generosity, faith, mildness and chastity." But if we abandon God's help, the result can only be "lewd conduct, impurity, licentiousness, idolatry, sorcery, hostilities, bickering, jealousy, outbursts of rage, selfish rivalries, dissensions, factions, envy, drunkenness, orgies and the like" (see Gal 5:19-23).

Because we have experienced at least the impulse to the latter in ourselves and have seen at least the appearance of them in others, we can come to appreciate how great is the gift of the Spirit. Because his fruits seem so normal and natural, we may tend to forget they can only be the gifts of God.

Our "remembering" is the gift of faith. We try to let it be wide enough and deep enough to suspect, at least, the infinite mystery that surrounds our lives. "The wind blows where it will. You hear the sound it makes but you do not know where it comes from, or where it goes. So it is with everyone begotten of the Spirit" (Jn 3:8).

Karl Rahner gives us a sense of this mystery of the Spirit: "Because God creates as God, he creates as Spirit everything in the world that is constantly new and fresh, free and alive, unexpected and mighty, at once tender and strong—the mystery of love. This is the Spirit of grace: God within us as our anointing and sealing, our pledge of heaven, our guest, comforter and advocate, the interior call, freedom and childhood, life and peace. . . .the secret power of transformation within us that presses forward to the resurrection of the glorified body" (K. Rahner and H. Vorgrimler, *Theological Dictionary*, p. 211).

11.

To Know Jesus Is to Know the Father, Son and Spirit: The Trinity

All similes limp, they tell us, and those we use for God limp the most. God as "Father" is one of them.

The idea of fatherhood is a good one, but the reality we see on earth is sometimes quite different. Some fathers abandon their children, beat them, ridicule or ignore them, damage them psychologically for life. Even good fathers have their limits. They get tired, they must often go away, sometimes they are helpless and, finally, they die.

To some people, then, the idea of God as "Father" is barren. So, for that matter, may be the notion of "Mother." But Jesus chose that word as the best way he could describe God. What we have to do, obviously, is to keep in mind only the positive qualities of fatherhood and motherhood (God is not male, of course), and forget all human limitation.

God is a father/mother who wants children more eagerly than any earthly parents ever yearned to see their love made visible in a new person. All that we associate with parenthood is infinite in God: begetting, pouring out, sustaining and protecting, guiding, encouraging. God is gentleness and strength, patience and justice. He gives birth, nurses and carries, waits and explains, lets go and welcomes back, forgives and heals.

God is *creator* and *redeemer*, to use the heavy words of theology. But the best word is still Jesus' word: *Abba*, which seems to form naturally on the lips of babies.

Someone once said that if he could remember only one verse of the Bible on that mythical island of shipwreck, it should be this:

God is love
and he who abides in love
abides in God,
and God in him. (1 Jn 4:16)

The prophets often had to warn people of God's absolute incompatibility with evil: that the consequences of their sin would overtake them and, thus, God would "punish" them. But the last word always echoed a parent's forgiveness and endless welcome. Hosea says it well:

When Israel was a child I loved him,
  out of Egypt I called my son.
The more I called them
  the farther they went from me. . . .
Yet it was I who taught Ephraim to walk,
  who took them in my arms;
I drew them with human cords,
  with bands of love;
I fostered them like one
  who raises an infant to his cheeks;
Yet, though I stooped to feed my child,
  they did not know I was their healer. (11:1-4)

Creation, an Act of Love. Science has taken all the poetry out of creation, leaving only an intricate pattern of molecules as lifeless as a clock. Genesis tells it better. The story God's inspired people composed to hold his creation in poetic grace is a masterpiece. The purpose of creation, it affirms, is the sharing of God's glory with human beings—not an abstract human race, but you and me and your Uncle Bill and old Mrs. Kim.

Take the time to make a list of all the truths contained in that simple story: the goodness of God, the dignity of man and woman, the beauty of creation, the unity of marriage, the holiness of the body, the freedom of our will, the call to responsibility and obedience, the hope for the future. . .

Why did God create us? God is infinitely happy in the "community" of Father, Son, Spirit. One of the things we must say is that he doesn't *need* us, objectively. The danger in making this necessary statement is that it may seem to make us a sort of minor hobby of God, like a million people a man might let into his stadium for a "show" while he drives off to seek his own diversion in Florida.

Lest we feel this way, God does all he can, considering human limitations, to make us feel the warmth of his love. He sends us people who are signs and sacraments of his love: loving parents first, for many of us a wife or husband, and genuine friends.

All these people give us a glimmering of the gift-and-response God wants in our personal and family relationship with him. He wants us to love him in each other, but he wants us gradually to experience a personal, intimate, conscious relationship of love with him, in Jesus and in his Spirit.

God could not make us any other way except with a built-in orientation to him. As a fish is made for water and the heart is made for love, we are made for God.

We are not "equals" with God as we are with our friends. But it is precisely in knowing the infinite grandeur of God that we discover how great our dignity is: This awesome Other is also the One within, closer to us than our own consciousness.

It is all God's initiative; yet, in the mystery of freedom, we must accept his power in order to make a response. To "seek God" is to allow ourselves to be found.

Why Suffering? We might as well face the age-old question: Why, then, is there suffering in the world? How can this good, loving God permit cruelty, sin, the senseless tragedy of the innocent?

We can "explain" suffering, of course. What God does, he does well. So, if he makes me free, he *really* makes me free. I can decide to do anything. In fact, I *must* decide what to do with my life, or I am not human. I am not forced to do either good or evil. I can search out truth and goodness and *choose* them. Or I can search out only what fattens my ego and flatters my body and *choose* these things.

Some people choose to be so selfish that others suffer. Now what is God to do? Wither the hand that is raised to strike? Deflect the bullet as it leaves the gun? Erase the vindictive or lustful decision?

Suppose God started to do that: There would be no stopping until every human being turned into a robot. And there is no love or joy in robots.

A good explanation? Yes, but don't try it on a mother holding a dead child.

God's "explanation" is the cross. Once he decided to make us free, he could not stop evil except by letting evil men stop the heart of his Son in death. This is the ultimate gift: God shows how much human suffering hurts him by coming to share it. We do not explain suffering; we conquer it by the power of the crucified and risen Jesus, the sign of a Father's tender concern.

Faithful, Just and Merciful. To the Jews, the greatest "quality" of God was not just his love, but his *faithful* love, his steadfast covenant love. No matter what unfaithfulness—adultery in their covenant relationship—they were guilty of, what pigheaded and perverse sinfulness, God was always the tender Father waiting to take them back. They knew he had to be just—it was their hope of relief for the injustice they themselves suffered. But they realized that his justice was his just-ness, his holiness, which simply could not coexist with evil. Sin could only wither away before the fire of his goodness, and the purifying fire was "punishment"—usually nothing but the logical result of their own stupidity.

But God's just-ness is his mercy. His all-knowing consciousness is not the suspicious eye of a detective, but a constant planning, if you will, how best to bring his free children to himself. His being all-powerful is simply a definition of God—he is limitless. But his power is never mere force. It is the relentless but gentle pursuit of the human heart, never intruding, but always calling.

God Is Holy. The word *holy* seems to cause us difficulty. Perhaps the difficulty arises when we try to apply it to ourselves, whereas it should be used only of God. To say God is holy is to say God is God. When the old Anglo-Saxons used the word, they meant whole, well, complete. "God is holy" means God is goodness without limit, love without limit, being without limit, etc. We cannot imagine that kind of wholeness. We do not know what it is *not* to be created, not to have a beginning, not to be limited. God's love is infinitely intense, overflowing, endless. His knowledge, power, forgiveness, justice, mercy are his love are his being are God, to imitate Gertrude Stein.

God Is One, but Triune. The New Testament has not changed the most fundamental of Jewish beliefs: "There is one God." Three gods would not be God, because one would limit the other. We all have a passion for unity because we sense that all things must go back to one source.

We come then to the same technical terms used in the case of Jesus: *nature* and *person.* God *is* one nature. His nature is to be God, divine. So in answer to the question "What?" we say, "God is the one infinite being who is the source of all being, all creation, all meaning."

But when we say "Who?" we answer, *but only because of Christian revelation,* that "God is Father, Son, Spirit—three persons in one God."

A person in this reference is obviously not an independent person such as each of us is. There are not three separate consciousnesses in God—there is only simple being, love, consciousness, life. There are not three intelligences, three wills, etc., in God.

How, then, do we explain that there is a "Trinity"—three divine persons in the one divine nature of God?

The first answer is, we don't explain it. We *believe* it because Jesus very obviously took it for granted all over the New Testament.

The traditional teaching of the Church, gradually developed, tells us that since God is one, all the creating and saving acts of God are acts of all the persons of the Holy Trinity. God is not "split up." Yet we do say that only the Son became man.

What is different about the three persons? The differences rest solely in relationships. The Father eternally "begets" the Son, though neither existed or acted before the other. This begetting is described as God's knowing himself with perfect consciousness. He expresses himself to himself perfectly, and this is the Word, the "only begotten" Son. (In a feeble comparison, we can express ourselves to ourselves. We "see" ourselves. Yet we are not two persons.)

Now, in God, everything is perfect. Therefore the perfect love that God has for himself as perfectly expressed in the Word causes another relationship. This love in God is a reality proceeding from the Father and Son, and it is called the Spirit. (Again, to use a feeble comparison, there can be a great welling up of love in us when we "see" ourselves for once divorced of all our sin and problems and precious in God's eyes, but this love does not become a separate person.)

But our words fail here. Best for us to simply use Jesus' way of speaking: We have a Father who loves us; he reconciles us to himself by giving us his Son made man; and he lives in us by the Spirit of his love. God is One, yet he is the mystery of three inner relationships.

Perhaps we can understand God best when we look into our own hearts and experience our inborn attraction to be with others. To love and forgive others is not an optional commandment pasted onto our lives to make them "nice." We are made like God, and God is, in a sense, a *community*. The very nature of God is to pour out love within his eternal life.

Meditating on the Trinity, we can say that the very nature of God is to be "with"—to know and love. God is not a solitary, lonely God, but a community of persons. If we want a final purpose for all human life, it is that we are called and enabled to "join the community." God above us (the Father) has become God with us (the Son, Jesus) and God in us (the Holy Spirit).

The Church, then, prays *to* the Father, *in* the Holy Spirit, *through* Christ our Lord. St. Paul expresses the mystery in a deceptively simple blessing: "The grace of the Lord Jesus Christ, and the love of God, and the fellowship [communion] of the Holy Spirit be with you all!" (2 Cor 13:13).

Part IV:
The Saving Work of Jesus in the World Today

12.

Jesus Living in His Members: The Church

The Church is a kind of sacrament
or sign and instrument
of intimate union with God,
and of the unity of the whole human race. . . .
Constitution on the Church, #1

Vatican II shocked some Catholics who hadn't done their history homework. They thought the Church was a tightly run ship, all orders from the captain strictly carried out, perfect discipline and order. There were obstreperous and sinful members, of course, but they were really "out," walking their own gang-plank.

Then the Church saw 2,000 bishops assembled in Rome engaging not only in dry discussion but in heated debate. A mischievous priest-reporter with the pen name of Xavier Rynne published accounts of behind-the-scenes maneuvering that would have done credit to a Democratic convention. People began to hear about a group of experts called theologians with varying and even contradictory opinions who seemed to have the ear of the bishops.

More surprising still, the bishops told the laity, "You're the Church too. Speak up!" And they did—with all the variety of Pentecost, but not always the peaceful spirit.

This variety of opinion was not really a new phenomenon in the Church, just more publicized. But this revelation of humanness in the Church made some people sad.

The greatest achievement of the Council was its *opening of the Church to the world*—Karl Rahner has called it a revolution that can only be compared to Copernicus' proving the earth goes around the sun, not vice versa—and its *deepening of the Church's consciousness of who we really are.* The Council painted a very idealistic picture. But, just as the bickering was nothing new, neither was the vision. It was a spelling out for our day of the implications of the gospel, the most idealistic document ever written. What is different, or "modern," is the open and courageous way the Church listens to all that is good in today's world and its applying the gospel to the concrete conditions of that world.

The greatest document of the Council was the *Constitution on the Church,* and it is that document we want to call upon to emphasize the heart of the matter: *The Church—all of us—is the sacrament of Christ.*

The opening words of the document could have been printed as poetry:

Christ is the Light of the world,
His radiance brightens the face of the Church!

Is that a description of the people you were with last Sunday at Mass? It is. It is, indeed, and all the sour cynicism about "hypocrites" and "I don't get anything out of it" does not change the fact. For Jesus was there, and his people were around him.

That's the greatest thing God ever had in mind for us. Certainly the Bride of Christ is not yet the unwrinkled beauty St. Paul speaks of (see Eph 5:25-27). Christ's bride gets younger, not older, and there are some blemishes that only the future will erase.

But Christ was not *visible* last Sunday. He disappeared a long time ago. Angels told his bewildered followers to stop looking up into the sky for him.

Jesus had come as the sacrament of God. If anybody wanted to know how God loved, forgave, yearned for human love, waited for erring children, all they had to do was look at Jesus. "Whoever has seen me has seen the Father" (Jn 14:9).

Jesus as sacrament was visible, touchable, hearable, flesh and blood: "an outward sign." But when you touched him or looked at his face, you touched God, you saw the radiance of divine love: "inward grace."

It hadn't been absolutely necessary for God to do this, but he wanted to be this close to us, to show our eyes as much as he possibly could.

But the sacrament disappeared. What now? Wasn't it still terribly important if not absolutely necessary that we still be able to "see" God?

It was, and Jesus took care of it. He left a new sacrament called the Church. The Church is the sacrament of Jesus just as Jesus was the sacrament of God. Jesus' radiance must shine on the face of the Church.

All the words of Jesus about the union of his people with himself, the mission of the apostles and all his followers to proclaim the Good News, the promise of his presence to the end of time, the power to forgive and heal—all his words are describing something visible, hearable, touchable: namely, that "body" of human beings whom God calls together to be the Body of Jesus.

There is no exclusiveness about this body. It is meant to include every human being on earth. Today it is a minority in the world. Perhaps it will always be. But it is an open community, lifted up among the nations to be the sign and instrument of Jesus' continuing work of salvation.

There is a momentous implication here: If Jesus said, "Philip, whoever sees me sees the Father," then the Church—that is, all who are gathered in unity around Jesus—must be able to say to the world in general and to each individual, "Whoever sees us sees Jesus."

That statement sounds arrogant, and none of us likes to say it. It's too great a responsibility, we're not worthy, etc. All beside the point. No matter how we distort his face to each other and to the world, Jesus has chosen to come visibly to the world through us. That's what Church means. We might even say Jesus can't help coming to the world through us, because he has joined his life to ours.

We have never shown Jesus to the world very well, but we have done it. Not only great saints but countless ordinary Christians, assembled for Eucharist or working in the marketplace, have brought Jesus visibly and effectively to each other and to the world. We have no choice, actually. There are no private cells in the Body of Christ where we can withdraw and enjoy private salvation. To be alone is to be a dead member.

Some people, however, scandalized by what they see as sin in members of the Church, say they can get along without the "organized" Church. They are just "Christians."

This is comparable to Jesus' saying, "My body isn't really important. My touching people, my words, my blood spilled, my flesh offered up, my risen body—forget all this and just concentrate on my 'spirit.' "

But we can't get to Jesus' spirit except through his body. To be human is to be spiritual-physical, visible-invisible. The Church is people, and people have bodies. These bodies have to *say* Christ-things, *do* Christ-things. And Christ-things are loving things, forgiving things—so the Christ-people must be a community, a called-together people, a visible body.

This opens the door to all sorts of messy failures: lying words and sneers, money-grabbing and sexual abuse, letting people starve and getting drunk. But it's the human condition. We couldn't strike each other if we had no fists, but we could not hold each other if we had no arms. There would be no slander or insults if we had no lips, but no comforting either, or sharing of feeling and need.

So Vatican II said the Church is "both human and divine, visible and yet invisibly endowed, eager to act and yet devoted to contemplation, present in this world and yet not at home in it" (*Constitution on the Liturgy, #*2).

Names for the Church

1) *The Mystical Body of Christ:* This is a concept developed by St. Paul. Christ and his followers form one Body: Christ is the Head, we are the members. All light, guidance, strength come from the Head. The Holy Spirit can be called the soul of this Body, provided we do not forget that the Holy Spirit is the Spirit of the *one* God.

Here is an attempt to picture the Mystical Body: When we receive Holy Communion, we each receive the living Jesus, body and soul, God and man. Now, imagine a whole parish, or a whole diocese, receiving Communion at the same time. Each person receives Jesus, yet only one Jesus is received in all. The one Jesus exists in all his members. He forms them into a living Body with him and with each other. Just as there is only one bread, so there is only one Body.

Each member of the Body has a function, just as in the human body. For Paul's striking application of this doctrine, see the entire Chapter 12 of 1 Corinthians; also Colossians 1:15-24 and Ephesians 4:1-16.

An amazing conclusion follows from this idea of the Church: Jesus needs us. We are the only way his hands can touch the sick or give bread to the starving. We are the only way people can see forgiveness in his eyes. Our feet are the only way he can walk the roads of modern civilization and proclaim the Good News.

2) *The Vine and the Branches.* This is Jesus' own comparison, spoken at the Last Supper (see Jn 15). The metaphor of the vine, in the sense of a supporting stem, may be a better one to express the place and function of Jesus than "head." The strong stem seems a greater support to the clinging tendrils than the head of a body, though obviously one must not be too literal. Jesus said:

"Live on in me, as I do in you.
No more than a branch can bear fruit of itself
apart from the vine,
can you bear fruit
apart from me." (Jn 15:4)

But also:

"My Father has been glorified
in your bearing much fruit
and becoming my disciples." (Jn 15:8)

3) *God's Family.* "You are fellow citizens of the saints and members of the household of God" (Eph 2:19). The greatest revelation of God is that he is *Father.* He makes us sharers in the life of his own "family" of Father, Son, Spirit. He gives us a brother, Jesus. Just as family members need and help each other, so do we. And those who need the most—the little ones, the crippled, the senile, the sick—receive our greatest care.

4) *God's Building.* Jesus was the stone that was rejected, but which turned out to be the cornerstone (see Ps 118:22). On this divine-human rock God laid the foundation—the apostles and Peter (see Mt 16:18; 1 Cor 3:11). "Through him [Jesus] the whole structure is fitted together and takes shape as a holy temple in the Lord; in him you are being built into this temple, to become a dwelling place for God in the Spirit" (Eph 2:21-22). Peter calls us "living stones" built into this temple (1 Pt 2:5).

5) *Jesus' Little Flock.* The Good Shepherd tells us, "Do not live in fear, little flock" (Lk 12:32).

"I know my sheep
and my sheep know me
in the same way that the Father knows me
and I know the Father;
for these sheep I will give my life." (Jn 10:14-15)

6) *The People of God.* Vatican II chose to emphasize this title. God makes

people holy and saves them "not merely as individuals without any mutual bonds but by making them into a single people, a people which acknowledges him in truth and serves him in holiness. He therefore chose the race of Israel as a people unto himself" (*Constitution on the Church,* #9).

The Council chose this title to emphasize the *community* aspect of the Church. It is a "fellowship of life, charity and truth" *(ibid.)*. The term *people* reminds us that we do not "join" the Church. Rather, we are called. The word *ecclesia* means "called out": The Church is the "called-together people," the assembly of God.

The Church and the Kingdom of God. The Kingdom of God is the *power of God* present to all human beings. This power offers salvation and also achieves salvation for those who respond.

God "rules" us by possessing our minds and hearts—and giving us the power to *choose* this self-surrender. God comes to us gently; we might almost say politely. He will not intrude. But, "Any who did accept him he empowered to become children of God" (Jn 1:12).

This gift of the Kingdom was given to the world in Jesus, in a way that can never be reversed. He inaugurated the Kingdom on earth, calling together a people made up of Jews and Gentiles, making them one in the Spirit.

By his death and resurrection, Jesus entered into the glory of the Kingdom, but he remains in his Church to the end of time. Then he will hand over the Kingdom to the Father, forever (1 Cor 15:24).

The Church is the initial budding forth of the Kingdom, though the Kingdom is broader than the Church. The saving power of God may be in many who have never heard of Jesus or the Father, those who through no fault of their own have no explicit knowledge of God but who sincerely seek "God," striving to do his will as it is known to them.

The Kingdom is "already" here, and it is "coming." Every day we pray, "Thy Kingdom come." The "Good News" (the literal meaning of *Gospel*) is precisely the coming of the Kingdom, finally and perfect in Jesus, then and now.

Entering the Kingdom. We have been talking about the Church as if it were a thing, something "out there." But, though God's action is primary, the Church and the Kingdom involve flesh and blood *people.* The Kingdom is for sinful people who want to be forgiven, purified and enlivened. And since everybody is more or less sinful, every human being on earth is invited.

To be a member of the Kingdom, the first essential is interior conversion, a change of heart, repentance for sin, and the determination to lead a new life.

"Born" Catholics may have trouble getting their minds around this. Converts have "conversion"; but many Christians are baptized as babies. How can there be a whole new life when one receives God's life at the beginning?

This is a real problem and there is no easy answer. What all of us must realize is that our whole life is an *endless conversion.* We are trying to become real converts. Whether or not we are baptized as babies, we must sooner or later—gradually (probably) or suddenly—come to the mind-shattering realization that Jesus is *the* Lord. We must come, as well as we can, to an Easter experience of knowing and being touched by the risen Jesus and then enter into a personal and conscious relationship of friendship-love-intimacy with him.

Most people don't think they've done this—though they probably have—in a substantial way. But we must not let this "humility" distract us from the urgent and gentle pressure of Jesus for a total self-giving.

The fundamental attitude of membership in the Kingdom is twofold: *poverty in spirit* and *whole-heartedness.*

First, members of the Kingdom are "the poor in spirit"—those nobodies drinking in the words of Jesus on the shores of the lake:

"How blest are the poor in spirit:
the reign [kingdom] of God is theirs." (Mt 5:3)

The "poor" have nothing, and they know it; so they accept everything from God. They believe Jesus when he said that only *little children* can enter the Kingdom (see Mt 18:3).

Second, members of the Kingdom have, or keep trying to receive, whole-heartedness. Jesus said, "Seek first his [the Father's] kingship over you, his way of holiness, and all these things will be given you besides" (Mt 6:33). Members of Christ base their lives on no other protection but this final saving Kingdom of God.

Nowadays someone is always telling us what something is "all about." Jesus is telling us that the Kingdom is what our life is all about.

Church: God's Ideal Made Real. The Church has plenty of problems and faults, and we must face them. But, happily, we can and must fall back on the ideal vision of the Church described in this chapter. If ever there was an impossible dream, it is the Church. God had the dream from eternity; it becomes reality in Jesus and in all who try to follow him or who, not knowing him, follow the true and the good as best they can.

At the Last Supper Jesus prayed for all who believe in him, present and future. In his prayer he described the Church:

"I have given them the glory you gave me
that they may be one, as we are one—
I living in them, you living in me—
that their unity may be complete.
So shall the world know that you sent me,
and that you loved them as you loved me." (Jn 17:22-23)

13.

Trying to Make Jesus Visible: The 'Outside' of the Church

There's a hangover from the ancient Greeks—certainly not from the biblical Jews—that still makes some people apologize for their bodies. Wouldn't it be nicer, they say, watching football mayhem on TV and munching Fritos, if we were not subject to such biological embarrassments as digestion (or indigestion), elimination, reproduction, coughing, sweating, muscle strain and ingrown toenails? Perhaps we could advance to being bionic men and women.

That same discomfort with bodily existence on a personal level gets translated into a discomfort with the *bodily,* visible, organized—and, therefore, imperfect—life of the Church: Why can't we have a Church without those "Sunday hypocrites"—a favorite harangue of non-goers. If only all Christians were like Mary and Joseph, all kids as obedient as Jesus, all popes like John XXIII (or Mother Teresa!), all bishops like the Beloved Apostle, all priests like the Cure of Ars, and all religious like Clare and Francis.

Unfortunately—rather, inevitably—we've had Peter, Judas and Ananias the liar; indulgence peddlers and popes who led armies; bishops who made Madison Avenue look shabby; priests who "ran" their parishes like Marine sergeants; and laity who have gouged the poor, stolen each other's spouses and turned the gospel over to Trappist monks.

We've had Christians—all of us, from first communicant to pope—who are more or less a scandal to each other and to the 70 percent of the world that doesn't even profess to be Christian.

Hopeless? No, just human. Not right, but understandable. We can't see the loving God directly, and he isn't always able to get through others to us or through us to others. We face imperious demands from our instinct for self-preservation and self-interest, from our feelings and flesh, from our questioning minds and restless wills. Chaucer has us right, more or less, in the *Canterbury Tales.*

If all this sounds like an apology for the Church, it is. Like every other human group, we are weak and sinful, always in need of healing, forgiveness, re-formation. As Vatican II put it: "While Christ, holy, innocent and undefiled, knew nothing of sin. . .the Church, embracing sinners in her bosom, at the same time holy and always in need of being purified, follows the endless way of penance and renewal. Christ summons the Church to continual reformation as she goes her pilgrim way. . ." (*Constitution on the Church,* #6).

The amazing fact is: God knows all about us and loves us anyway. The ironic thing is: We the sinful are called to be Jesus' instrument for healing all sin. We are, as in the title of Henri Nouwen's book, "wounded healers."

We are, as human beings, the Body of Christ—and we have an "outside" for all to see. We are part of the "scandal" of the Incarnation. Jesus took our human nature; he joined us. He is gladly "stuck" with us, and he is willing to suffer all the bad publicity we give him.

For, in spite of "the gates of hell"—that is, the power of evil—the Church, soul and *body*, is succeeding because she is the Body of Christ.

This chapter should not really be separated from the preceding one—as if the good and holy Church were the Body of Christ, and the visible, "organized" Church is really something else. There is only one Church, just as there is only one Jesus, God and man.

In order to understand why the "outside" of the Church—the visible, organized part—is important we have to ask the question: What is the Church for? The Church's purpose is to do *in flesh and blood* what Jesus did and does. Jesus is Priest. Jesus is Prophet. Jesus is King. So the Church has the commission and the power to *continue the priesthood of Jesus*—in all its members, each according to his or her vocation. The Church has the commission and the power to *continue the prophetic* (speaking for God) *work* which Jesus did and does—again, in all its members: the hierarchy in its way, the laity in its way, all in Christ's way. And the Church has the commission and the power to *continue the kingly rule of Christ*—the most problematic of the three, because it includes washing others' feet as well as "binding and loosing."

Since the laity have received a new birth of freedom from Vatican II, let's consider how they fit into this scheme first.

The Laity. *Layman* has a negative meaning, and changing to *laypersons* (peace to Gloria Steinem) doesn't help much. Even the dictionary contributes to the conspiracy. A layman is someone who is *not: not* a clergyman, or—second meaning—*not* an expert in some field.

The Council tried to counteract this notion by a fundamental statement: "All the faithful of Christ of whatever rank or status are called to the *fullness* of the Christian life and to the perfection of charity" (*Constitution on the Church,* #40). "One and the same holiness is cultivated by all" (*ibid,* #41).

In other words, there are no second-class citizens in the Church. A priest is not holier because he is a priest; a layperson is not less holy because his or her vocation is to be involved in secular affairs. We are all called to receive the one and only holiness: God's.

All Catholics learn somewhere along the line that the Church's job is to teach, sanctify and rule. This is what is meant by "sharing in the three offices of Jesus: prophet, priest, king." Now the Council reminds all laypersons that popes and bishops and priests are not the only ones who do this.

As St. Peter said, we have all been made into a "royal priesthood, a holy nation" (1 Pt 2:9). This is not a denial of the ministerial priesthood—that of ordained priests—but an affirmation of what Baptism does. The baptized *can* "offer spiritual worship." They have the privilege of being able to participate in the Mass—unlike, for instance, a non-believing spectator who happened to wander into Church.

Laypersons are prophets, not necessarily in the pulpit, but at home, at the hairdresser's, at the union meeting, at cocktail parties and funerals and rap sessions. Christ's Word comes through them in a way it may never come through bishops and priests.

Christ's kingly mission is to "subject" all to himself. But he does this not by force but by *service.* So laypersons serving their fellow human beings can lead them to the King through their humility and patience.

The Council emphasized that "a secular quality is special to laypersons. By their very vocation, they seek the Kingdom of God in temporal affairs" (*Constitution on the Church,* #31).

The laity are now exercising greater influence in the Church and taking their rightful place in ministry. Laypersons serve as religious education directors, lectors, ministers of the Eucharist, members of parish councils and members of the various committees that advise these councils.

But lay ministry is not a totally new movement. We have always had multitudes of laypersons teaching in and running Catholic schools, or being quietly prophetic in public schools; serving in parishes as ushers and members of various church societies or organizations to aid the poor; and bearing powerful witness as just plain everyday Christians living their lives in the world.

The Apostles and Their Successors. Jesus chose 12 leaders for the new Israel, the fulfillment of the promises to the 12 tribes of old. He sent them as his visible representatives, first to his own people and then to the world.

As the apostles began to die, a structure to replace them gradually developed. The New Testament names "overseers," "elders" and "deacons" ("those who serve").

In varying degrees, these three orders of ministers (bishops, priests and deacons) have the power and authority of Jesus backing them up:

"Full authority has been given to me
both in heaven and on earth;
go, therefore, and make disciples of all nations.
Baptize them in the name
'of the Father,
and of the Son,
and of the Holy Spirit.'
Teach them to carry out everything I
have commanded you.
And know that I am with you always
until the end of the world!" (Mt 28:18-20)

And in John's Gospel:

"Then he breathed on them and said:

88

'Receive the Holy Spirit.
If you forgive men's sins,
they are forgiven them;
if you hold them bound,
they are held bound.' " (Jn 20:22-23)

Sternly, Jesus described the characteristics of authority in the Church: "If anyone wishes to rank first he must remain the least one of all and the servant of all" (Mk 9:35). And, still more pointedly, at the Last Supper, he said:

"But if I washed your feet—
I who am Teacher and Lord—
then you must wash each other's feet." (Jn 13:14)

So the leaders of the Church are to proclaim the Good News, teach all that Jesus commanded, bring Jesus' forgiveness of sins and guide the Church on its way ("bind and loose")—and be servants of all. They are to make disciples by being witnesses of Jesus' power, love, forgiveness still visible in the world.

The Pope. It is evident from the Gospels that Jesus gave Peter a special place among the Twelve, so much so that one anti-papal writer has said that the "unwarranted power" of the pope began in the New Testament itself!

Jesus said to Peter alone, after his strong statement of faith in Jesus as the Messiah: "Blest are you, Simon, son of John! . . . I for my part declare to you, you are 'Rock,' and on this rock I will build my church, and the jaws of death shall not prevail against it. I will entrust to you the keys of the kingdom of heaven. Whatever you declare bound on earth shall be bound in heaven; whatever you declare loosed on earth shall be loosed in heaven" (Mt 16:17-19).

At the Last Supper, even as he foretold the denial of Peter—and thus accepted the fundamental weakness of the man (and men) in the office—Jesus said, "I have prayed for you [Simon] that your faith may never fail. You in turn must strengthen your brothers" (Lk 22:32).

Finally, after his resurrection, Jesus singled out the penitent Peter, asked him three times if he loved him, and three times commanded him to "feed my sheep" (see Jn 21:15-17).

Jesus gave a general commission of evangelization and witness to the whole Church; a special commission to the apostles; and a singular commission to Peter. He is the *visible center* around which the unity of the Church can be maintained. He is the unique feeder of the sheep, the unique source of strength for his brothers and sisters.

There have been 262 popes (the word is from the Latin *papa*, or *father*) and there will be more, because the service Peter performed is necessary until the end of time. A relative few were a disgrace (and their sins have been amply publicized!), but the great majority have served the Church and the world well. Even a world that is touchy about any kind of authority has expressed admiration for the leadership, wisdom, graciousness and service of our recent popes:

John Paul II and John Paul I, Paul VI, John XXIII and Pius XII.

The style of any one of them may not be congenial to all Catholics. They have their normal share of human weakness and temperament; they are unable to shake all the dead weight of entrenched custom. But they have done Peter's work for Christ, and they have done it well.

Papal Infallibility. While the climate of ecumenism has softened religious tensions considerably, infallibility remains an interdenominational problem, not only on the theological level—where there is hope—but also on the emotional level where our egos shout, "Nobody tells *me*."

Let us first be very clear what we are talking about when we say "infallibility."

First, infallibility certainly does not mean impeccability—that is, freedom from sin. The pope goes to confession like anyone else. And he can be as wrong as anyone else about the weather, the future of the dollar and the outcome of the Rome-Milan soccer game.

What, then, is the infallibility Catholics claim for the pope?

Let's take a look at history. We have this Spirit-guided group of people who can't wander too far off the track because Jesus has promised to remain with them and enlighten them by his Spirit. But they do manage, being human, to get picky or opinionated and back themselves into tight corners. Someone has to speak with enough authority to settle the argument, to respond to an error serious enough to throw the Church off the track. Jesus *is* truly God. Jesus *is* truly man. God does absolutely forgive our sins. And so forth.

Back in Jerusalem the primitive Church trusted the Apostles to come to some kind of agreement as to whether or not circumcision—a tremendously sacred law of the Jews—should be required of Gentile converts. Throughout history, the Bishop of Rome, usually with those of his brother bishops who could attend a Council, was trusted by the Church to settle things. The Reformation made the question of papal authority (not to mention infallibility) a burning issue. But it was not until the year 1870 that the doctrine of papal infallibility was finally defined.

The First Vatican Council said that, within the faith of the whole Church, the infallible teaching of a pope is the concrete expression of that faith *in certain very restricted circumstances.* The pope speaks infallibly when (1) he means to use his authority for the whole Church; (2) and definitely decides, as a matter of obligation of faith for the whole Church; (3) a matter of faith or morals; (4) using words which expressly say he is calling upon this power promised by Christ to Peter.

Pope Pius XII met these requirements when he defined the Assumption of Mary in 1950. The same can be said of Pius IX's declaration on the Immaculate Conception in 1854.

Notice that Vatican I spoke of the pope having "that infallibility with which our divine redeemer *willed to endow his Church* in final decisions." The whole Church is infallible in its faith. Pope John Paul II commented on this: "To believe in the infallibility of the Church does not mean—in any way—to believe in the infallibility of man, but to believe in the gift of Christ; in that gift which allows fallible men to proclaim infallibly and to confess infallibly the truth revealed for our salvation!"

How would any pope exercise this function? He is obliged to do what every other human being must do: exercise the virtue of prudence. With the utmost intensity he must use all human means of discovering the true faith of the Church, by study, prayer, consultation, deliberation. He does not receive any private revelation. He does not take a Gallup poll, but neither dare he ignore the long tradition of faith in all the members of the Church. He teaches them, but also makes concrete what is already their fundamental belief.

It is also the teaching of the Church that the *whole body of bishops, in union with the pope,* can exercise infallibility in teaching. Such teaching would normally take place in Church councils. But Pius XII defined the Assumption of Mary apart from a council.

It is necessary to begin the discussion of infallibility with all these if's, and's and but's because of the controversial nature of the doctrine. We begin like lawyers, which is fine; but we must end the discussion as believers. We will never "prove" infallibility to be true in a debate. Protestant and Catholic theologians are meeting each other to discuss the subject in charity and honesty, and that is the best hope we have.

But Catholics believe that the positive side of infallibility is the Holy Spirit, who can not be tied down in lawyers' or theologians' language. We simply presume that the Spirit of Jesus fills the Church, head and members, and illumines the faith of all.

The infallibility of the Church is something positive and beautiful; something to be thankful for.

Magisterium. Obviously there is another kind of teaching which does not fall within the strictly defined area of infallibility. This is called the "ordinary teaching" (magisterium) of the Church. In our day this will usually be found in papal encyclicals (letters to the whole Church on important matters). In recent decades, for instance, great emphasis has been placed on social justice in encyclicals from Leo XIII (*Rerum Novarum*) to Paul VI (*Progress of Peoples*). Paul VI also issued an important encyclical, *Humanae Vitae* (Human Life), which stated the Church's teaching on sexual morality in marriage.

Dissent. *Humanae Vitae* serves to focus on an agonizing problem that has arisen for many Catholics, one which cannot be swept under the rug. Usually the problem is seen as a conflict between two obligations: What, then, if a Catholic in good conscience—that is, after prayer, consultation and serious deliberation—is unable before God to assent to an ordinary teaching of the Church, such as on contraception? (This supposes that he or she has tried to be as open as possible to the teaching, has respected its weight and reasoning, its widespread acceptance, its history.)

The Catholic in these circumstances assumes the serious responsibility of humble dissent. Obviously we are not talking about mere whim, or self-serving

91

narrowness, or, still less, sinful stubbornness. The agonizing nature of such decisions is often the fear of being guilty of precisely these faults. But it must be said that dissent in clear conscience is possible. In their commentary on *Humanae Vitae*, the American bishops took note of this real possibility. Archbishop John Quinn of San Francisco brought the matter into the open at the 1980 Synod in Rome. (See also Chapter 22.)

Bishops. Except for infallibility, a bishop is for his "church" or diocese what the pope is for the whole Church. A bishop cannot function apart from the Church and the pope, of course, but he is not merely a delegate or helper. He is one of the successors of the Twelve, an authentic teacher of faith, the sign and center of unity in his diocese. He is not independent of the rest of the Church, or its faith and law, but he is the "local Apostle."

Catholics do not belong just to the worldwide Church; they belong to a "local Church," which refers primarily to a diocese: the Church of Denver or Pittsburgh, Sioux Falls or Santa Fe. Any community around an altar under the ministry of the bishop is a symbol of the oneness and the love of the Body of Christ. Vatican II says, "In these communities, though frequently small and poor, or living far from any other, Christ is present (*Constitution on the Church*, # 26).

Like the pope, the bishop exercises the priestly, prophetic and kingly office of Christ. He cannot be in every church of the diocese, but "every legitimate celebration of the Eucharist is regulated by the bishop" (*ibid.*).

The bishop of a diocese is assisted by a presbyteral council, or a priests' senate. He is responsible for not only the spiritual but also the temporal welfare of the diocese. Like the pope, he must delegate some functions to others.

Priests are assistants to the bishop. They too are meant to be centers of unity and charity in the ultimately "local" community where the "whole" Church is present when the Eucharist is offered. We will consider their office in the chapter on the Sacrament of Orders (Chapter 21).

Laws of the Church. All societies have laws. Families have rules and regulations (in by midnight, no snacks before dinner, homework before TV). The purpose of law, including the law of the Church, is to guide people to a common goal. Law safeguards the rights and privileges of each person. Law also directs people to their duties and obligations.

The body of Church law is called Canon Law. Just as family rules change when circumstances change, so do the laws of the Church. The most recent update of Church law occurred in 1983.

Many Catholics were shocked when Pope Paul VI repealed the law of Friday abstinence for much of the year. (They should have read the whole document, which was a restatement of the continual need of all Christians for penance.) They had equated this Church law—made by the Church and therefore changeable by the Church—with the law of God.

On the other hand, one sometimes hears Catholics speak of some laws of God as "Church rules" which should be changed. When the Church presents its teaching on abortion or contraception or divorce, it is not pushing its own regulations, but what it believes to be the law of God. Pope Paul did not ban contraception the way the Senate bans TV in its chambers. Rather, he saw the law of God demanding certain conclusions.

Like it or not, the Church is not a democracy. It is a visible community with a visible head. The pope is neither a dictator nor a counter of opinions. Like any prudent person he must listen to anyone who can help him come to awareness and insight; but he is the single leader who must uniquely serve all.

Who Belongs? We learned a new word from Vatican II: *ecumenism.* Strictly speaking, it refers only to the movement toward unity among Christians. But the spirit of Vatican II also reached out in welcome to non-Christians.

The Council said, first, that the unique Church of Christ *subsists* in the Catholic Church, although holiness and truth can be found outside her visible structures. In some real way, all Christians are joined with Catholics by the Holy Spirit, whose gifts and graces are given to all the baptized. Therefore, those who "believe in Christ and have been properly baptized are brought into a certain, though imperfect, communion with the Catholic Church" (*Constitution on the Church,* # 15).

The bishops of Vatican II also recognized others related in various ways to the People of God. First, the Jews, "the people to whom the covenants and the promise were given. . . .This people remains most dear to God." Next, the Moslems, who "along with us adore the one and merciful God who on the last day will judge mankind" (*ibid.,* #16).

The term *anonymous* Christian is not used, but the Council did say, "Nor is God himself far distant from those who in shadows and images seek the unknown God, for it is he who gives to all men life and breath and every other gift, and who as Savior wills that all men be saved." Further, "those also can attain to everlasting salvation who through no fault of their own do not know the gospel of Christ or his Church, yet sincerely seek God and, moved by grace, strive by their deeds to do his will as it is known to them through the dictates of conscience. Nor does divine providence deny the help necessary for salvation to those who, without blame on their part, have not yet arrived at an explicit knowledge of God, but who strive to live a good life, thanks to his grace" (see *Constitution on the Church,* # 16).

And most importantly, returning to those who belong to the *visible* body of the Church: "He is not saved, however, who, though he is part of the body of the Church, does not persevere in charity" (*Constitution on the Church,* # 15).

The greatest ecumenism, and the greatest witness to the genuineness of the Church, always rests on Jesus' words:

"This is how all will know you for my disciples:
Your love for one another." (Jn 13:35)

Love within the Church cannot be held within its visible boundaries. The simple love its members display is the greatest apology for their faults and the strongest argument for the unity Christ desires.

14.
Jesus Worships in His Church:
Eucharist, the Radiating Center

What does it mean to talk about "the international situation," "the state of the economy" and "unemployment levels"? Certainly the last phrase would mean more if you were out of a job! But even then you would want to hear about the actual *persons* who are causing *your* unemployment or who are working to relieve it.

We can't communicate without abstracting. It's a great gift to be able to look at a hundred trees and know what "tree" is. But if we get lost in talking about "treeness" and never look at a living, breathing *tree,* we are missing the real world.

So also it is necessary and helpful to talk about "grace" and "the supernatural" and the "the sacraments." But we must beware of making them *things* existing by themselves. Going to confession to "get more grace" can have beautiful meaning; it can also sound like gathering some extra gold bars.

"The sacraments" can be a phrase that escapes reality, too. A sacrament can seem like a stereo system. "It" is all there waiting, plugged in to 110 volts, needing only a human hand to press a button, insert a tape, adjust dials. One can then leave the room and "it" will play by itself.

In order to de-emphasize this almost unavoidable view, I would like to begin our consideration of the sacraments by talking about actual living persons acting together, consciously and faithfully. After we have made their experience our own, we can speak about "what" all "sacraments" "do."

Eucharist in the Ideal Church. Forty, or 1,000, or five people smile at each other as they take their places around a simple altar. A woman has lost her husband during the past week, and those near her embrace her silently, one by one. A baby cries, an old man is helped forward and given a seat next to the altar. A priest who has been moving through the group stands at the altar, and silence falls. After a minute or two, he extends his arms as if to hold us all and says, "Father, we thank you for calling us together to praise you with Jesus.

94

We thank you for bringing us again to his saving death and resurrection and for renewing your Spirit in us. Nourish us again, heal the wounds of our sin, deepen our love and forgiveness for each other. Open our hearts, now, to your living Word. We pray through Jesus our Lord."

The whole group answers "Amen!" and looks expectantly to a young man who goes to the altar, reverently picks up a Bible and reads slowly and confidently. Again a relaxed silence falls.

A woman sings a short refrain, "This is the day the Lord has made," and we repeat her words. Then she sings, softly at first, several stanzas of a psalm: "I will bless the Lord at all times. . . ," pausing a little between verses. The group sings the refrain after each verse.

The Gospel is Jesus' words about the seed that must die in order to bear fruit. After its proclamation, the priest sits down, leans forward and seems unable to find words. Then he looks all around him and says, "When John died last week, we sang with hope, because he had loved and prayed with us, and we knew his lifelong willingness to be joined to Jesus' death and resurrection. Today, Jesus asks us again to continue our dying and rising. He gives us power to die to everything that is not his work and to rise in faith and hope and love to be with him. This is his gift to us. We offer it, in him, to the Father."

A husband and wife bring bread and wine to the altar. The priest prays that they may become the body and blood of Jesus.

"Lift up your hearts!" And the answer comes, strongly, "We have lifted them up to the Lord!"

"Let us give thanks. . ."

The "Holy, Holy" rises joyfully. The simple words of the Eucharistic Prayer go on: "Let your Spirit come upon these gifts. . . . Take this, all of you, and eat it. This is my body which is given up for you." The eyes of all are as one, piercing the bread. "The cup of the new covenant is my blood. Drink it, all of you." There is a little pause. Our heads bow with Jesus on the cross, and we see his face radiant with Easter glory.

"Christ will come again!" The last words are prolonged, as if no one wants to part with them.

"Father, we offer you Jesus, we offer ourselves in Jesus' childlike trust and obedience. Bring us closer together with him and with each other, so that we may be the one Body and show your kindness to the world.

"Bless all your people, who span the earth making you visible under our earthly father, the pope, and our bishop. Take to yourself brothers and sisters who ate at this table and have gone through the veil in faith. And make us, gathered here, worthy to be with Mary and all your children who are gathered with you, in Jesus.

"It is through him and with him and in him that we who are one in your Spirit can offer you this perfect gift of honor and glory."

"Amen! Amen! Amen!" We sing our faith. Yes, that is what we want: to be the one Body, each concerned for every member, always dying with Jesus, always rising, joyful in offering his trust, his obedience, his worship.

He taught us to pray. Children around a table, we call to our Father and bless his name. The bread we ask for, the nourishment that will keep us alive forever, already lies before us. "Save us, in the great trial."

The loaf is broken, a piece for each person present. The body is not broken, but shared. Its separate pieces come together in the bodies and spirits of all present, making us the living Body. It is a fearful responsibility, a divine generosity. We sing our faith, our love for each other, our trust, and our joy.

Then it is over, quickly, and we go back—perhaps to our cells in a Roman prison, or to the kitchen for coffee and cookies, or home for breakfast. The Mass is over, the Mass has just begun. The pain of dying and the assured peace of rising thread our days.

What Happened? There are people who are irked at idealistic presentations. Better to be practical. What really happens to all those people who crowd into churches on Sunday? What kind of books do they need? When does one stand, sit, kneel? When is it a mortal sin to miss? How close together can we schedule Masses and be sure the parking isn't a mess?

Thank God for practical people. They save their communities from buying mythical oil wells in Zanzibar, from attempting Handel's *Messiah* at the 7:30 a.m. Mass and from trying to build a church with local elm trees.

But there is no need to apologize for the idealistic. We are personally involved in an event that reaches far beyond idealism. We are part of a divine action. We don't go to Mass to watch, but to act. And *our* acts are the least: God acts first, right now, in Jesus. To be very practical, we shouldn't miss the point.

Live and in Person. We have seen what Jesus *did:* lived, died, rose. What does he *do* now, today? At this Mass?

The Jews cherished a saying which shows what a liturgical-sacramental celebration does: "Not with our fathers did he make this covenant, but with us, all of us who are alive here this day" (Dt 5:3).

They certainly weren't denying what God had done in the past. They were saying that the past is present. God acted back there in history. But there is no "back there" with God. There is only *now.*

When Jesus said, at the Last Supper, "Do this in memory of me," he was not inviting a sort of wistful remembering of something long ago, like pleasantly basking in the memory of a childhood picnic or of a kindly doctor, long since dead, who saved our life.

Jesus does not die and rise at each Mass. Calvary and Easter are not repeated. Rather, his one sacrifice and victory is made present—we are brought into union with it, time is annihilated. As the Mass is repeated throughout history, this happens to more and more people at more and more times.

At the Easter Vigil, one light is struck from flint in the darkness. This symbolizes the resurrection. Then the flame runs through the church as through stubble, as all the candles of the people are lighted from the one source. *It is one fire.*

Fire is a good word here. We may tend to think of "presence" as some-

96

thing factual, impersonal, dead. All the kids may be "present" in class on the day of the first snowfall, but their eyes are on the window. Two people can be seated at the same table and cut off from each other. In the room where you are, chairs and pictures and lamps are present, but they are not present *to* you.

It is the living risen Jesus, raised above all human limitations and pain, who is present with us: not like a visiting official, but as our closest friend; not impersonally, but sharing an intimate meal; not condemning, but forgiving.

This Jesus, eternal God and our brother, shows us the heart of Calvary and Easter through his attitude, his spirit, his trust, obedience, generosity, total love of the Father. Eucharist is to make us, as a Body and as individuals, *like him.*

Lord, Save Your People. Jesus does not save us as individuals, but as members of his Body. We are not just *people*—unconnected and isolated arms and legs—but we are *a people,* in fact, *the* people of God.

God saves the world by undoing Babel, which happened when *a people* became just *people,* all doing their own thing. They did not love each other so they did not love God. They did not love God, so they did not love each other. Babel babbles—no communication because no community.

"God in Christ was reconciling the world to himself" (2 Cor 5:19). The whole world is meant to be one family in Jesus. Jesus came to bring all of us "into the circle," which is what re-concile means. (We pull our chairs back from the circle; we don't want any part of the meeting. We're not interested in *them,* just in ourselves. Jesus reforms the circle, inviting us to pull up a chair again.)

In the first burst of enthusiasm after Pentecost, we find an "ideal" Christian community—a model, so to speak, of Jesus' whole purpose. As Luke reports in Acts: "The community of believers were of one heart and one mind. They devoted themselves to the apostles' instruction and the communal life, to the breaking of bread and the prayers. A reverent fear overtook them all, for many wonders and signs were performed by the apostles. Those who believed shared all things in common; they would sell their property and goods, dividing everything on the basis of each one's need" (4:32-34).

(There's no denying some troubles in that community. The selfishness of Ananias and Sapphira (see Acts 5:1-2) pops up today, too. But this is still the authentic picture of Church.)

God calls his people together. *Ekklesia,* the Greek word from which we get English words pertaining to Church (for example, *ecclesiastical*), meant an assembly of citizens called together by the town crier. We do not "go" to Church, as if it were our idea. We are privileged to be called. We have received an urgent message from the King.

Jesus makes us into his people, again and again. But he doesn't start "from scratch" each time. At our initiation into the Church, we are brought into an already existing community, the Body of Jesus. The Mass is the expression of a love already existing among us, nourishing and reconfirming that love. And as we visibly converge on the altar, like spokes of a wheel, we "make" the visible Jesus today, his Body. Only he can give us the power to love and forgive each other, and as we do that together at Eucharist, we discover he is in our midst.

The Last Supper. Jesus has consciously and willingly accepted his death. He has deliberately come to Jerusalem to die. It is his choice, the final, perfect giving of himself to the Father. Now, before the agony begins, he celebrates his death and resurrection in the family meal his people have celebrated for a thousand years.

His spirits are high. In a few hours, the coming horror will rise to the surface, and he will shrink into the earth at Gethsemane. But now he says, "I have greatly desired to eat this Passover with you before I suffer" (Lk 22:15).

Passover is the most sacred time in the Jewish year. At the meal, a child ritually asks, "Why is this night different from all other nights?" The answer is a grateful recalling of the greatest moments of Jewish history—till now.

When they were slaves in Egypt, God gave the Jews a special meal: an unblemished lamb. Some of its blood was to be put on their doorposts; then they were to eat the lamb with loins girt, sandals on their feet and staff in hand, like those who are in flight (see Ex 12:11).

The angel that struck the firstborn of the Egyptians "passed over" the homes marked with the blood. Then God led his people out of slavery—the Exodus, the escape, the way out, the rescue—and brought them to the desert. He fed them with manna. And on a sacred day at Mount Sinai, he ratified a new covenant with his people: "If you keep my covenant, you shall be my special possession, dearer to me than all other people. . . .You shall be to me a kingdom of priests, a holy nation" (Ex 19:5-6).

Moses offered the sacrifice that ratified the covenant in a dramatic liturgy. Taking the blood of animals, he poured half onto a stone altar which represented God. Then he sprinkled the other half on the people saying, "This is the blood of the covenant." Blood meant life: By God's gracious gift, his life was joined to the life of his people.

Now the Lamb of God is about to pour out his blood on the altar of the Cross. In an amazing irony, the hateful wish, "Let his blood be on us and on our children!" (Mt 27:25), will come true. The New Moses will pour his own life-giving blood out of his crucified body to give his life to his people.

Jesus carefully follows the Passover ritual. But when the time comes to eat the unleavened bread, he speaks words never heard before: "Then, taking bread and giving thanks, he broke it and gave it to them, saying, 'This is my body to be given for you. Do this as a remembrance of me.' He did the same with the cup after eating, saying as he did so: 'This cup is the new covenant in my blood, which will be shed for you'" (Lk 22:19-20; also see Mt 26:26-28; Mk 14:22-24; 1 Cor 11:23-26).

The constant faith of the Church has always taken the words of Jesus literally. "It has always been the conviction of the Church," said the Council of Trent, that there is a "marvelous and extraordinary change of the whole substance of the bread into Christ's body and the whole substance of the wine into his blood, so that only the species [external appearances] remain." Or simply: What was bread and wine is now Jesus.

But the meaning is essential to the fact. The Last Supper made present the reality of Calvary and Easter even before they happened in time. The body that would die and be glorified, the blood that would become the life of his people, already lies in the hands of the disciples and touches their lips. Jesus is irrevocably committed to his death and resurrection. The Eucharist of the ages is already before the Father.

In the same way our Eucharist is Jesus' making present the fact and the meaning of his death and resurrection. It is always, as it was then, a new Exodus, led by a New Moses. It is a new and transformed Passover meal, a holy sacrifice uniting God and his people. It is the new and perfect covenant, eternal and unshakable.

The Transformation of the Community. It is not just bread and wine that is changed. *We* are changed, transformed/purified, enlivened. It may not always be possible to feel the fire that runs through the assembly, but we must be open to its transforming power.

Jesus certainly doesn't want a group of bored "disciples" standing outside the door while he goes in and makes arrangements for our release. We're not just getting out of prison; we're getting out of human slavery to evil, untruth, greed, lust, cruelty, mindlessness, boredom. We're being rescued from human suffering.

But this process is not merely negative. There's no way we can be forgiven without being made more human. So Jesus has to make us human—loving, thirsting for truth and wisdom, open, forgiving—in order to have something to "sacrifice" to the Father in authentic worship.

Jesus, of course, is the perfect Adorer of the Father. But the only criterion of how I love God is the way I treat my neighbor. So the sign of true adoration is true community. Jesus can only be our "Amen" to God if we join his "Amen" as sincerely loving brothers and sisters.

In a certain community of priests, a maverick homilist once said, "We do not dare to continue this Mass if we don't intend to stop treating each other like strangers!"

One Loaf, One Cup. In an ancient Eucharistic hymn, the first Christians prayed: "Just as this bread which was once scattered grains on the hillside has been gathered into one loaf, so may the Church be gathered into one Body" (Didache).

Like the gathered grain is the one cup of wine, the product of many grapes. Wine is the symbol of festivity and fellowship. We are nourished, but we are also delighted.

Bread and wine—it is the meal of the deathly poor, indeed, but also the banquet of the children of God, a foretaste of the eternally happy table of the Messiah: "Taste and see how good the LORD is" (Ps 34:9).

A Holy Sacrifice. The popular notion of sacrifice centers on giving up something valuable; often it has a note of penitential discipline. But the understanding of sacrifice in the Bible—and in early Christian theology—centers on the literal Latin meaning of the word: to make holy.

St. Augustine's definition of sacrifice was "every work done in order to achieve unity with God in holy communion." St. Thomas Aquinas says that the suffering of Christ is a sacrifice precisely because it is the expression of his love for us and for his Father. Sacrifice is primarily a matter of the heart and involves total self-offering. And Jesus was wholly open in love to his Father.

So the Mass is the one perfect sacrifice in the world. Jesus offers himself—and we are offered with him. Sacrifice is the way Jesus makes us holy. By his blood we have divine life.

The Mass is both meal and sacrifice. Jesus is both priest and victim—if we remember that the meaning of the latter word is "set apart, holy." The whole purpose of his sacrifice is to unite us with him. Paul says, "I have been crucified with Christ, and the life I live now is not my own; Christ is living in me" (Gal 2:19-20).

Jesus makes us holy by standing before us and saying, "I hand you my life. I hand you this bread and wine to be your life. I want you to know what it is to die that others may live."

Christ Will Come Again. At the beginning of this chapter we spoke of an ideal Mass. This straining toward the best is implicit in the Eucharist: We are—perhaps unconsciously—straining toward the Kingdom in its perfect fulfillment, the way it will be in heaven. Heaven begins on earth, in the union of Jesus and his people. We are already the community of the faithful joined to the heavenly Eucharist Jesus celebrates with all who have gone before us in faith. They are gathered around the Father in happiness—and we are that same gathering. When Jesus spoke of himself as Bread of Life, he said,

"If anyone eats this bread
he shall live forever." (Jn 6:51)

Forty, or 1,000, or five people smile at each other as they leave the altar to become a widening circle of Jesus' presence in the world. They go back to their cells in Buchenwald, strengthened and peaceful against the day of their being offered up; back to the kitchen for coffee and klatsch; back to a thousand homes where life will have hope and courage and dignity.

"Follow the way of love, even as Christ loved you. He gave himself for us as an offering to God, a gift of pleasing fragrance" (Eph 6:5:2).

15.
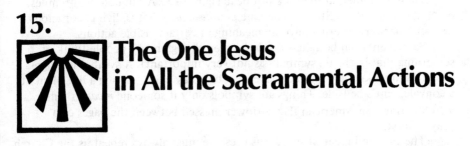
The One Jesus in All the Sacramental Actions

The Eucharist as discussed in the last chapter can be taken as a model of all the other sacramental actions of the Church: Baptism and Confirmation, Reconciliation and Anointing of the Sick, Marriage and Orders.

For a working definition, which will be expanded, let us say that the sacramental actions of the Church are visible signs of God's saving love. Jesus "makes" these signs by means of his community, the Church. Faith-filled entrance into these signs is the means of salvation and holiness of individuals and, therefore, of the community.

God Alone Brings Us to the Altar. Our human tendency is to congratulate ourselves on the great things we do for God—such as faithfully going to Mass on Sunday. The fact is, we could not approach or partake in the Eucharist if we were not invited and empowered by God. Our covenant-friendship with God is his gift, not our achievement.

We have the privilege of being born again into God's own life. "Going to confession" is possible only because God calls to us. Christian marriage is God's special consecration, not merely something comparable to what a justice of the peace can effect.

God Acts in Jesus. Recall the tremendously important fact that Jesus is the Sacrament of God. In him we see God in human flesh. We know what God is like by looking at Jesus, by listening to him.

But Jesus is no longer visible. So he gave the world the *sacrament of Jesus,* his visible Body, the Church—a group of people *who do what he did,* not just in imitation, but with his power acting through them. They continue his saving actions today.

Each Christian around the altar represents Jesus in a unique way. The priest has been given the vocation of representing Jesus as the Head and Center, a visible center around which the Church can gather. Every man and woman and child there, by Baptism, is a sharer in Jesus' priesthood, enabled and called to full, conscious and active participation.

If sacramental life begins to pall from repetition, faith can revive the astounding fact at the center: Jesus meets us personally and applies now, through his Spirit, the healing and enlivening power of his death and resurrection.

Jesus Acts Through Signs. The traditional definition of sacraments is that they are "outward signs of inward grace instituted by Christ."

These sacramental signs are not dead signs, like "Albuquerque, 46 miles," or "Luebering's Paint Store." They are *people-signs*—that is, living, conscious, faith-full persons entering into the meaning of certain visible actions.

Sacraments can be called *symbols* (even though many people think of something that is "just a symbol" as not very important). A symbol is a sign-with-feeling: a kiss, an embrace, sharing a birthday cake, putting a live plant at a convalescent's bedside. Things are symbols only if someone *means* them: wedding rings, an American flag, a flower pressed between the pages of a prayer book.

The first and greatest sign Jesus uses, we must always repeat, is the Church gathered in faith and love. Within this fundamental sign, however, Jesus and his Church chose other signs. First, in the Eucharist, Jesus chose the oldest "natural sacrament" of the human race—a family meal. For Baptism, there is water, the symbol of cleansing and, more importantly, of life and death—we cannot live without it but we can drown in it. Anointing with oil suggests the suppleness and strength of athletes' muscles as well as the healing ointments put on the bodies of the sick. Hands laid on people in Orders is a kind of embrace, showing the desire to share power, love, healing. The vows of bride and groom are the sign of their lifelong and exclusive commitment to each other.

Why Seven? Every person, every action, every thing in the world can be a sign, a symbol and a "sacrament." Words are symbols. Emily Dickinson speaks of the "sacrament of summer days." Every Christian is called to be a sacrament of Jesus' love and healing today.

The seven sacraments, however, are the events in which the *crucial moments of salvation history* are brought to bear on *critical situations in our lives:* in the Eucharist, a summing up of all salvation; in Baptism, birth; in Confirmation, facing up to responsibility; in Penance, the terrible human need for forgiveness; in Anointing, facing the inherent weakness of the body; in Marriage, the forming of the essential building block of society; in Orders, the need for a center of unity and proclamation of Jesus' words.

One final purpose of a determined set of visible signs as we have in the seven sacraments is this: *We can be sure.* Of course we know God loves us—as you might "know" your spouse or friend loves you. But if he or she gives no external sign of love—if there were never any word or touch or gift or smile— you would conclude there is no love. Once deeply loved, we may be able to go on if we are forced into loneliness or isolation. But just being human means we need to be *reassured* all the time.

The signs of God's love made by his community in the sacraments are absolute assurances of God's love. I am absolutely certain God welcomes me at the Eucharistic table or forgives my sin because his Church does.

We may get some idea of the assurance of the sacraments by recalling an expressway trip. We are fairly sure we're on I-75. We saw the sign when we started. We couldn't have missed a turn, could we? But there hasn't been a sign for a long time . . . ah, there's one—I-75!

But this is a mere "dead" sign. Sacramental actions are living signs, like embracing, holding someone's hand, comforting a sick child. They "contain" human and divine action and feeling.

Sacraments Demand Community. The Church is never so much the Church as when it is gathered together for the liturgy. In fact, that is the only time one can find the Church, otherwise it is invisible, merged with the world.

We have already stated many times that the community of the Church makes Jesus visible. What needs to be stressed, further, is the presence of the community for the celebration of *all* the sacraments.

Sometimes only a priest can be present to an individual for the sacramental action—a lonely sick person, the only person who comes to confession. Or the Baptism of a baby may be attended only by two sponsors. These circumstances may be unavoidable, but they are not the normal way the Church should act. A genial priest may be able effectively to communicate a whole parish's welcome. But in any case it is the whole community's love that is to be made visible.

In Baptism, the *whole* parish—at least the part represented by all who are, say, at one of the Sunday Masses—welcomes the new member. In Confirmation, those who have already given witness in the Spirit—and perhaps have some scars to show for it—add their own "confirmation" to that of the Spirit. In Penance, the sinner is joyfully received back by a community which continues the forgiving spirit of Jesus; in Anointing, at least family, friends and neighbors represent the great community of the Church which asks the sick person to join his or her suffering to the ongoing dying and rising of Jesus. In Marriage, the community is happy to see a new "little church" beginning and promises its support and encouragement. At an ordination, the congregation welcomes one sent to proclaim the Word to them.

The spirit and attitude of priest and all the other members of the community is very important. A listless priest and/or a bored community can make the individual sacramental actions look like magic, mumbo jumbo. If a number of individuals happen to coincide at Mass, but show no interest in each other, they certainly do not give the "sign" of the loving Jesus continuing his work. If a priest is mechanical with a penitent, if the parish shows no interest in a new baby's Baptism or a young couple's marriage, the impression can be given that something merely official or magical happens.

A word must be said here about a phrase that has caused a lot of misunderstanding about sacraments: *ex opere operato.* This means that the worst priest in the world, provided he has at least a minimum intention of exercising his priesthood, cannot *stop* the love of God coming to his people through sacramental actions. In other words, the *worthiness* of the minister is not an essential factor. However, the sign-value of the minister and the worshiping community is important if the fullness of God's saving action is to be experienced.

It is the ongoing community which makes possible sacramental action. We do not start "from scratch" every Sunday. We come to *express* the faith and love which God has already developed within us; and we come to be *renewed and strengthened* in that life. Hence the sacraments are both causes and effects. A celebrating community is alive when it comes and more alive when it disperses. In all the sacramental actions—not just Eucharist—unity and charity are of the essence.

God Speaks. An important new emphasis in sacramental celebration is the reading of God's Word. This was always done at Mass, of course, and at Anointing. Now it is an integral part of the other sacraments as well.

For instance, readings similar to those in the Liturgy of the Word at Eucharist are now part of communal penance celebrations. Even at the reconciliation of just one penitent, a reading from Scripture is to be made. Why?

It is a reminder, at least, that *we* are not the prime movers. This is God's sign, and God wants to tell us the *meaning* of his signs. God's initiative is heard in his Word. God's gentle assurance, or his unavoidable warning, are part of his call.

'Inward Grace.' Grace is at the heart of Christianity, and should be as clearly understood as anything divine—and therefore mysterious—can be.

First of all, grace is not an "it," even though we refer to "it" that way. There is no such thing as "grace" stored in a vast heavenly container, from which God sends out various "amounts." It is a shame that we human beings think of grace that way, because we thereby reduce "it" to a measurable commodity like money or ice cream.

Grace is actually the loving God offering himself to us in a relationship of friendship. God offers us a sharing in his own life, whereby our love becomes possessed by divine love, and our consciousness (faith) by divine wisdom. God's grace is not something separate from God, as a person's gift is separate from the person. Grace is God calling us into his own intimate life— not just to any kind of relationship but into his very nature. Grace is God personally coming to us. This God-life is hidden now (though its effect, in good people, is beautiful to behold). But someday it will blossom into face-to-face vision and union with God.

The "it" problem comes from the fact that we speak of grace as the *result* of God's coming—our accepting the relationship, our "allowing" God to enter into our lives. (But even this is God's doing. As the Sacramentary says, "Even our desire to please you is your gift.") From this viewpoint, then, we think of grace as something "in" us. Yet it is not a something so much as a *quality* of our being. It is God giving us the power to be united with him, the power to choose to accept and continue a loving relationship. Truly, grace enables us to be "born again" into a "new" life infinitely superior to mere human life.

In Jesus, we have unparalleled grace. That is, *as man*, he allowed himself to be totally possessed by his Father's love. His very food was to do the Father's will. He was totally graced. He was the primary sacrament of God's gracious loving.

Each sacramental action means the pouring out of the one love of God in accordance with the particular purpose of that sacrament. The sacraments separate out the one love of God into its various aspects like a prism separates light into the colors of the rainbow. So we see the one love of God as life-giving, healing, reconciling, strengthening, enabling.

But we must not make the sacraments the only source of God's grace. These are the peak moments, the high points in the Christian community's life. They are moments, as it were, of *visible* grace, of *assured* grace. But God simply loves all people *all the time.* As Gregory Baum has well said, the first means of grace is life. Every moment, every person, every situation is a kind of sacrament. Coming through each one is God's offer of strength, God's reassurance, God's call to truth and love—to himself.

It is our *life* that is graced. We are never without the presence of the saving God.

Worship. Do we think of getting married as worshiping God? Or going to confession? That is the emphasis the Church is trying to get us back to.

The sacraments are indeed God's signs. If he did not "make" them, we would be helpless. But we must enter into them, and into their *meaning.* And when God acts, it can only be to bring us to himself, the only source of life and happiness. When that happens, what is the obvious thing to do? To thank God, *to treat him as God*—that is, as the only Good, the only Love, the source of all, Father and Savior. This is worship.

When God leads us through sorrow to a new dedication to him, total trust and faith and obedience, this is the worship of our lives. When anointing calls upon the sick person to put complete trust and hope in God, or when Christian marriage places a lifetime into God's hands—this, too, is worship.

This is not just staid, somber, "official" worship, but the joyful worship of those who are fully aware of the privilege of being God's people, who can come with a deep joy and peace even to the funeral of a loved one, and who can go away from the altar, if necessary, to the ovens of Auschwitz.

Someone has suggested that a very simple definition of any sacrament is *saving worship:* The love of God comes "down" to us, and our perfect worship goes "up" in Jesus.

Straining Toward the Future. In the back of our minds, at least, we realize that any sacramental action of Jesus comes from eternity where he is already "at the right hand of the Father." Yet the life of the Church can only be lived *today,* of course. To live in the past or in the future is to miss the grace of the present moment. But it is still true that, as Paul says, "Here we have no lasting city" (Heb 13:14).

We may not neglect any possible improvement of the human condition, in medicine, science, education, art, etc. But we are straining forward to the day when we will see God face to face, when we will see the risen Jesus and be united to all our families and friends and the whole people of God.

Those who have "gone before" are part of every liturgy. The praise of the earthly community is the same as that of Mary and the saints in heaven.

Summing up, then: God calls us to sacramental acts. They are the acts of God, in Jesus and in the Spirit; they are acts of the Church; they are acts of each individual. They are acts of faith and worship. They are the acts of a visible sign, a community, using visible signs itself. God speaks to us in human words, and our hearts are filled with his life, called grace. We worship and we are saved. We face the present with peace and the future with hope.

So the Christian community is called to give "signs of life." From a human viewpoint, it is a fearful responsibility. Only God gives our sacramental actions meaning. If the first "sign"–the union of loving Christians–is not an evident sacrament, many will feel that the seven particular sacraments are meaningless ritual.

It is easy to describe Sunday Mass as a bore. Thousands of people do. But Jesus came to make, not to find, the perfect community. He found sinful men and women and offered them forgiveness, healing, new life, faith. It doesn't happen magically, and it doesn't happen instantly. The last day a Christian community gathers around an altar, there will be something awry. There will still be a ferment of resentment in some hearts. Not everybody will be "open" to his or her neighbor.

But it will still be the Mass. All the glorious things said of it will be true.

And for the people there, painfully on their way to becoming "Christ come to full stature" (Eph 4:13), it will be a *sign*–of hope.

16.

Jesus Welcomes Strangers Into His Community: Baptism

Suppose a stranger happened into the place where the Eucharist was being celebrated by the same group we met in Chapter 14. Suppose, further, that this man or woman was moved by the obvious love these people had for one other. The stranger might sense the peace of the assembly, perhaps an atmosphere of humbleness as well as joy.

What would the community do for the stranger?

Again, let us paint the ideal picture. The gathered Christians would first of all welcome the stranger as a person with respect and ease. They would then offer him anything possibly needed: food, clothing, shelter.

If the outsider sooner or later asked, "What is it that you have? Why do you act the way you do?" they would say, "Stay with us and see."

In this way the "catechumenate" would begin (or rather, in this case, the "pre-catechumenate"). The word *catechumenate* comes from the Greek and means "instruction." Catholics learned in their "catechisms"—the same word—that far back in Church history the first part of the Mass was called "the Mass of the Catechumens." Catechumens were people being prepared for Baptism.

Because a time came when infants were almost the only ones being baptized, the catechumenate faded for a time from the experience of the Church. "Taking instructions" to become a "convert" replaced the catechumenate. An individual (sometimes a class) would meet with a priest weekly for two or three months for instruction in the doctrines of the Church. If all went well, Baptism followed.

The bishops at Vatican II called for the restoration of the catechumenate and, after years of preparation, the new rite was given to the Church in January, 1972. It is "something new again" for many Catholics. Their instinct is right, for the respected liturgist Father Aidan Kavanaugh, O.S.B., has said: "This document may well appear to a writer a century from now as *the most important result of the Second Vatican Council for the life of the Church.*"

Why? Because it will—or should—bring home to both catechumens and "born Catholics" the radical and shattering implications of what it means to be "born into Christ." It points to the only possible way of approaching the Christian life: total, lifelong, deepening "conversion."

In Christian countries the most frequent celebration of the sacrament, obviously, will still be for infants. We will return to this matter later. But the emphasis on the catechumenate will serve to point up what must be the lifelong process whereby these baptized infants are brought to full commitment to Christ.

The catechumenate takes place within the Christian community. Special people are of course involved—bishop, priest, deacon, sponsors. But the whole community (parish) is called to be concerned for this identifiable group of catechumens. The catechumens are a designated group; they are known and loved for what they are, new "children" coming to birth. They are the object not only of the prayers but also the personal attention and encouragement of the community.

The *Rite of Christian Initiation of Adults* (RCIA) directs the faithful to "be ready to open up the spirit of the Christian community to the candidates, to invite them into their families, to engage them in private conversation, and to invite them to some community gatherings." Members of the community should be present at the various celebrations of stages in the catechumens' process of being brought to Baptism, especially the special Lenten ceremonies. As the new Christians are baptized at the Easter vigil, Christians "should renew their own baptismal promises in their hearts." In the time after Baptism, they should welcome the newly baptized with charity and help them to sense the joy of belonging to the community of the baptized.

Each candidate has a sponsor who knows and helps him or her. The sponsor is the witness to the community of the "morals, faith and intention" of the candidate. It is the sponsor's responsibility to "show the catechumen in a friendly way the place of the gospel in his own life and in society, to help him in doubts and anxieties, to give public testimony for him, and to watch over the progress of his baptismal life."

The bishop or his delegate admits the candidates. Priests attend to the pastoral and personal care of the catechumens, providing for their catechesis with the help of deacons and catechists.

The preparation of catechumens covers several periods. The first is a period of inquiry (the *pre-catechumenate*). The community—priests and laypersons—begins to introduce its belief and its life to an interested person.

The *catechumenate* begins with a public ceremony in which the catechumens profess their intention to become a part of the community and the community, in turn, welcomes them to the Church. During this time, catechumens are instructed more deeply in the faith, grow more familiar with the community's way of life, participate in the Liturgy of the Word and begin to take an active part in the community's activities.

The third stage *(election)* begins the day the catechumen is chosen for Baptism by the Church. It usually coincides with Lent, a period of intense purification and enlightenment for all believers, but especially for those preparing for Baptism. Special rites are celebrated within the Sunday liturgy, offering the catechumens the support of the community's prayers and introducing to them the words Christians cherish: the Creed and the Lord's Prayer. The culmination is the high point of the Church year: the celebration of Baptism at the Easter Vigil.

Finally, the period of *mystagogia*, or post-baptismal catechesis, draws the newly-baptized into full participation in the community.

Sacramentals of Baptism. At various points in the process of the catechumenate, special ceremonies gradually unfold the meaning of the sacrament. The Sign of the Cross is made on the forehead of the candidates by the priest and sponsors or catechists when they are accepted as catechumens. They may take a new name. The candidates are welcomed into the church building. Special oil is blessed for the anointing of the catechumens, a sign of strength. Special ceremonies are held for them on the third, fourth and fifth Sundays of Lent.

After Baptism each new Christian is anointed on the crown of the head as a sign of new dignity shared with Christ as priest, prophet and king. A white garment is placed on each, and the priest prays, "You have become a new creation and have clothed yourselves in Christ. Take this white garment and bring it unstained to the judgment seat of our Lord Jesus Christ, so that you may have everlasting life."

Finally, the sponsors light a candle from the Easter candle, representing Christ newly risen, and hand it to the newly baptized. "You have been enlightened by Christ. Walk always as children of the light and keep the flame of faith alive in your hearts."

Evidently something very serious is going on here! And "born Catholics" are moved to say, "If so much is asked of these catechumens, what should I be asking of myself? What does it mean that I am a baptized Christian?"

What *does* it mean?

New Life in Christ. St. Paul speaks of the Gentiles being *grafted* onto the vine who is Christ. A grafted branch bears leaves and fruit from a new "rich root" (Rom 11:17). The new Christian begins an entirely new life. He or she is a "new creation" (2 Cor 5:17), called to be as different from the old self as the new Adam was from the old.

Another word not familiar to us has a powerful meaning: *incorporation.* Baptism makes us members of the Body *(corpus)* of Christ. We become living members through which the life of Jesus flows and acts.

The stranger who wandered into our ideal community soon felt the warmth of Jesus in his members and heard his call. Baptism is the concrete assurance of that acceptance. It is the stranger's personal decision to be accepted and become no longer a stranger, but one who is joined to the whole community of Christ—both this visible one right here and the community of Jesus in the whole world—a living member, needing and needed.

Another word seems somehow unworthy of Baptism: *initiation.* But it means more than joining a club; it means to make a beginning. There are three sacraments whereby one is fully initiated into the Body of Christ: Baptism, Confirmation, Eucharist. The new Christian celebrates all three of these sacraments with the community at the Easter vigil.

Baptism is a "*Christ*-ening," a beautiful word we have flattened into "christening." It means being made able to grow to the maturity of Christ. Each of us is a unique person, and each of us has a unique, unrepeatable relationship with Christ—a source of the infinite variety and beauty of the Church.

In Jesus we enter into the life of the Trinity, baptized "in the name of the Father and of the Son and of the Holy Spirit."

We are the "adopted" children of the Father because, unlike in a mere legal adoption, he begets in us a sharing in his own life. Beyond all understanding, we become "sharers of the divine nature" (2 Pt 1:4). We live and move and have our being in the very life and love and power of God. St. John exclaims:

See what love the Father has bestowed on us
in letting us be called children of God!
Yet that is what we are. . . .
What we shall later be has not yet come to light.
We know that when it comes to light
we shall be like him,
for we shall see him as he is. (1 Jn 3:1-2)

Baptism is the concrete assurance of these gifts of God. It is also our acceptance of God's love. It is our declaration of unconditional self-giving. We become God's property. We always were, of course, but now we make it joyfully voluntary.

The voluntariness is a gift. We do not "decide" to come to Jesus; he calls us. This is dramatically expressed in the ritual dialogue at the very beginning of the catechumenate:

> *Celebrant:* What do you ask of God's Church?
> *Candidates:* Faith.
> *Celebrant:* What does faith offer you?
> *Candidates:* Eternal life.

Being "in Christ" becomes the prime value of life. No one and no thing is more important. Now there is only one way to look at all Christians: They are all graced by Christ. Everything else—being pope, working miracles, having children, being crucified—is secondary. As Paul says, for all who have been baptized into Christ, "There does not exist among you Jew or Greek, slave or free-man, male or female. All are one in Christ Jesus" (Gal 3:28).

Water: Death and Life. Whether Baptism is administered by means of immersion or by pouring water over the candidate's head, its meaning is the same: We die and rise again. In the early Church Baptism was conferred by immersion (as in many Churches today). After the long period of preparation, the climactic moment came. The candidates were led, one by one, down the steps of a baptismal pool and immersed beneath the surface of the water. They disappeared, "drowned." Then they were raised up, literally and grace-fully, and led up the steps on the other side of the pool—new Christs.

This is what Paul is referring to when he says: "How can we who died to sin go on living in it? Are you not aware that we who were baptized into Christ Jesus were baptized into his death? Through baptism into his death we were buried with him, so that, just as Christ was raised from the dead by the glory of the Father, we too might live a new life" (Rom 6:2-4).

We are close to divine mystery here. We are brought into the dying and rising of Jesus himself. We are enabled to join his willingness to lose everything, even life—in total trust of the Father. With him we are raised to new life—he to glory, we to grace now and glory ultimately. When Paul says, "I have been crucified with Christ," he is not speaking of physical suffering (though that finally became a result of his union with Christ), but of a death to everything that was not the attitude of Christ, as his next words indicate: "The life I live now is not my own; Christ is living in me" (Gal 2:19-20).

Forgiveness of Sin. The stranger who came to our Eucharist is a symbol of all the alienation in the world. To sin is to become a stranger to God, wandering like Cain in a vast and empty wasteland. But in Baptism, received in faith, God forgives all sin.

In the beginning, the human race estranged itself from God by deliberate sin. As a result, we are all born in the condition of "original sin." It is as if our grandfather once owned the state of California and lost it in a poker game. It is not our fault we will not inherit the property; but we have no claim to it just the same. Likewise, our earliest ancestors lost the spark of divine life that was given them at creation.

Being born in the state of original sin does not mean we are being deprived of any "rights" by God. It is the mystery of human solidarity that no one person can do anything without affecting everyone else. If that condition seems unfair to us, let us remember that God's love surrounds every human being more powerfully than the condition of belonging to an alien race.

God wills the salvation of every human being. What he wills, he effectively achieves. Nothing—not the death of a baby before Baptism, not ignorance, not living in a place where Jesus' name has never been heard—nothing can stop God from offering salvation to every human being. How? We don't know. We are simply sure that if we are concerned, God is infinitely more so—and will take care of it admirably.

What of those who through no fault of their own do not know Christ or God or who conscientiously reject a distorted concept of God that has been offered them? The bishops spoke clearly at Vatican II: "Nor does Divine Providence deny the help necessary for salvation to those who, without blame on their part, have not yet arrived at an explicit knowledge of God, but who strive to lead a good life, thanks to his grace" (*Constitution on the Church, #* 16).

Almost certainly, God's grace-life enters a catechumen months or years before the actual hour of Baptism, through what is called "baptism of desire."

God does not have moments. He does not decide he will forgive someone next Tuesday; he *is* forgiveness. So the moment anyone accepts the healing love of God, all sin is forgiven.

Why, then, the sacrament? Because *we* need external signs. This is the whole rationale of all sacrament and ritual. We need to see and feel and experience concretely what we are sure of in our heart, but which is not yet fully human because it has not been expressed in the flesh. The sacrament is the absolute assurance, through the action of the Church, of God's forgiveness.

Forgiveness is the first part of the Good News, the first result of Jesus' dying and rising: "This is my blood. . .to be poured out in behalf of many for the forgiveness of sins" (Mt 26:28). The first forgiveness the Church brings is not that of Confession but Baptism.

When Paul encountered Jesus on the road to Damascus, Jesus told Paul to go to the Gentiles "to open the eyes of those to whom I am sending you. . . ; that through their faith in me they may obtain the forgiveness of their sins and a portion among God's people" (Acts 26:18).

In Peter's Pentecost discourse, forgiveness is the first effect of Baptism he cites: "You must reform and be baptized, each one of you, in the name of Jesus Christ, that your sins may be forgiven; then you will receive the gift of the Holy Spirit" (Acts 2:38).

Conversion—reform—is a lifelong process. Baptism is not a once-and-for-all completion of our union with God. It is a beginning, just as the birth of a baby is a beginning. It is a decisive and unrepeatable moment, indeed, but it needs to be filled out in literally millions of moments to follow. We are not "converts" but "people being converted." In Baptism God reveals our true (final) image, and we begin to let him make that image real in ourselves.

Infant Baptism. The ongoingness of baptismal conversion is precisely the argument for baptizing infants. If the Church could have started with the adult candidate at the moment of birth, it would have done so, for this would have meant 20, 30, 40 more years of training and example.

The important factor in infant Baptism is the community and, within the community, the parents and sponsors. They share the responsibility for bringing this baby to the point where full Christian commitment will be his or her totally voluntary choice.

Appealing as it may seem at first, the argument that it would be better to wait until the age of say, 21, seems to lose all force when the question is pressed: "Wait for what?" No child can be brought up in a value-free atmosphere. Parents' and society's values are constantly being impressed on the child.

It would be unthinkable to wait until a child is 21 to insist on bathing, eating properly, being honest, respectful and caring. So it is unthinkable to Christian parents that Jesus be kept a stranger from their children. They want them to experience, gradually and according to their capacity, the meaning of God's gift of eternal life.

This is a delicate process, of course. Religion should not (and cannot) be "rammed down the throat" of anyone. Faith cannot be taught; it can only be "caught" from others in whom it burns bright. Children are the "catechumens" of home and school and, gradually, the "big" Church.

Infant Baptism has one other advantage: It is a clear statement that salvation is entirely God's work. His love is freely bestowed before the child can possibly do anything to seem to deserve it. Long before a baby has come to know the Christian community, the community says, in St. Paul's words: "You are strangers and aliens no longer. No, you are fellow citizens of the saints and members of the household of God. You form a building which rises on the foundation of the apostles and prophets, with Christ Jesus himself as the capstone" (Eph 2:19-20).

17.

The Spirit of Jesus Sends Forth Witnesses: Confirmation

Confirmation is the second of the three sacraments of initiation. Its focus is the Holy Spirit, already given in Baptism, but "now" given for a *special purpose.*

The two words, *already* and *now* point up a minor difficulty in understanding the sacrament: How can the Holy Spirit be given twice?

The difficulty did not exist for the first Christians. In the early Church (as in the restored catechumenate), Baptism, Confirmation and Eucharist were one celebration, one rite of receiving new members into the community.

In later history, entire cultures became Christian and most baptisms were of infants. Christian initiation was divided into two parts: baptism with water by a priest and anointing by a bishop. Since the bishop obviously could not be present at all baptisms, the anointing gradually was seen as separate and postponed (along with First Eucharist) to later life.

Obviously God cannot be parceled out in time capsules. One who is baptized becomes a temple of the Spirit, the home of the indwelling Trinity. No "part" of the Holy Spirit is held back at Baptism to be given in Confirmation. Every celebration of a sacrament is a sign from the one God of the one continuing, infinite love that is poured into our being.

Neither is Confirmation a sign of Catholic adulthood. Its celebration does not mark a mature commitment to Christ. Reaching such a commitment is a lifelong process; it can neither be delayed until 21 nor "finished" at 71.

Baptism and Confirmation are still almost impossible to separate in meaning. Each happens only once; each calls for a continuing unfolding of the Christian life. We probably have to be satisfied with the general statement that Baptism makes us alive in Christ, members of his family, given holiness and called to holiness. This implicitly calls for the activity that Confirmation stresses: witnessing to this faith with courage, in the power of the Holy Spirit.

Sealed With the Spirit. When Confirmation is celebrated, the bishop takes fragrant oil (chrism) on his thumb and makes the Sign of the Cross on the forehead of the one being confirmed, saying, "Be sealed with the gift of the Holy Spirit."

The perfumed oil (olive or any suitable plant oil) is the sign both of what the Pentecost prayer calls the "sweet refreshment" of the Spirit and of the strength the Spirit gives. (Oil may not immediately suggest strength to us today, but athletes still use "rubdowns" to make their bodies limber and strong.)

To be "sealed" is to be authoritatively marked or stamped as the property of someone. In Confirmation the Spirit claims and empowers a Christian as a responsible and, if you will, "official" representative of the Church before the world. He or she is to take responsibility for bringing Jesus to the ends of the earth.*

The newly confirmed Christian now says what Jesus said of himself:

"The spirit of the Lord is upon me;
   therefore he has anointed me.
He has sent me to bring glad tidings to the poor,
   to proclaim liberty to captives,
Recovery of sight to the blind
   and release to prisoners,
To announce a year of favor from the Lord." (Lk 4:18-19)

Paul sums up what we are celebrating in this way: "God is the one who firmly establishes [confirms] us along with you in Christ; it is he who anointed us and has sealed us, thereby depositing the first payment, the Spirit, in our hearts" (2 Cor 1:21-22).

Thus Confirmation stresses the power of the Spirit to make Christians witnesses of Jesus to the world. It turns the Christian *outward* to face the world with courageous testimony—in whatever way—to the Good News of Jesus.

Confirmation is to Baptism what Pentecost is to Easter. Again we should not make too great a separation: John tells of Jesus conferring his Spirit on the evening of Easter Sunday; Luke locates the event 50 days later. It is one and the same giving.

In Acts, written by Luke, Jesus tells his apostles to wait in Jerusalem "for the fulfillment of the Father's promise. . . .Within a few days you will be baptized with the Holy Spirit. . . .You will receive power when the Holy Spirit comes down on you; then you are to be my witnesses in Jerusalem, throughout Judea and Samaria, yes, even to the ends of the earth" (Acts 1:4-5, 8).

Luke describes the transforming Pentecost experience in terms of fire and wind—the way the Old Testament describes the coming of God, for example, at Mt. Sinai. Something like a strong, driving wind filled the house where the disciples were. "Tongues as of fire" descended on each one and "all were filled

---

*Three sacraments cannot be repeated: Baptism, Confirmation and Orders. They are said to "engrave" upon our person a certain "character" or distinguishing mark. (The word *character* literally means a mark engraved on stone, or a mark to indicate ownership.) While the Church has never determined the precise nature of this "indelible mark," theologians have generally taught that it has to do with priesthood—that of the laity and that of priests. A baptized person is simply different from, say, a good Moslem who happens to be at Mass. The Moslem may be far holier than the Christian at the moment. But he is not a member of the worshiping community. He has not been given the power to make the offering on the altar a sacred sign of the worship of God and of oneness in love with Jesus the High Priest. Without flaunting superiority, Christians are "set apart."

with the Holy Spirit. They began to express themselves [witness] in foreign tongues and make bold proclamation as the Spirit prompted them" (Acts 2:2-4).

The rest of the Acts of the Apostles is the story of this bold proclamation under the guidance and power of the Holy Spirit. We might almost say that Acts is the "Confirmation book" of the New Testament, and that the sacrament makes Pentecost a permanent event in the life of each Christian.

What Does It Mean to Witness? An entire document of Vatican II, *The Church in the Modern World*, might be used by confirmed Christians as a textbook on witnessing to Christ: "Inspired by no earthly ambition, the Church seeks but a solitary goal: to carry forward the work of Christ himself under the lead of the befriending Spirit. And Christ entered this world to give witness to the truth, to rescue and not sit in judgment, to serve and not to be served" (#3).

To mention just a few examples of Christian witness to the world might suggest nonexistent limits. Any genuine activity for the benefit of others can be done only with the power of the "befriending Spirit." A mere skimming of the topics treated in *The Church in the Modern World* shows the unlimited field for action: the problem of change, humanity's deeper questioning, the dignity of the human person, the problem of atheism, social justice in the world community, marriage and the family, the proper development of culture, economic development, politics and the Church, war and peace, the international community.

Catholics can find many groups for activity, both local and private as well as Church-wide and formal. But no one needs to do anything special—except to do the special thing which his or her talent and circumstances call for. The person dying of cancer witnesses to Christ as well as the pope; a child who prays in innocence is breathing in the Holy Spirit. The couple who "simply" love each other faithfully and courageously and endure the joys and sorrows of family life are telling the world of the Spirit's presence—and the world hears, even when it seems to be looking the other way.

Christians are daily telling the world that there is Good News. They are making visible the reconciliation God works in Christ and the transforming of creation into the Kingdom.

Personal Experience of the Spirit. In biblical symbolism the number seven stands for fullness, completeness, perfection. Hence to speak of the "seven" gifts of the Holy Spirit is to emphasize not the number, but the fullness the prophet attributed to the promised Messiah:

> The spirit of the LORD shall rest upon him:
> a spirit of wisdom and of understanding,
> A spirit of counsel and of strength,
> a spirit of knowledge and of fear of the LORD,
> and his delight shall be the fear of the LORD. (Is 11:2-3)

(Translating the first mention of "fear of the Lord" as *piety* made the gifts seven in number.)

Likewise, St. Paul's list of the *fruits* of the Holy Spirit is his tumbling of words upon words to express the limitless benefits of that Spirit: "The fruit of the spirit is love, joy, peace, patient endurance, kindness, generosity, faith, mildness and chastity" (Gal 5:22-23).

Gift in Greek is *charisma,* which means grace, favor, kindness, gift. In recent years the "charismatic movement" has become a prominent and sometimes bewildering part of Catholic life. The movement stresses certain particular gifts (charisms) of the Spirit (see 1 Cor 12:4-11), especially speaking in tongues and prophesying.

Charismatics speak of "Baptism of the Spirit": an intense religious experience of the Spirit. This is not the first Baptism of the Spirit which all Christians receive sacramentally, but a felt release of the Spirit's power, a deeper realization of the presence of Jesus, greater strength in prayer and greater zeal to witness.

Like all movements, this one has not been without its problems—the place of authority in charismatic communities, the danger of fundamentalism in Bible teaching, the temptation to elitism. But "you can tell a tree by its fruit" (Mt 7:20), and the Church can rejoice that thousands of lives have been dramatically changed by the charismatic experience.

Those who find the movement either threatening or excluding them have to look to their own willingness to be open to whatever gifts the Spirit may give them—particularly, as the Council says, those which are less dramatic and more ordinary. St. Paul reminded the charismatics of Corinth that the litmus test of the Spirit's presence is the gift which "surpasses all the others"—love (see 1 Cor 13).

Every Christian is called to experience the presence of God as fully and consciously as possible. But it is also a commonplace of all Christians' experience—the saints' especially—that this can mean many foot-slogging days and dark nights. Faith lives on trust.

18.

Jesus Brings Sinners Back to the Father: Reconciliation

"Nothing is a sin anymore!" has become the worried comment of a significant number of Catholics. The Church seems to have become very lenient—or at least many Catholics have decided to be rather lenient with themselves.

One cause of the new outlook, among many contributing factors, is this: While the "requirements" for mortal sin are still the same (serious matter, full awareness, full free consent of the will), these have now come to be seen in their full depth of meaning. "Full awareness" means at least an implicit knowledge of the fact that my sin is actually rupturing my relationship with God; "full consent" means that, knowing this, I go ahead anyway, with a freedom that is not seriously damaged by emotion. Mortal sinfulness is seen as a kind of life-choice. It isn't something people can "zigzag" in and out of.

Pope John Paul II called a synod of bishops in 1983 to consider the problems facing the Church in the Sacrament of Reconciliation ("confession" is only part of the sacrament). They wrestled with the subject for weeks. Later the Pope issued an exhortation that summed up his own conclusions and those of the bishops.

As if answering the complaint that "nothing is a sin anymore," he describes the evil that is rampant in the world: the trampling of the rights of the human person, above all the right to life and to a decent quality of life; the attack on freedom, especially that of professing one's faith; racial discrimination, violence, torture, terrorism; the piling up of weapons in an arms race which spends billions that could ease the undeserved misery of many human beings. The Pope sees divisions in a shattered world: between individuals and groups, nations and blocs of nations. And he says that the root of all these things lies in our inmost self. In the light of faith we call it sin.

The Pope uses two Bible stories to illustrate the meaning of sin. In erecting the tower of Babel, humanity sought to be powerful without God— a rival of God, in fact. We find the same rivalry in Eden, when human beings set themselves up as being somehow self-sufficient, as powerful as God.

All through history this has been sin, in all its forms: exclusion of God, the rupturing of relationship with him. Sin is the disobedience of a person who by a free and knowing act does not recognize the sovereignty of God over his or her life, at least when the sin is committed.

All Christians need, in view of all this, a renewed sense of sin—a spiritual thermometer whereby we are sharply aware of the seeds of death contained in sin, as well as the thousand disguises under which sin hides itself.

The Meaning of Sin. In a previous chapter we tried to describe the Church at its best at Eucharist. The community returns to try to re-create that ideal every Sunday. At the same time, it is a community that always needs to be saved because it is always a weak and sinful community. Some members of the Body may have become lifeless; others are seriously ill; all may have at least a slight fever.

How does sin happen in the very body of Christ? A gradual lessening of warmth between members occurs, aided by repeated experiences of the limitations and faults of others; a willingness not to look too hard for the truth or at the truth grows. One by one people slip into a life that is partly a lie, a disorder they will not face; they are overtaken by the heady wine of freedom, the satisfaction of pleasure divorced from purpose. Things become little gods instead of creations; people become things for use and enjoyment apart from the great purposes of life.

And so it is possible gradually to move back from the circle of the community and from the Lord who gives that circle a center.

Sin is a way of life. It is an attitude that grows—just as love develops in giving and receiving. Nothing human is instantaneous. What happens at 12:00 was already begun at 11:59 and at 9:00, growing toward fullness yesterday and last week and perhaps last year. The growth is not unnoticed—for then there would be no fault—but it is not admitted.

Often I choose sin by default: I do not do the right and reasonable thing. I need not stamp my feet and shake my fist at God—I just don't decide to do the good thing. I will not do what the words of Jesus are calling me to do. His meaning is obvious, but I refuse to hear. There is a terrible scene in *Leave Her to Heaven* in which a woman sits calmly in a rowboat, her eyes hidden by sunglasses, watching a rival drown. She sits very still, watching, doing nothing. Sin*fulness* becomes *this* sinful act, gradually, just as one can become drunk by letting his glass be filled again and again and never objecting.

It really isn't serious for a while. This is literally true but has led to the foolish view that something is "only" a venial sin. But nothing is just "a" sin; it is a point along a ramp going down. All sin is a gradual slipping from life to death, so gradual that when one crosses the line it is scarcely noticed—for the willingness to cross the line was present long before. The woman who watched her rival drown had come to be a murderess by many slow, sly steps.

So the community we spoke of is not ideal because there are empty places at the table. Some may have moved their chairs to private cliques (Paul had trouble with that at Corinth). Some, in John's words, must hear Jesus say, "You have turned aside from your early love" (Rv 2:4).

Church: The Reconciling Community. By the very fact that Jesus joined people into a visible Body to be his sacrament, he "automatically" created the Sacrament of Reconciliation. For the Church is the sign of Christ's love, and therefore of God's endless willingness to forgive. The Church is given the ministry of reconciliation not just for the rebirth of Baptism, but—such is the "bind" God gets into by being God—for the 70 times seven times one may lose the life once gratefully received (see Mt 18:22).

The community—somebody—must carry out the ministry of reconciliation in such a way that sinners can first be sure they are welcome back. To the sinner—miserable and alone in the most crowded room, caught in the trap of greed or hate, cold stubbornness or pride, lust or mere self-sufficiency—someone must bring back the memory of the Father's table.

If sinfulness is a way of life, so is the life of grace. A new—the former—way of life must be entered.

First, and hardest of all, must come the admission of sinfulness: not a "mistaken judgment" or a "forgetting" or an "I didn't think. . . ," but a simple, factual statement, with the Prodigal Son, "Father, I have sinned. . . ; I no longer deserve to be called your son" (Lk 15:21).

Real sorrow must follow—not just remorse for the self-inflicted pain and misery (for punishment is built into sin itself) but a genuine sorrow that God's love has been ignored, his trust betrayed. Something holy and valuable has been spoiled. A consecrated body-spirit, a mind made for truth, freedom made to love, a body made to share and show the spirit's faith, a heart meant to experience the beauty and purity of life—all have been infected, abused, prostituted.

The sinner turns back to God for healing and new life. "God, in Christ, was [and is] reconciling the world to himself" (2 Cor 5:19). God brings the sinner back to his table, knowing how he or she has hungered for that place. God gives the determination to change, the power to take the necessary steps, to *leave* the foreign country where the inheritance was squandered, to do practical things like repairing and restoring and apologizing.

The Sacrament of Reconciliation is the sign from God that the sinner is absolutely forgiven. The sign is the welcome of the community, the kindness of the priest, the certainty of acceptance, the grace of God made visible.

Confession. One who has been truly guilty of mortal sinfulness must ordinarily confess the sinfulness to a priest, individually and privately, even though God's forgiveness has already been given and experienced. (*Ordinarily*—unless, for instance, one is unable to confess because of physical or moral impossibility such as sickness, the danger of being overheard, etc.)

This is a sticking point for many—once for Protestants, now for some Catholics. Why go to a man, the argument goes, when God has already acted? Or, in the words of the more liturgically-minded, why do we need anything more than the community's forgiveness, expressed in its welcome?

We are speaking, remember, of one who truly separated himself or herself internally from the Body of Christ. It seems only common decency that one does not resume a place at table as if nothing had happened. Even the most loving of families would expect something more than that.

Confessing, like any external physical act, makes the interior act fully human. If a resolution or feeling is genuine within me, it will out. It may not even be fully *mine*—of me, this body-spirit unity—until I have done something

119

external, until I have created words that make me realize what I truly mean.

Confessing is a "public" statement (even in the privacy of the confessional or reconciliation room) that (1) I am truly a sinner; (2) only God can forgive my sinfulness; (3) I want and accept God's forgiveness; (4) I mean to do something about my sinfulness.

Confessing involves saying the three most difficult words in the human language: "I was wrong"—not just "in error" but *sinful.* It is not meant to be a humiliation—the priest goes to confession too—but a healthy statement of fact. Once said, the words are lost in the mercy of God. True confession means the end of guilt and guilt feelings.

Most important of all, the voice of Christ himself becomes audible in confession—speaking to us individually about our individual sinfulness. It is the sign which, being human, we desperately need.

The actual words of absolution said as the priest holds his hands over the head of the penitent are:

> God, the Father of mercies,
> by the death and resurrection of his Son,
> has reconciled the world to himself,
> and sent the Holy Spirit among us
> for the forgiveness of sins.
> By the ministry of the Church,
> May God give you pardon and peace.
> And I absolve you from your sins
> in the name of the Father,
> and of the Son,
> and of the Holy Spirit.

The New Rite. Vatican II called for a revision of the rites of the sacraments to make their nature and purpose clear. In the case of the Sacrament of Reconciliation, the revisions are not all that new. There is a new emphasis, however, on three things: (1) the internal—the full, deep—meaning of sinfulness and grace; (2) the Word of God; (3) the community. Let us begin with the last.

On a particular day the community gathers to celebrate the Sacrament of Reconciliation (a communal penance service). The sinner who has been away comes back. It is no humiliation to return, for now the pain of self-imposed isolation is over. The sinner confesses privately to the priest in the course of the sacramental celebration, and God gives the assurance of forgiveness through the priest's words of absolution. The community welcomes the sinner back to the table.

But even when only priest and penitent meet (in private confession), the community is there. The priest represents the reconciling community.

The confessor must make a judgment, for the Church. Ninety-nine times out of a hundred the judgment is that the penitent is truly sorry. But it is possible that a priest may be forced to conclude that a given person is nowhere near real sorrow or purpose of amendment. The priest has the great responsi-

120

bility to try to show the sinner the love as well as the truth of God; but he cannot make a mockery of the words of absolution and pretend the sinner has really returned to community life when in fact it may merely be a case of empty ritual.

Besides this emphasis on community, the revised rite insists that the Word of God be an integral part of every sacramental celebration. The Bible is a kind of sacrament of God's actual living word to us *today*. It is not a collection of choice sayings, an interesting religious anthology. The reading of Scripture in sacramental celebrations is, or should be, a striking emphasis on the fact that the sacraments are God's actions, God's self-communication, and involve some definite expectations on his part.

So the reading of Scripture focuses our minds on God's presence and *action*. The words of Scripture are a communication from God, and a personal response must be given. In this sacrament, it is God giving reassurance, healing, forgiveness—but, insofar as necessary, a restatement of his will and a wholesome warning.

Finally, there is a renewed emphasis in the new rite on deepening our awareness of the full meaning of sin and grace. Confession need not be made face to face, but this method gives priest and penitent a better chance to get beneath the surface of sin to its roots and to make the reconciliation a felt and grace-full experience.

The priest is not a psychiatrist. He is a fellow Christian who can help the penitent see things in faith again and make personal the present love of God. He can sympathize as well as speak the unyielding truth.

It is easy to make fun of the old "grocery list" confession, but who knows what depths of real sorrow and full awareness of the grace of reconciliation and of the need of penance accompanied that "list"? At any rate, the emphasis today is where it always has to be—on the motives and attitudes that run beneath the surface, the traits of temperament that are the filter of both sin and virtue.

It is hoped that the sacramental rite can help even so-called "venial sinners" sense the seriousness of sacramental reconciliation. Even if I have not left the table, I may have pulled my chair back: I can't stand this person, or I don't want to share with that one, or I don't want to have to adapt to that one. I am thereby refusing to love my neighbor, and the life of the community is made a little less healthy. The pulse and flow of the life of the Body has been restricted.

When a community gathers for the sacrament, each member is saying to all, "I have hurt you by what I have done and what I have not done. Show me the forgiveness of Jesus." And each member also says to all the rest by the very coming together, "I offer you the forgiveness of Jesus, who calls us to be one in him." This is reconciliation, turning away from sin and turning to God by joining the community again, or joining it more generously.

'Penance.' Finally, there is a "penance" to be done by each individual after celebrating the sacrament. It is not "satisfaction" in the sense of "making up" to God for our sin, for we can never do that. We can only accept his forgiveness.

Penance is letting God change my life, particularly in the area in which I have sinned. An individual's "penance" is balm for his or her particular needs and difficulties: to learn charity by performing an act of kindness for a person the penitent dislikes, for instance.

Thus the healing of Christ is given to all who have thrown aside their baptismal garment, or have soiled it; who have let their candle go out or burn low; who have wiped the oil of their dignity off their brow.

> If we acknowledge our sins,
> he who is just can be trusted
> to forgive our sins
> and cleanse us from every wrong. (1 Jn 1:9)

Reconciliation Is Worship. The celebration of the sacrament ends with a proclamation of praise to God. Sacraments are worship, and the most natural thing for a reconciled sinner to do is to be happy about the mercy of God. This is not like leaving a courtroom where one was barely acquitted and perhaps subjected to humiliation. Rather it is the celebration of the family, especially the reunited members. No longer does it matter what I was or what I did. Shame and scandal are forgotten. Joy comes from what I *am:* loved to life by God.

19.

Jesus Heals the Whole Person: Anointing of the Sick

Sin is not the only flaw in our ideal community; sickness of every kind also exists there. We are not spirits who merely drag our bodies along, but amazing creatures whose total well-being and happiness is physical-emotional-spiritual. Our bodies are really a part of us, and so, therefore, is all the sickness and suffering that bodies entail. No part of God's wise and generous creation can be ignored.

The body was certainly not beneath the notice of Jesus, as if he came to speak only "spiritual" things. Almost the first thing he did in his public life was to go down the street and heal the sick. Much as we may shrink from using the phrase, Jesus is *the* "faith healer."

Health—wholeness—remains a prime Christian concern. As the bearers of Jesus' ministry, we must reach out to those who are in pain. If we must wait for Mass because we are needed at a sickbed, then the Mass must wait—for an hour, a day, a week.

Taking a broader view for a moment: Just as it would be un-Christlike to tell a man in terrible pain to wait for his medicine until we finish the Eucharist, so it is a contradiction in terms to celebrate the saving death of Jesus and be unconcerned about the pain of our brothers and sisters anywhere in the world: the starving, the malnourished, the prisoners of tyranny, the poor crushed under greed. (Suffering can be borne gracefully only after the experience of God's love visible in others; not before.)

Our physical, emotional and spiritual health is *one*. If there is a disorder in one area, there is a disturbance in all. Physical sickness can be, to say the least, a great distraction. It may present great temptation to discouragement, bitterness or even loss of hope. When the body is trussed up with tubes and bottles and wired like a machine while the *person's* feeling and agony are ignored, sickness is dehumanizing.

With the mindset of the Old Testament, Jesus approaches a human being as a unity. He came to save *us*, not just our souls. (That is why *bodily* resurrection is part of salvation.) When he sent his disciples out to proclaim the Good News, and the corresponding need for repentance, they also "expelled many demons, anointed the sick with oil, and worked many cures" (Mk 6:13).

Besides the general mission of healing which Jesus gave the Church, the particular Sacrament of Anointing is described in the Letter of James: "Is there anyone sick among you? He should ask for the presbyters of the church. They in turn are to pray over him, anointing him with oil in the Name [of the Lord]. This prayer uttered in faith will reclaim the one who is ill, and the Lord will restore him to health. If he has committed any sins, forgiveness will be his" (5:14-15).

As we have seen, "sacramental grace" is the one love of God applied to a particular situation. Serious illness is one of life's most critical situations. Salvation must be brought about in these circumstances too.

Faith says that suffering can be a spiritual experience, a time when God draws us closer to himself and when we understand our whole life more deeply. Suffering by itself, however, is worthless. The whole plan of God is to rid his children of every kind of pain.

Yet suffering seems not only inevitable but even the noblest part of many people's lives. Obviously only faith can reconcile these opposites, making suffering a test but not a temptation. Only the power of God's love can enable us to share the trust and generous love of the suffering Jesus.

Does Jesus Still Heal? Before we go on, we must face the nagging questions: Does Jesus heal the sick *today?* Are the healings by people like Kathryn Kuhlman and Oral Roberts genuine or imaginary or hypnotically induced? Why have most of us never heard of, still less experienced, a miraculous healing?

We might as well admit it: We may not have enough faith. Notice James says that "the prayer uttered in faith" will reclaim the sick person. Jesus did not work miracles in his hometown because of the people's lack of faith (see Mt 13:54-58). If we really don't expect God to do anything, nothing will happen. If we expect mere magic, nothing will happen. Genuine faith, even if it can only repeat, "I do believe! Help my lack of trust!" (Mk 9:24), sees God working in the world through the Body of Christ. It is not surprised at anything.

But after admitting that we may be wanting in faith, we must also realize that this is not the only reason why prayer and sacrament fail to effect miraculous cures. Mother Teresa no doubt prays with great faith every day for many sick people, even particular sick people. We all know people with pure, humble faith who pray for the sick and "nothing happens." What can we say?

The sacrament of the sick is a sign of God's absolute victory over all evil in the death and resurrection of Jesus. Looking at the total history of the world "from eternity," we can be absolutely sure that all evil will be destroyed: sin, death, suffering, sickness. We have no doubt whatsoever about this.

Is it watering down the sacrament to say that the physical healing may not occur until the Lord raises the body of the sick person from death to eternal and total "health"? The anointing of a sick person's body is the signed promise of God that Jesus' healing will come. We may wish and hope and expect that it come immediately; but we need not be disturbed if healing is delayed.

What the Sacrament Does. As the body of a sick person is anointed, the Church prays:

> Through this holy anointing
> may the Lord in his love and mercy help you
> with the grace of the Holy Spirit.
> May the Lord who frees you from sin
> save you and raise you up.

Through the sacrament the whole person is brought to health—now or ultimately.

The essential first healing is forgiveness. Suffering and death are the result of sin—humankind's sin, not the sin of the sick person (though my sickness may sometimes be the result of my abusing my body, my emotions or my mind). The great Healer always heals the worst sickness first.

The sacrament gives the strength to face the temptations and anxieties of sickness. Serious sickness brings us face to face with the fact that we are fragile creatures. Even though *this* sickness may pass, ultimately we will fail to save our bodies from death. Facing that knowledge, we can either be depressed or we can put ourselves with trust into God's hands, knowing he will give us the strength to suffer, to die and to rise when the time comes. His grace creates in us confidence, trust and peace in spite of pain and a gloomy prognosis by the doctor.

The sacrament joins us to the suffering and victorious Jesus. We are given the light and strength to make Paul's words our own: "Even now I find my joy in the suffering I endure for you. In my own flesh I fill up what is lacking in the suffering of Christ for the sake of his body, the church" (Col 1:24).

Nothing is really lacking in the sufferings of Christ. But he has left a place beside him for us to join his *spirit* in suffering, his absolute trust of the Father and therefore his redeeming power. We can no more think of suffering as our particular punishment than we can imagine a vindictive God "satisfied" by Jesus' suffering. Suffering is in possession, as it were. It is unavoidable. Ours is to win over it by maintaining our peaceful faith. If we do that, the "prayer of faith" will indeed save us.

The sacrament is God's absolute assurance that this pain, this desolation has been transformed in the suffering and death of Jesus and that we are already joined to his resurrection and victory. The complete concrete fruits, healing and joy, will infallibly come. When we shall taste them, we leave in God's hands. Hence the words of Vatican II to the sick, exhorting them "to contribute to the welfare of the People of God by associating themselves freely with the passion and death of Christ" (*Constitution on the Church,* # 11).

The sacrament should be celebrated in conditions that are as "normal" as possible. Being sick is not normal, of course. But the time for the sacrament is as early as possible in the sickness, not when death is close and the patient is sedated almost beyond consciousness. The sacrament is not some kind of magic to be mumbled over an unconscious person. The sick man or woman should be given the best opportunity to exercise faith consciously and to be aware of the support of family and friends.

Again, the Community. In the ritual of anointing, the Church repeats what it says of all sacraments: The presence of the community is very important, not only for psychological reasons of support, but for the loving reassurance that makes Christ visible. "The family and friends of the sick and those who take care of them have a special share in this ministry of comfort" (*Rite of Anointing,* # 34).

Sometimes it is impossible to gather the community: A priest may be called to the hospital bed of one who has no immediate relatives; nurses are busy; no friends or other parishioners can be found. The priest is the comfort of the whole Church. But normally "the Church" should be there.

Death. It will take perhaps two or three generations to eradicate the notion that when the priest is called to anoint the sick, it is also time to call the undertaker. The old name of the sacrament was Extreme Unction, the last anointing, "the last rites." Vatican II asked that the sacrament be called "The Anointing of the Sick."

But the old name was not without foundation. Serious sickness is a signal, perhaps decades ahead of time, that our hold on life is precarious. Humanly speaking, we are alone and helpless before death. Mortality is part of our inheritance.

But Jesus made even death a beautiful and deliberate act of trust and love. Death was the symbol of the fatal power of sin until Jesus made it the focus of the opposite power—God's power to create and re-create, to heal and raise. Jesus' death was the most voluntary act he ever made. It summed up his life of absolute trust in the Father. He literally handed himself over in the dark to his Father. His Father embraced him and he was alive again, fully free and whole, victorious and all-powerful.

Some psychologists say we begin to come to terms with death early in life. As Christians we try to rise above the natural fear of dying by a life that is basically love and trust. We would do well, though, deliberately to make an act of trustful dying far ahead of time. One way of doing this is expressed in a prayer I found on a well-worn piece of note paper in a saintly old lady's prayer-book: "Lord Jesus, trusting in you, I now at this moment willingly accept whatever death you may send me, with all its pain and darkness, for I know it is my coming to be with you forever."

Here we see the full meaning of healing. We may be restored to health *now*, in view of a longer preparation for our final salvation; or healing may be a holy death in the Lord, who is our final health and salvation, and who will infallibly give us total health forever.

20.

Jesus at the Heart of Married Love: Marriage

Recently a middle-aged woman came to me in shock. After 33 years of marriage, her husband had just announced that he was leaving her. This was his response to their teenage daughter's pregnancy. (Life is always stranger and crueler than fiction.)

Now these two blows were tragic enough. But this woman expressed another worry, vivid in her feelings in spite of the greater sufferings: Should she stop being a minister of Communion in her parish?

She was sure, from her experience, that some would think it improper for her to continue, even though she was completely innocent as far as the divorce was concerned. I was reminded of another case in which a mother received three poison-voice phone calls berating her for allowing her pregnant and unwed daughter to remain at home!

These are examples of a total absence of community and total ignorance of what a parish is called to be. They reflect an externalism that has no heart— the very thing Jesus condemned the most: pharisaical "scandal."

The community aspect of the sacraments is doubly important in the case of marriage: First, there would be no community if there were no faith-full married Christians; second, married Christians need the support of the community to remain faith-full.

We know this instinctively. Baptism may unfortunately be celebrated with only a few people present; and Penance may, also unfortunately, be an isolated experience. But weddings always bring a crowd of friends and relatives. In a sense, this is the Church community giving approval and support. It is a kind of natural "parish" for the couple.

But perhaps the friends live far on the other side of town and relatives return to Coshocton and Seattle. What then? Perhaps nothing but what is described by a rather ominous term: "the nuclear family," husband and wife and children alone in a sea of strangers. Perhaps they do not even know the names of the people in the next apartment.

So, let us go back to that community gathered around the altar for Eucharist. Today we are celebrating the wedding of Jim and Helen.

What do we *mean* when we celebrate the sacrament? What do we say to them—and to all the husbands and wives struggling to communicate their feelings to each other, to put their lives on the line each new day, to maintain love and patience when the fire burns low? What do we say to those deserted by their spouses, or hurt by infidelity? What do we say to all the fathers and mothers present, those with children pulling straight A's and those whose sons are already crippled by drugs and whose daughters reject the faith that was "rammed down their throats"?

We again say something *ideal, impossible, Christian.* We say that sacramental Christian marriage is like the human-divine life of Jesus himself: God-like love flowing into (and through) the limited "container" of our human nature.

In Jesus, there were no limitations of selfishness, no moral obstructions— only the physical limitations of flesh, space, time. In married Christians, there are also moral limitations, the not-always-successful struggle to love freely and generously. But the similarity to Christ's life is there, nevertheless. Day by day, "for better or worse, in sickness and in health," the patient effort of Christian couples to be faithful to each other and to the ideals of Christ is the constant making of the Church, the Body of Christ. Christian couples' love gathers into itself all that is beautiful about "natural" love and transforms it in a personal couple-relationship to Jesus.

It is possible that a couple want to be married without considering the Christ-relationship. They would just as readily be married by a justice of the peace, except that their Catholic families would be upset, or because they like the church or the reception hall.

Now, this may be a "good" marriage. The couple may love each other very deeply just as, say, two atheists may love each other. We are not ridiculing this love; we are just saying that if it has no relationship to Jesus it is not *Christian*.

We are all at different stages of faith. Perhaps that couple has a glimmering of what they are called to do in faith. Perhaps their love will develop, and they may "catch on" to what it's all about. We cannot judge the interior disposition of anyone. But we cannot water down the sacrament, either.

The Presence of the Divine. All genuine love is divine. For if it is genuine, it springs from the presence of God at the heart of all who love.

> God is love,
> and he who abides in love
> abides in God,
> and God in him. (1 Jn 4:16)

We have to say that if love fills one's whole life, it is fully graced love, even though it is not consciously Christian because of ignorance or immaturity.

But Christian married love is called to be *consciously* Christian, *consciously* Jesus-related, *consciously* divine. The grace of the sacrament is the one love of God enabling a couple to live a Jesus-conscious life in all the circumstances of marriage.

Veteran marrieds may smile at this—tolerantly or cynically. But Christians can say no less.

It took a while for the Church to realize the depths of Christian marriage, it is true. At first Christians were married by whatever secular form was in use. But gradually it became evident that there was something special about the love of Christian husbands and wives. The sacrament was not created, then, but discovered.

Some Catholics have heard St. Paul's words about Christian marriage so often that they flow over them like water off an oilskin: "This is a great foreshadowing; I mean that it refers to Christ and to his Church" (Eph 5:32). It sounds "tacked on" to what everybody knows is the "real" and thoroughly human experience of marriage.

Again we must say: We are not talking about just any marriage, no matter how beautiful, but Christian marriage. And again it must be said: No condemnation of couples who have not reached even the most minimal stage of Christian awareness is intended. God bless them, but let's not talk about the sacrament as if it is something that happens magically by repeating the words "I do" in front of someone who happens to be a priest.

The Meaning of Christian Marriage. What has our (hopefully ideal) community (with the help of the couples' parents, of course) taught Jim and Helen over the years about marriage?

They have taught them, by the example of daily living and sometimes in words of faith, that Jesus is the inspiration and the empowerment of married love; that all the pleasure and pain of marriage, the highs and the lows, have a part in the redeeming love of Jesus that is saving the world. They have demonstrated that the deeper their faith is, the more they can love each other; that the more they open themselves to the unknown depths to which God is leading them, the more they can be willing to venture with trust into the mysterious growth areas of human relationship. They have professed that communion with each other is communion with God, and communion with God is enriched by the experience of human love in all its forms.

Jim and Helen realize that Jesus' love is a love for individual persons, not just a generic love spread thinly over all. The whole Church is made up of families, and the love within families is the symbol and actuality of Jesus' love for the Church, and the Church's love for Jesus. One feeds the other; one is impossible without the other.

Most of all, they realize that they cannot maintain their love without being inwardly possessed by the love of Jesus. That is, they know that if they had to find fulfillment *only* in each other, they would not find it.

Faithfulness in Marriage. The greatest thing the Jews could say about their God was that Yahweh loved them with a steadfast covenant love. They might change, or sin, or abandon God, but he could not abandon them.

To put it in the lowest terms, God is "stuck" with us. It's his choice, but it is a choice that calls for a lot of forgiveness, patience, that marvelous attribute called "long-suffering," and waiting. But God loves us anyway, not reluctantly or with a love that has grown merely official from the wear and tear of our unfaithfulness, but with both the fireworks-love of the young and the steady-burning love of the mature.

The essence of any Christian marriage is to reflect God's love in a lifelong commitment. If the worm of tentativeness is in the apple on the wedding day, there is no real marriage—only a tryout.

So the Christian couple is undertaking a fearful thing: to have and show and share the very love of Christ to each other for life, and to "create for God"—pro-create—faith-full children.

We used to use a horribly inadequate word for Christian marriage: *contract*—something that is possible between the bitterest enemies. *Covenant* is a better choice because in that we are imitating God. He "wedded" himself to us for eternity, and he will not turn back. Jesus' humanity is the pledge of that. Married couples enter into God's eternal faithfulness because there is no other way for their love to be divine and complete.

This means infinitely more than not committing adultery. It means making life together a shared adventure with intimations of eternity. Everything has eternal value, everything is "for good."

The word for this quality of Christian marriage is "indissoluble." This does not mean love cannot die, but that the very nature of living Christian love simply makes "another" married love as impossible as having two heads. This is not merely an external law, but a condition of having Christian married love in the first place.

Jesus himself said it: "What I say to you [in contrast to the former permission to divorce] is: everyone who divorces his wife—lewd conduct is a separate case—forces her to commit adultery. The man who marries a divorced woman likewise commits adultery" (Mt 5:32).

Jesus is not just talking to people who have reached the stage where adultery becomes appealing. He is saying that married love can think of nothing less than having the faithfulness of God.

Bible scholars have long puzzled over Matthew's phrase, "except for lewd conduct." Now, Jesus is certainly rejecting the easy-divorce principles of some of the religious teachers of his day. He is not "allowing" remarriage because of immoral conduct on the part of husband and wife. He must mean, the scholars point out, a marriage that is not a marriage—an illicit union, a mere living together.

'Annulments,' Separation, Pauline Privilege. When a marriage is not fully a marriage, as in the case of a non-consummated union, the Church has always claimed the right to annul. What is often *mistakenly* called "annulment" today is something quite different. Technically, it is called a "declaration of nullity," that is, a Church court finds that there was "nullity," *no marriage,* from the beginning. True marriage never did exist, for one or more reasons: for example, because of force or fraud, psychological immaturity, emotional disorder—whatever did, in fact, prevent the "consent" from being the full and free consent required for the lifelong covenant of Christian marriage. The Church in these cases is not changing its doctrine, merely deciding about *facts.*

Separation is sometimes legitimate. Uncondoned adultery is such a reason—though forgiveness is always an option. If life becomes intolerable because of physical, moral or emotional abuse, there is no obligation to continue living together. It may be necessary, in some cases, to obtain a civil divorce, so that the innocent party can be assured of obtaining his or her rights. This does not, of course, mean freedom to remarry, since the previous marriage bond still exists.

The following words of St. Paul are the basis for the Church releasing a person from a non-sacramental marriage for the sake of his or her faith: "If any brother has a wife who is an unbeliever but is willing to live with him, he must not divorce her. And if any woman has a husband who is an unbeliever but is willing to live with her, she must not divorce him. . . .If the unbeliever wishes to separate, however, let him do so. The believing husband or wife is not bound in such cases. God has called you to live in peace" (1 Cor 7:12b-13, 15).

So, when a partner in a non-sacramental marriage will not live "peaceably" with the other party, who is thereby kept from practicing the faith, the Church invokes these words of St. Paul to annul the marriage.

Sacrament of Daily Life. One professor of theology used to treat marriage first in his course on the sacraments because it so fundamentally enters into all aspects of life. That is to say, God's love enters the lives of husband and wife in every kind of situation. The particular "crisis" or "decisive point" to which this sacrament looks is *all life.* One might say this of Baptism, in that the life of God is given simply for living. But the grace of marriage focuses that baptismal power on the day-to-day, nitty-gritty, earthly-divine elements of life which married persons face.

No offense to the single. One can lead the full baptismal life without being married—and do so devotedly, heroically. The very nature of sexuality—"male and female he created them" (Gn 1:27)—shows the essential incompleteness of every person, absolutely needing to be filled by love and friendship, whether in marriage or in single life. But obviously married life, with its tremendous responsibility for children and its intimate, exclusive and lifelong relationship, involves experiences which singles do not have.

God's gracing of matrimony is a pointed reminder that everything human has been consecrated—making a living, going on a picnic, holding a sick child, exploring all the pleasures and enrichment of sexuality, building a new home, putting up with the old car, facing emotional, physical and moral problems, failing and succeeding, forgiving and starting all over again.

When Beginnings Are Shaky. In the United States, the diversity of Churches inevitably leads to marriages between Catholics and Lutherans, Jews and Episcopalians—even atheists and Christians.

Leaders of all faiths, I believe, must say that it is better for a person to marry within his or her own faith. If marriage is the sharing of life, it should include the sharing of the deepest values of life. It is hard to imagine a fully Christian marriage where husband and wife do not share the Eucharist. Perhaps two Christians will not be affected by differences on matters like papal authority, infallibility, some of the sacraments, Church tradition—but it seems impossible to do this without a quite vigorous faith (which of course should be there in the case of any Christian marriage).

But there may be a bigger problem than that of difference of belief—the *apparent* absence of much Christian belief at all. The priest must sometimes agonize over whether or not to concur with a couple's decision to marry. He cannot celebrate a sacrament that is almost certainly not a sacrament in any real sense of the word; for instance, when the only reason a couple wants to be married at St. John's is the fact that it is a "stylish" church. On the other hand, he cannot demand full maturity in those who by definition are called to grow.

That leaves a large gray area in between where he must weigh the possible harm of a commitment that has very shaky foundations and the possible benefit of a beginning surrounded by a supporting, praying community.

Equality in Marriage. Poor St. Paul has been boxed in with the male chauvinists, and it's not really fair. He did reflect the culture of his time, as we all do. (Future ages will be horrified at our blithe abuse of natural resources.) He certainly did not see women as inferior to men: "All of you who have been baptized into Christ have clothed yourselves with him. There does not exist among you Jew or Greek, slave or freeman, male or female. All are one in Christ

Jesus" (Gal 3:28).

In marriage he counsels husbands and wives to give themselves equally—wholly—to each other. "A wife does not belong to herself but to her husband; equally, a husband does not belong to himself but to his wife" (1 Cor 7:4). Even the often quoted verse, "Wives should be submissive to their husbands as if to the Lord" (Eph 5:22), is preceded by a word to *all:* "Defer to one another out of reverence for Christ" (Eph 5:21). And no less is demanded of husbands. They must love their wives "as Christ loves the church" (Eph 5:25).

Children. Mutual communion in love is so intimately connected with that other purpose of marriage, the procreation of children, it is impossible to separate them. Love is by nature creative—otherwise we would not be here. This divine instinct makes people who truly love each other want to see that love *embodied* and shared. It is only because mother and father love each other that there is any hope they will have "normal" children, that is, persons who can experience life as God made it to be.

It is as important to help children *experience* being Christian, if only in a minimal way, as it is to teach them Christian concepts and definitions. This of course is part of the whole "change" in the world and in the Church from an emphasis on the objective to an emphasis on the subjective, from "what" to "why," and from external form to internal meaning.

Fathers and mothers can never delegate their responsibility to others. Everyone else—priest, nun, teacher—is a helper for them. Parents have the primary privilege and responsibility of "teaching" religion to their children. Actually, they succeed or fail at this "automatically," or rather, inevitably. That is, they are exposing their children to day-long experiences, and these experiences are either Christian or they are not. If they are, then the child has experienced the meaning of Jesus before any words or definitions are learned. Those experiences of love and forgiveness, respect and sharing, a common table and common prayer—are the greatest—and really the only—"education" parents can give their children. Parents must trust that their marriage in Christ gives their lives power.

The day may come when their children will either sinfully or misguidedly reject these values. So be it. They must take their lives into their own hands and decide. Parents can only do what God does: offer truth and love and ultimately allow freedom to make its choice. The community shows the concern of Jesus in helping parents in this task.

And Still the Community. The law of the Church requires that Catholic couples be married before a priest and two witnesses. This sounds very cold and legalistic. It means that marriage is a great concern of the community. The priest is to make a judgment—and he can be helped by any number of community members—as to whether the couple is indeed free to marry and whether they are prepared to live a Christian married life.

Every new marriage is a new unit of the Church beginning—for there would be no "big" church without all the little "domestic churches" of family life—and the community is concerned that it be a responsible unit, not just a couple whom civil law declares to be married. The two witnesses stand up for the community, but there should be many more than two. Again, not just to "make it legal" but to show the support and prayer and welcome of the community—and to promise that support for the future: in warm friendship, for every Sunday, for times of financial or emotional strain; when children come or tragedy strikes through death or disgrace or desertion.

The deserted wife mentioned at the beginning of this chapter must not have received (or noticed) the message of community love from her parish. All those "little churches" of Christian marriage should have given most when she needed it most. Marriage—and those suffering broken marriage—can only survive by feeding on and passing along the divine love at the heart of the sacrament.

21.

 Jesus Continues His Priesthood: Orders

The ideal community of Jesus, the Church, contains an amazing variety of individuals. The love of God shines through them like colors through a prism. But the richness can be sustained only if there is comm-*unity.* Jesus must be the center, the Head, the only source and model of Christian life.

The whole Church makes Jesus visible. The priesthood makes Jesus visible as Head and Center. The unity of the Church gets its visible support from the gathering of Christians around his visible representatives in the priesthood. (In this chapter we use the word *priest* to include bishops, who have the fullness of the priesthood, for priests, and for deacons within the limits of their sacramental function.)

Recall that a sacrament is first of all a *sign.* The sacramental ordination of a priest is a sign Jesus makes through the action of his Church. In this case, it is the public "sending" of a person to make Jesus visible in the Church as Head of his Body, a *center* around which the Church can find its unity.

In a culture where the only authority usually recognized is that of competence, not appointment, the ordination of a man may seem to say that he is "better" than the rest of the Church. A priest should be a true disciple of Jesus. But, to put it crudely, Jesus has to have *somebody,* so he picks this man! It could be anyone, but it must be *someone*.

The Church is not a group of unrelated individuals, but a Body, a living organism, a unity which needs a center. The priest is, for his Eucharistic community, a public center from which Jesus wants the Good News proclaimed; a visible center around which the community gathers for Eucharist and other sacramental celebration; and a center from which unified guidance can come. The priest is the means of sacramental union with Jesus.

No one knows better than a priest that he is unworthy to make Jesus visible as Head of the Church. But it must be done. The Church must hear "This is *my* Body" and know that it is Jesus truly speaking. A sinner must know that Jesus is personally forgiving and healing him when he hears "I absolve you from your sins."

What Priests Do. Jesus sent his apostles and their successors and helpers to proclaim the Good News in his name, to celebrate the Eucharist and the other sacraments, and to guide and shepherd the People of God. This "sending" is the origin of the new *Christian* priesthood, and these three functions of the priest are the three great offices of Jesus: prophet, priest, king.

Vatican II reminded priests that their *primary duty* is the proclamation of the gospel of God to all. In this way they fulfill the Lord's command, "Go into the whole world and proclaim the good news to all creation" (Mark 16:15). Through this Word the spark of faith is struck in those who do not yet believe, and it is fed in the hearts of the faithful. The Council lists four ways in which priests proclaim the Word: by their own "honorable behavior, by actual missionary preaching, by handing on and explaining the faith, and by their trying, in the light of Christ, to deal with contemporary problems." Priests do not teach their own wisdom—but God's Word, "to summon all men urgently to conversion and holiness" (*Decree on the Ministry and Life of Priests, #4*).

If the primary task of the priest is to proclaim the gospel, the *source* of that preaching *and its apex* is the celebration of the Eucharist, "the very heartbeat of the congregation of the faithful over which the priest presides" (*Ibid, #5*).

Radiating from the Eucharistic celebration in the midst of the community, the priest's office of pastor, guide, shepherd is concerned above all with peaceful unity—in charity, in doctrine, in service. "They gather God's family together as a brotherhood of living unity and lead it through Christ, and in the Spirit, to God the Father" (*Ibid, #6*).

He has the responsibility of handing on the authoritative teaching belief of the Church, and thus sometimes of pointing out doctrinal error.

In specific detail, there is almost no end to what a priest may be called to do. Nowadays, he is getting more and more help from the laity, as is proper. In a changing world, he can only try to be open to changing needs in the spirit of the Good Shepherd.

Bishops. Priests, though they work fairly independently, are helpers of the bishops, who represent the apostles whom Jesus sent as his primary representatives. Bishops have the fullness of the priesthood. Sacramentally, the main difference between bishops and priests is that the former can ordain other bishops and priests and are, by the office, *the* official proclaimers of the Word in their dioceses. A bishop is *the* spiritual father of the Church over which he has been placed to serve.

Deacons. Deacons share in the office of Jesus the priest "in the ministry of the *liturgy,* of the *word,* and of *charity."* Vatican II lists these offices of a deacon: to administer Baptism, to care for and dispense the Eucharist, to assist at marriages, to bring Holy Communion to the dying, to read the sacred Scripture to the faithful, to instruct and exhort the people, to preside at the worship and prayer of the faithful, to administer sacramentals, and to officiate at funeral and burial services. He is also dedicated to duties of charity and administration (*Constitution on the Church,* # 29).

Problems. Wherever there is authority, there is going to be trouble. The priesthood has the problem of involving two totally different kinds of authority: first, what might be called jurisdictional, that which has to do with *government* and *law* in the Church. We have discussed this in an earlier chapter.

In this area popes and bishops have usually been at the storm center, either because of their own faults or because of the human aversion to being told what to do. But pastors, too, are now learning the joys and sorrows of democracy from parish councils and worship commissions. And even ordinary priests are more and more frequently hearing that new imperative mode in the English language: "Father, would you like to use these readings today, and these prayers of the faithful?"

A second problematic kind of authority is that connected with the "power of (holy) orders." Just what authority belongs to a sacramentally ordained bishop, priest or deacon?

Among Protestants, the names of denominations indicate their solution to the problem. Congregationalists hold that Christ is the only head of the Church, and all sovereignty rests in the congregation. Luther stressed the common priesthood of the faithful, and the doctrinal basis for Lutheran "ministering men" has not always been clear. Presbyterians (from *presbyter,* "elder") reject both episcopal authority and congregationalism. As the name implies, the Episcopalian church, as well as the Methodist offshoot, is under the authority of bishops. Baptists place authority in all the baptised in the local congregation.

In the Catholic Church, the recognition of the dignity of the laity has naturally led to many questions about their function. How many of the functions of the priesthood today could or should be exercised by laypersons? Lay pastoral care programs are being sponsored by many dioceses. These will bring more and more laypeople into such activities as teaching, counseling, spiritual care for the sick, hospital chaplaincies, administrative offices, spiritual direction, leadership of prayer groups. In the liturgy, they are becoming increasingly active as ministers of Holy Communion, lectors, cantors and catechists.

This can only be seen as a healthy development in the Church. Priests who have exercised most of the years of their priesthood before the cultural explosion of the 60's find the transition hard. But, despite unavoidable blisters from the new shoes, most priests welcome the "rise" of the laity. They were doing too many different things, anyway.

The Law of Celibacy. Priests of the Latin rite (as compared with the Eastern Catholic rite) are bound to celibacy, that is, not to be married. This practice began in the fourth century and was being gradually extended to the whole western Church by the 12th. Priests of the Eastern Church may marry, but usually they must do so before receiving the diaconate; they may not marry later.

The law of celibacy has no essential connection with priesthood. It is a law of the Church, and the Church could change the law if it wished. Individual priests may therefore be excused from the law and allowed to marry, having received permission no longer to be active priests.

Why celibacy? If we start at the most practical level, it is a matter of time and possibly economics. There would no doubt be advantages to a married priesthood, but there is also no doubt that a celibate priest has time to be available, mobile, and committed to a degree that no responsible married man could be. (See 1 Cor 7:32-34).

On the level of witness, anyone (not just a priest) who lets himself or herself be thus publicly designated as freely and faith-fully living a celibate life is giving a *sign*. The sign may not be impressive to many, and it may be obscured by human weakness and fault. But in itself, voluntary celibacy for Christ points to the need for every Christian to have one fundamental relationship before all others—with Christ. Gospel celibacy is not a putdown of marriage. It gives a *different* witness. Marriage glories in the holiness of the Incarnation, this life now; it is said to be an *incarnational* witness. Celibacy in faith is a witness to the other world, already present. It is, if you don't mind the big word, an *eschatological* witness.

Women Priests? The question of the possible ordination of women to the priesthood has been urgently raised by some Catholics in recent years. The pope and the bishops have resolutely rejected the idea for theological reasons. These reasons are not accepted as convincing by many proponents of equal rights for women, who claim that it is not a matter of doctrine, but of cultural inheritance. The question will no doubt continue to be argued, and Catholics will continue to have varying opinions.

The Divine Office. Bishops, priests and deacons are joined by members of religious orders and laity in what is called the Liturgy of the Hours or, in ordinary parlance, saying the Breviary, or the Divine Office. The purpose of this prayer, which is largely taken from Scripture, is to make the whole course of of the day holy. The "hours" are Morning, Daytime Prayer (at mid-morning, noon, or mid-afternoon), Evening Prayer and Night Prayer. By thus distributing the prayer through the day (and in some monasteries and convents during the night), the Church is "ceaselessly engaged in praising the Lord and interceding for the salvation of the whole world" (*Constitution on the Liturgy*, #83).

Religious Communities. A religious "order" or community—Sisters of Mercy, Dominicans, Brothers of Mary, Poor Clares, etc.—is a religious group of men or women who live in community, under a common rule, observing the vows of poverty, chastity and obedience with the approval of the Church. Religious orders find their distinctive spirit from their founder: Ignatius of Loyola for the Jesuits, Francis of Assisi for the Franciscans, Teresa of Avila for the Carmelites. Some orders are "clerical," that is, composed entirely or largely of priests. (These are not the same as "diocesan" priests, those ordained to serve a diocese.) Others are entirely lay. A man may be a priest *and* a Benedictine, or he may be a Benedictine only. It is an unintended insult to such brothers, "regular" members of an order, to ask why they do not "go on" to become priests. They have a wholly different function. They are, among men, what sisters are among women.

Each religious institute may have a particular kind of work, but the fundamental purpose of all is to be living reminders of eternal values to the rest of the Church. There is obviously a negative element to vows: one does not have property of one's own, one does not marry, one does not have absolutely free disposal of one's activities. But this "giving up," if done with a free spirit and buoyed by a joyful community life, is a reminder to all—like the celibacy of priests just referred to—of the "other world" whose values must underlie the most secular of activities. Religious brothers or sisters are not better than others. They just have a different function in the varied beauty of the Church.

Part V:
Our Grace-full Response to the Commandments of Jesus

22.

'With All Your Heart': Morality and Conscience

What do you do when you have experienced someone's love for you? When deep within you are filled with peace and security because someone has given you trust and generosity and unselfishness?

You want to *respond* in a way that will give the other the same happiness you have. Love begets love, not by measuring who gives or gets more but by a simple, free *response*.

As Jesus said:

"Therefore you shall love the Lord your God
    with all your heart,
    with all your soul,
    with all your mind,
    and with all your strength." (Mk 12:30)

Jesus is quoting Deuteronomy (6:5 and 10:12). This is no new commandment, therefore. It is, we might say, the most fundamental law of nature: that the creature turn back to the Creator with its whole being, with *everything*. God cannot ask for anything less than truth. And the truth is, we owe him absolutely everything; he has given us everything. God cannot love half-heartedly, or even with only 98 percent of his heart. Neither can his children. The Great Commandment is not an arbitrary rule but the law of our own human nature.

The Bible uses four words to express our whole being: *heart, soul, mind* and *strength*. We all know what these words mean and imply in everyday relationship: "Put your heart into it!" "Have a heart!" *Heart* means generosity, enthusiasm, feeling, passion and compassion. We have "soul music" and someone is the "soul" of kindness." *Soul* is life, spirit, breath. Our *mind* is something we make up or lose; it is our intention, awareness, purpose, decision. Finally, our *strength* is our power or our ability.

If we put all these things together, we know what we are called to be, and we know the elements that are involved in all human goodness and evil. Without too much forcing, we may even reduce the four terms to two: *heart-strength* to signify our feeling and our freedom; and *mind-soul* to express our consciousness, our awareness, knowledge.

Heart-Strength

What does our heart have to do with responding or not responding to the love of God, with being morally good or morally evil, with being in the "state" of grace or mortal sinfulness? Obviously everything.

Jesus had a lot of trouble with some of the Pharisees, as we have seen, because he kept emphasizing the heart, the interior, and they kept emphasizing external observance. He told them, for instance, "A good man produces goodness from *the good in his heart;* an evil man produces evil *out of his store of evil;* each man speaks from his *heart's abundance"* (Lk 6:45; emphases added). And on another occasion, again rejecting their excessive harping on external and ritual purity, Jesus said: "Woe to you scribes and Pharisees, you frauds! You cleanse the outside of cup and dish, and leave the inside filled with loot and lust!" (Mt 23:23).

Notice that Jesus speaks of something already in the heart before the good or evil act is done: there is a "store" of something there, even an "abundance." Modern theologians have coined a phrase that says the same thing in more abstract language: *fundamental option.*

What it all means is this: each one of us gradually *becomes* consistent in our way of life—fundamentally good or bad. We multiply decisions and, gradually, these decisions become one big decision—our way of life, our "heart," our "abundance," our "store." On that basis alone can we judge ourselves; and on that basis it becomes impossible for us to judge others.

The man or woman who has built up a way of living, responding, deciding that is aimed at total love of God—a fundamental option for God—is the one in whom all the glorious promises of God are being fulfilled. God truly lives in such a person; he or she is "in" the state of grace, is alive with God's life, has real faith, hope, love.

If we think of our lives as a line going from base-zero—an infant, neither good nor bad—to full life in Christ, we see the story of growth. When does one cross the line from being a non-moral infant or child to being a mature—better, *maturing*—person who freely and consciously chooses to accept God's love and life? It is as gradual and unmeasurable as the growth of a tree. This growth cannot be judged by anyone but the person involved—and God. What may look like the genuine thing from the outside, may not be. What may look like its absence may be a false impression.

But it should be evident that our true goodness takes its root, as Jesus said, in our "heart."

Mortal Sinfulness. As with a good "heart," so with an evil one. One decision after another produces—gradually, then finally—a big decision that is a fundamental choice, *a way of life,* that represents our values. "Where your treasure is," Jesus said, "there your heart is also" (Mt 6:21).

One only gradually slides into what St. John calls the "second death" and what catechisms have called "mortal" sinfulness—that is, the death of our relationship with God.

We may still be doing externally good things. The adulterer has not yet done anything overt. But, Jesus says, "if a man looks at a woman lustfully, he has already committed adultery with her in his heart" (Mt 5:28; *Jerusalem Bible*). People who have long since gone over the line interiorly may still be going to Church; but, "This people pays me lip service, but their heart is far from me" (Mt 15:8).

It is very hard—indeed, it is impossible—to judge the interior guilt of anyone else, precisely because we don't know where they are on the "ramp"—and whether they are headed up or down.

This is not to say that single acts are not sinful; or that external order, the keeping of laws, should not be a serious matter to any Christian. But no single act is committed in isolation from the rest of a life, apart from years of growth—or non-growth—in understanding and love. No one *suddenly* becomes an adulterer or an embezzler or a slanderer. Certainly no one enters mortal sinfulness abruptly. It is simply impossible psychologically and, therefore, morally.

Because this is so, I cannot judge the *guilt* of anyone's actions but my own. I can and I may judge the emotions and some of the reasons why somebody does something: obviously this person wants to be chairperson of the committee so badly she can taste it; obviously this man has a bossy, domineering temperament; obviously this boy "likes" this girl. But I cannot judge the moral goodness or evil of any of their actions.

Yet even while I cannot judge the guilt, I must deal with externals. Society cannot say, "Since we don't know the moral guilt of this bank robber, we will have to let him go." The bank robber can be convicted of a *crime* with complete certainty; but it is possible that he committed no serious sin. It is possible that his heart was drowned in fear or anger to such a degree that his fundamental goodness was temporarily blocked out.

Mind-Soul

Separating mind and heart is a dangerous business. It's like separating hydrogen and oxygen: you end up not having water. Each of us is *one* body-spirit, one free, intelligent, feeling being. Yet we speak of "knowing" as being different from "feeling" and "deciding."

Here we meet our conscience.

Conscience. Let us set aside for the moment two common usages of this term: We speak of "examining our conscience"—that is, remembering our *past* actions and considering their goodness or evil. Second, we speak of "forming our conscience"—thus taking it to be something that needs to be refined and sharpened for the *future*. Neither this past nor future orientation of conscience is the focus of our discussion here.

Conscience, rather, is our ability and our obligation to seek the truth and decide for the truth *now*. Ultimately, conscience is a decision or a judgment made in the light of our knowledge. It is a decision about the *here and now*.

To sin is to be aware of what God is really calling us to do here and now and to refuse (or simply to omit) to do it. To be a child of God and a follower of Christ is to have *discovered* by serious *deliberation* what the loving and Christlike thing is *here and now, deciding* to do it, and *doing* it.

Sometimes the impression is given that conscience is automatic. Sometimes it is: For instance, I have an impulse to take revenge; but the impulse is so alien to my love of God I immediately reject it. But more often the situation is cloudy: Should I stay with this sick person or not? How long? Should I move to a new job? Should I report this drug addict? Should I say this, or that, or nothing? When should I speak up against what seems to be unfairness? When be tolerant? How much money should I share with the poor?

Sometimes it is not even clear how the law applies, or if it applies. I may not bear false witness. But is it false witness to give good references to a person who desperately needs a job but who is not entirely competent? The commandment tells me not to kill. Must I let a maniac keep killing others if the only weapon I have to stop him will cause his death? I must not steal. Is it stealing to "tote" when one gets less than the minimum wage?

Prayer is not enough when good advice, discussion, authority and expertise is available. One cannot expect the Holy Spirit to insert decisions into our mind. The Spirit floods all of life with the light of the great truth of God's relationship with us. We know with absolute certitude the *spirit* with which we are to proceed. But the Spirit must not be subjected to our itch for magic, or made into a supernatural computer from which automatic answers can be obtained by pressing a few keys of prayer. Prudence is *our* job.

It has been suggested that there are four "D's" that make up the act of conscience. The first is to *dig* for facts. What's involved? Who? When? Where? Why? What will be the results? What does Jesus say? The Church? My friends? My enemies? The experts? Common sense? What do I sense through prayer?

The other "D's" are to *deliberate* between the alternatives, to *decide* one way or the other, and to *do* what has been decided.

A judgment of conscience always involves a bit—or a lot—of risk, depending on the amount of certainty I can acquire. But God accepts my good will in seriously approaching the question. I may turn out to be "technically," or objectively, incorrect or imprudent. I really shouldn't have bought the Edsel, or moved to Hoboken—but my decision was prudent—that is, I did all the things that truth and love required. (To make a very long story very short, this means that "God's will" is what I prudently decide!)

Sometimes conscience can only choose the lesser of two evils. Sometimes I may have difficulty deciding whether the good result I seek is worth the bad that will incidentally accompany it. And always a higher law makes lesser laws stand aside: "The Sabbath was made for man, not man for the Sabbath" (Mk 2: 27).

Conscience is not very often automatic. It is the ongoing moral task of our lives. Just as our heart and strength is gradually built up to become a store and an abundance, so our mind and soul gradually acquire habits of making either morally good or morally evil judgments.

To do good, for a Christian, is to see everything (at least subconsciously, by habit) in him who is the Light of the world. To sin is to shut out the Light. Jesus quotes Isaiah to describe a sinful conscience:

". . .they have firmly closed their eyes;
otherwise they might see with their eyes,
and hear with their ears,
and understand with their hearts,
and turn back to me,
and I should heal them." (Mt 13:15)

It has been said that Jesus merely brought the good or evil in people to the surface:

"Everyone who practices evil
hates the light;
he does not come near it
for fear his deeds will be exposed.
But he who acts in truth
comes into the light,
to make clear
that his deeds are done in God." (Jn 3:20-21)

The Challenge: Mercy. Our hearts and minds are mysterious, even to ourselves. We are not as free as we might be; we often obstruct light. We can only keep trying to be liberated from all that enslaves us, from all ignorance and prejudice. That is salvation—being saved, freed, rescued.

But as we go our way, we must stand under both the judgment and the mercy of God: "God reads your hearts" (Lk 16:15). That may be our greatest consolation—or our condemnation. We are not deceiving ourselves if we see that we were not entirely free in a certain thought or action, or we were not aware of the full meaning of the action. (And this holds for our good acts, too!) To reach the fullness of sin or goodness, we must be fully free and fully aware of the meaning of what we do.

And if we can be merciful to ourselves, we certainly must be so to others. As far as they are concerned, only the "mercy" side—not the "judgment"—is available to us.

Many people are damaged both in their awareness and in their freedom. Perhaps denied love in childhood, or kept in a state of perpetual anger or fear by the injustice of others, they are simply not fully free. Emotional sickness can also cloud both mind and will.

Jesus takes note of the differences in people's awareness in this parable: "The slave who knew his master's wishes but did not prepare to fulfill them will get a severe beating, whereas the one who did not know them and who nevertheless deserved to be flogged will get off with fewer stripes. When much has been given a man, much will be required of him. More will be asked of a man to whom more has been entrusted" (Lk 12:47-48). By the same token,

144

less will be asked of one to whom less has been entrusted.

Law

Emphasis on the interior may lead to de-emphasis on the exterior. But we are not angels. We are *body*-spirits, and our lives have sharp corners that may injure others, or take up their space, or consume their food. I am free, but so are you. Respecting each other's freedom imposes limits on both of us.

Laws are needed for organization in any society, even one of thieves. Laws try to ensure the peace and security of community life. They protect rights and define duties. They point out areas of moral danger.

But law, by nature, must be general and simple. It cannot take all circumstances into consideration.

This is the essential difference between civil law (at least in the U.S.) and the law of God and the Church. There are no exceptions in Anglo-Saxon law. Even if you need the money to save your child's life, the Internal Revenue Service will penalize you for not paying your taxes. Even in the middle of the desert and with no other cars within miles, you can be arrested for going through a red light.

But God's law is always directed toward the highest possible good, even if that means setting aside one of his specific commands. Thus my neighbor's need for first aid on Sunday morning outweighs my obligation to attend Mass; my desperate need for food takes precedence over your property rights.

Even God's positive laws (those which command us to *do* something, rather than avoid evil) may be morally or physically impossible to observe: I simply cannot take care of this person any longer; I cannot fulfill a promise now; in these circumstances, I cannot take back the stolen purse. Why? Because I would suffer greater harm than the situation warrants. Jesus excused David for eating the holy bread which only the priests were permitted to eat, because "he was in need and he and his men were hungry" (Mk 2:25).

Under God's law, the higher good also supersedes any human law, ecclesiastical or civil, unless disobeying the law would cause harm to the whole community. For example, if my refusal to give up a job for which I am incompetent but which I desperately need would mean the loss of federal funds for a project, my job must go. Likewise, if my refusal would mean contempt for God or goodness (I may not engage in immoral acts even to save my life or that of others).

How big a reason do I need to be excused from the law *now?* My reason— my physical or moral impossibility—must be as serious as the law itself. For instance, I do not need to have something as serious as scarlet fever to be excused from Mass this Sunday; but neither does soreness from yesterday's picnic excuse me. I need not go through a blizzard to bring the evening paper to my mother; but I must run the risk of infection to save the life of an abandoned sick person.

In all this, we see the need for a sensitive, humble conscience. To say that one may sometimes be excused from the law is not to say we should make a career of looking for excuses. On the other hand, to worship the law and neglect its purpose and the human needs of others is to fall into the legalism of the Pharisees, so angrily denounced by Jesus. "Woe to you scribes and Pharisees, you frauds!" he said. "You pay tithes on mint and herbs and seeds while neglecting the weightier matters of the law, justice and mercy and good faith. It is these you should have practiced, without neglecting the others" (Mt 23:23).

Wholeness in Action. Spirit and meaning is not enough; external rule-keeping is not enough. With our *whole* persons we are to love God—with our whole heart, our whole mind, our whole soul and our whole strength.

We keep the highest law in mind *first:* following Jesus in total faith and trust and love for God and neighbor. Then we try our best to sort out all the tangled circumstances of life and bring the spirit of Jesus to bear. We want his light to shine on our whole life—all persons, all circumstances, all possibilities. We want our hearts to be ruled by the generosity of Jesus himself.

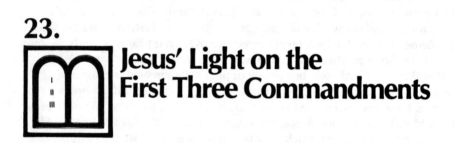

23.
Jesus' Light on the First Three Commandments

There are no rules to define love's responses, though love always finds concrete expression. Those who have not yet experienced God's love need rules—guard rails, as it were—to keep them from hurting themselves until they catch on to what life is about.

So there are commandments for all of us who seem never to catch on completely to what God is about, to what his love is all about. Sometimes we experience a transfiguration, a peak moment when we feel the awesomely tender love of God within us. At other times we need the guard rails, when we seem barely able to do the minimum.

So the Christian life is a strange combination of two things. On the one hand we experience the zeal of which John spoke: "The anointing you received from him remains in your hearts. This means you have no need for anyone to teach you" (Jn 2:27). On the other hand we need to be as hard on ourselves as the most cold-blooded business analyst: "Where are the results? What proof is there that you are Christian? Are you doing even the minimum—keeping the rules?"

These two outlooks may be behind the polarization in the Church today. Some say that if you don't *mean* what you do, if there's no love in it, what's it worth? Others argue that if you don't *do* what you say you mean, what good is your airy talk about love?

Thus you have people complaining, "They don't teach the Ten Commandments anymore," and calling for more discipline, more authoritative teaching. And you have others pleading for depth and spirit and deep personal relationships with God and with our neighbor.

At least these two groups may keep each other honest!

The 'Commandments' of Jesus

As Christians, we must base our lives primarily on the commandments of Jesus, which obviously include the Ten Commandments. Jesus said, "Do not think I have come to abolish the law and the prophets" (Mt 5:17). But Jesus came to bring the law—all law—to perfection.

The new law is his own Spirit and spirit. Jesus is our Law. And following that law will take us miles beyond the Ten Commandments, which are only the minimum, the guard rails of morality.

The whole New Testament is the commandment of Jesus. His life, his spirit, his death and resurrection, his presence with us—that is our law of life, the standard whereby we make generous responses of love and conscientious decisions.

Spirit, not analysis, binds friends. That is to say, two people who love each other do not sit down and *chart* their love. One would never say to the other, "Today I will work on trusting you; tomorrow I will concentrate on being generous to you; and Sunday I will zero in on faithfulness." Rather, they want to be all these things at once, as expressions of one spirit, one love. At times, they may send many words tumbling over each other, trying to express the *one* love: "I love you. I trust you completely. I will stay with you through thick and thin. What is mine is yours. You light up my life."

It is the same in our relationship to God. We speak of "different" virtues (faith, hope and charity) but they do not live in airtight compartments. One supposes the other; none can survive without the others.

So, in this chapter, we will discuss several things together, because they belong together and are all concerned with the one love that must fill our lives. That is, we will combine the *first three commandments* of God and the fundamental virtues of *faith, hope* and *love.* These first three commandments concern God directly; so do the virtues. And Jesus' "commandments" bring them to perfection. True, it is impossible to separate love of God and love of neighbor; to separate the first three Commandments from the other seven. But since we cannot talk about everything at once, we think first of our relationship to God.

A Matter Between Friends. We begin then, with the supposition that the commandments are a matter between *friends.* The fact that this friend is God does not affect the freedom of love. But in this case there is no equality between friends: God is the total giver and we are total receivers. The friendship begins when this loving God-man Jesus says to us, because he loves us: *"Follow me."*

"Follow *me*. Not just any one thing, not just any one teaching, not just any one rule. But *me*, as a person. Make my spirit your spirit, my attitude your attitude. You don't have to do what I did—be a carpenter, walk around Palestine. You will probably not have to die the same way. But I have no choice but to ask you to die to everything but me. I love you. I died for you and I live for you. Trust me."

Now the "greatest" commandment has a new meaning: "You shall love the Lord your God with all your heart, with all your soul, with all your mind, and with all your strength"—and now the "new" commandment of Jesus: *"And follow me in doing this!"*

In other words, Christians do not start with the law, even the law of the Ten Commandments. We start with Jesus, and fulfill all law in his spirit.

Another "commandment" of Jesus, if we may call it that, is to believe that in loving him and our neighbor we are made part of the community of God, the Trinity. "He who loves me will be loved by my Father" (Jn 14:21). He asks us to believe that "the love of God has been poured out in our hearts through the Holy Spirit" (Rom 5:5).

This is less a commandment than a reassurance. Jesus is saying, "Don't be afraid to believe that it is God, not just a man, who loves you. You are valuable, you are important, you are loved. Live with this assurance. Then all other things—all obedience—will be added to you."

The whole Christian life is a matter of responding to the love and friendship of God as we experience it in Jesus and through his Spirit. It is unthinkable—except when we let down our end of the friendship—that we should reduce friendship merely to "fulfilling our obligations." When friends start doing that, they become strangers fulfilling a contract.

The first thing Jesus asks—a commandment, if you will—is that we have a personal relationship, an "encounter," a friendship with him, and experience his love. How do we do that? Only by being loved by other human beings: family, friends, the Christian community.

With All Your Heart. Is there such a thing as a "minimal" friendship? Can you tell me how much I "have to do" to be your friend, or give me a list of obligations so that when I have fulfilled them I don't need to bother further? Anyone who has ever loved and been loved—in marriage, family, community—knows that this is the sign of a dying or dead friendship. We make up the list, not our friend—and we make it as long as we possibly can.

Love is like fire. It cannot be confined. If you put walls around it, with no outlet, it dies. Therefore the God who knows all about love can only ask us to love him *totally*. Jesus was not being domineering, only truthful, when he said, "None of you can be my disciples if he does not renounce *all his possessions"* (Lk 14:33; emphasis added). Nothing, no treasure of mind or body or bank, can be more important than our friendship with Jesus.

People may complain about the lack of absolutes today, but this is one absolute: "Love me absolutely." This is what love of God is.

There's a nameless saint in the Gospels, a poor widow who had only two copper coins to her name. It was, in Jesus' words, "every penny she had to live on." She put them into the treasury of the Temple, and Jesus loved her. "I assure you, this poor widow has put in more than all the rest. They make contributions out of their surplus, but she from her want has given what she could not afford" (see Lk 21: 1-5).

Isn't this unrealistic? Idealistic? Impossible? Yes, of course. How deep a friendship would you have to have to give up your last two pennies? Yet that is the kind of absolute trust Jesus asks of his followers.

This trust is like that of the birds of the sky and the lilies of the field. Birds don't have barns, and wild flowers don't have garment factories. "Yet your heavenly Father feeds them. Are you not more important than they? . . . Your heavenly Father knows all that you need. Seek first his kingship over you, and all these things will be given you besides" (Mt 6:26, 32-33).

Notice that Jesus doesn't ask us to abandon our intelligence or our daily work. He just says that there must be an absolute priority in our lives: the kingship of the Father. Those who would follow Jesus must want absolutely to be possessed by the love of the Father and to live by the power and wisdom of God.

The First Three Commandments

First Commandment. *"I, the LORD, am your God, who brought you out of the land of Egypt, that place of slavery. You shall not have other gods besides me" (Ex 20:2-3).*

What has Jesus done to this commandment? We "keep" it now by having the absolute love of Jesus for his Father and an absolute trust in Jesus himself, who alone leads us out of every kind of slavery. Jesus tells us that his friendship must precede all other loves. Anything less than total love is a lie, love given to other "gods"—other sources of power, pleasure, love, happiness.

If we really have experienced friendship with Jesus, all the *details* of the commandment become obvious. No one thinks to *buy* a real friend's care or concern (magic, superstition), and the last thing to do would be to abuse or dishonor someone or something connected with the friend (sacrilege).

Second Commandment. *"You shall not take the name of the LORD, your God in vain (Ex 20:7).*

In the biblical mind, the name *is* the person. ("My name is *me*," said a contemporary Arab to explain why he did not want me to write down his name, thus "possessing" him against his will.) Even for us it is unthinkable to use a friend's name to back up a shady deal or to support a lie. One speaks a friend's name with love. Our admiration shows through when we speak the word.

The name of God is *God.* Jesus tells us we are reborn in Baptism in the name of the Father and of the Son and of the Holy Spirit. We are reborn in

God. We are friends at the table of the Trinity. It should never enter our mind to dishonor God, who is his name.

Third Commandment. *"Remember to keep holy the sabbath day" (Ex 20:8).*

Jesus restored the Third Commandment to its purity. It had been strangled in all kinds of specifications that became more important than its real purpose: entering into God's "rest." Jesus cut through the red tape with, "The sabbath was made for man, not man for the sabbath" (Mk 2:27). He did not mean it wasn't made for honoring his Father, but that external acts of worship could wait for an hour or a day if one's neighbor had some urgent need.

Jesus fulfills the Third Commandment by giving us the perfect gift with which to worship the Father—himself. The Eucharist is at the heart of the Christian life, and the Sunday liturgy is where the Body of Christ is most clearly visible on earth today.

If the question must be put and an answer must be given, participation in Sunday worship is indeed a *serious* obligation. For whom? It is a *happy* obligation for friends and lovers who are always "much obliged." (If I cannot make a planned visit to my friend, I call him or her and say I am sorry. And I really am.) It is a *burdensome* obligation only if it is not part of wanting to follow Jesus in his friendship to his Father.

(This is the only one of the Ten Commandments that is not natural law, that is, which is not a precept which any reasonable person could come to recognize even without revelation.)

The First Three Virtues

The total commitment of friendship also tells us what the first three virtues are. The absolute friendship *is* faith. It is giving ourselves to God through Jesus in a way we cannot give ourselves to any human being. It is total trust—in the dark, if necessary. It is a risk gladly taken—"Whatever you say." It is burning all the bridges behind us. It is believing God's Word as we can believe no human being's word. But it is more than that. It is entering into a dynamic relationship which grows and deepens as experiences multiply.

Faithful friendship merges into a confidence that is unshakable—hope. I trust my friend. I trust an absolute friend absolutely. It is not wishful thinking—like hoping I win the Irish Sweepstakes or hoping I don't have to give a speech. It is, rather, *expectation* of what I do not yet see: I expect God to be the perfect friend and to give me the power to be a worthy friend in return. I am absolutely certain of forgiveness, patience, generosity, faithfulness. I can *expect* these.

I may have a terrible temptation to abuse this hope by simply presuming on God's friendship without reciprocation. But it does not seem possible for anyone who has known God in Jesus ever to despair of his forgiveness.

As for love, what else is friendship but love? What else is absolute friendship but absolute love? It is "naturally" so on God's part, and the purpose of human life is the attempt to let God make our love absolute in return.

Jesus' First Recorded 'Commandment'

"After John had been arrested, Jesus went into Galilee. There he proclaimed the Good News from God. 'The time has come,' he said, 'and the kingdom of God is close at hand. Repent, and believe the Good News' " (Mark 1:14-15; *Jerusalem Bible*).

Thus Matthew and Mark summarize the beginning of Jesus' public ministry. Jesus gave people ample reason to understand, however dimly, that in him the Kingdom had indeed come. They could sense, from his whole personal presence, that he brought good news, indeed *the* Good News. Only when we sense this can we repent.

In fact, the word *repent* has been weakened by joking use in imitation of countless preachers. We must go back to what the word literally means: "Change your outlook, change your way of life!"

Change *from* what? Change *to* what?

Many "converts" have never turned from God. Their whole lives have been nourished by God's Word, at least as it comes to them through a sincere conscience. They have never had to "turn" from a seriously sinful way of life. But they did have to be changed from mere human beings, members of a race alienated from God, to a "new creation," living the life of God himself. Gradually, or all at once, they understood the love of God, the evil of sin, the privilege of grace; and their lives became a process of constant change for the better.

For those who really have turned away from God with full consciousness and freedom, these words are indeed the first commandment: "Repent, and believe the Good News." They are life-or-death words. When Jesus was asked whether the Galileans whom Pilate murdered were being punished as sinners, he said, "Certainly not! But I tell you, you will all come to the same end unless you reform" (Lk 13:5).

This is jolting, and Jesus meant it to be. A good doctor does not shield a patient from essential danger. It is useless for us to pile up all sorts of supposedly meritorious practices—going to Mass every Sunday, scrupulously avoiding adultery, murder and robbery—without even seeing our fundamental selfishness, superficiality and self-sufficiency. It is useless to "go through" sacramental ritual—Baptism, Eucharist—unless we let God thoroughly change our heart, our whole outlook and way of life. Or rather, unless we let God fill us with the determination to enter seriously upon this lifelong process.

But notice the positive and reassuring love of God which surrounds the strong words of Jesus about repentance: "the good news of God"; "the time of fulfillment" (of God's promise of salvation); "the reign of God is at hand." God can only be a loving Father, Jesus can only be one who heals. And the Church—you and I—must be the witness of this.

How Can Anybody Keep These Commandments? Since we are considering the first and fundamental commandments, we should also consider the first heresy: "If you try hard enough, you can save your soul. If you work at it, you can be holy. You can put God in your debt."

It is hard for us to believe that our virtue is not our own—though we find it easy to let our sin be somebody else's fault. After all, we say, nobody helped me stay honest and pure and sober. I was the one who got up in the dark and went to Mass, or said my prayers. I deserve the credit.

God does give us credit for freely doing what he asks us to do. But the most basic fact of life is that without him, we can do nothing. I cannot do a single good act without power flowing into me from God. It doesn't come from "outside," like current through a wire; but from the heart of my being, where God lives. It is not just a psychological "inspiration"—though it should be that, too. It is God offering and giving us the power to make courageous and generous decisions and to do the good thing.

If I "die" to my intense desire for revenge, the power of Jesus (whether I am conscious of it or not) joins that "death" to his and gives me another little share in his resurrection. The *Sacramentary* says it best: "Even our desire to please you is itself your gift." Or, as Scripture has it:

"It was not you who chose me,
it was I who chose you
to go forth and bear fruit.
Your fruit must endure." (Jn 15:16)

24.

Jesus' Spirit in Us Responds to the Father: Prayer

Prayer can hardly be called a commandment. If a husband and wife have to be commanded to talk to each other, they are nowhere near being candidates for the Couple of the Year Award.

Besides, it wouldn't work. Perhaps you can make people say words to each other, but you can't make them communicate. That comes only when they really want to share something with one another. Communication is another name for love.

When Jesus talked about prayer he spoke about its unsuspected depths, and about God's side of the communication.

Prayer as Gift. God speaks first. Prayer is not something we do in order to "get to" God. Prayer is God's gift to us. We cannot pray unless God opens our minds and moves our hearts and attracts us to himself.

That's surprising at first, and a bit deflating. We usually think of prayer as *our* business. But it's also a great relief. We are indeed responsible adults who must "make it" through each day; yet we are God's children, with our hand in his, walking along with him in total and peaceful dependence.

St. Paul says it with his usual directness: "The Spirit too helps us in our weakness, for we do not know how to pray as we ought; but the Spirit himself makes intercession for us, with groanings that cannot be expressed in speech. He who searches hearts knows what the Spirit means, for the Spirit intercedes for the saints as God himself wills" (Rom 8:26-27).

So prayer is what the Spirit does in us, and the Father knows what the Spirit means—and what we mean.

Who did this praying best? Jesus, of course. The Spirit drove him into the desert, to deep communion with his Father, for 40 days. Luke tells us that he often retired to deserted places to pray. We glimpse Jesus at prayer in some of the crucial events of his life: after being baptized, before choosing the apostles, alone on the mountain when people wanted to make him king and, above all, when he was in the agony of fear in Gethsemane.

"He kept saying, 'Abba [the tender but strong word of a son or daughter], you have the power to do all things. Take this cup away from me. But let it be as you would have it, not as I' " (Mk 14:36). An angel appeared to Jesus to strengthen him—the comfort of his Father. Then, "in his anguish he prayed with all the greater intensity, and his sweat became like drops of blood" (Lk 22:44). (One of the best ways we can pray is to enter into Jesus' *feelings* on various occasions in his life, for his human feelings are our human feelings.)

The first purpose of our prayer is to learn to pray as Jesus did. In describing the Transfiguration, St. Luke says, "While he was praying his face changed in appearance" (9:29). In Jesus' case, it was the divine glory shining through. In our case, it should be the *spirit* of Jesus possessing our minds and hearts.

Prayer, the Most Personal Thing We Do. There are no two sets of fingerprints alike in the world, and of course no two persons alike. Nor are there any two pray-ers alike. God has a unique relationship with each of us—just as we have unique relationships with every one of our friends. It's not just that our love is deeper for some; but each relationship has a different tone and spirit, a different style.

In prayer I am alone with God. Me, as I am, nothing hidden and nothing uncared for by a loving Father. The problem is not praying, but getting ready to pray. Once I can come to this face-to-face consciousness of God's presence, the response called for is evident. Unless I have been misguided somewhere along the way, I can be confident, calm, secure. I know my sins, but shame is not my prime emotion. I feel gratitude, assurance and true humility in the sense of total and perfectly willing dependence.

Prayer does not require a set of directions, any more than two friends need a script. This is not to ridicule certain suggestions made to keep our minds on the track, or rather, to keep us quiet enough to hear what God is saying. But it has been well said that once we have followed Jesus' advice and gone to our room and shut the door (see Mt 6:6), it doesn't matter what we say. It's probably best when we don't say anything.

Jesus warned against thinking that the value of prayer depends on the quantity of words we manage to speak. "In your prayer do not rattle on like the pagans. They think they will win a hearing by the sheer multiplication of words. Do not imitate them. Your Father knows what you need before you ask him" (Mt 6:7-8). Then he taught his apostles the Our Father.

Prayer is best when it is simple. It is simple when it has only one purpose: to "be still and know that I am God" (Ps 46:11; *RSV*).

The Pestering Petitioner. If this story were not in the Gospels, we would never dare make it up. Jesus teaches persistence in prayer with the example of a man who gets unexpected guests in the middle of the night.

With true Eastern hospitality, the man wants to set food before them. But he has no bread. Ah, a friend lives down the street. He goes to the friend's house and knocks on the door. There is a sleeping mat against the other side of the door. The whole family has been settled down, sardine-like, for hours.

It would be a major operation even to get the door open. So, the friend says, "Please come back in the morning. Go home, go to sleep." But the empty-handed host, no doubt secure in this friendship, keeps pounding on the door. Finally, Jesus says, the head of the house capitulates, throws off the covers, scoops the children from in front of the door, and shoves a loaf out into the darkness (see Lk 11:5-9).

Jesus says we must pester the Father in the same way, perfectly aware that he cannot get exasperated.

But petition him for what? At what is our persistence aimed?

"Hallowed be thy name, thy kingdom come, thy will be done on earth as it is in heaven." Perhaps not exactly what we had in mind. (At least we would have put the "daily bread" first.) And what does it mean after all?

In our best moments—moments of real prayer, whether all alone or on a crowded bus—we want first things first. We do love our Father—his Spirit empowering us, Jesus giving us the example—and like all who love we want first of all what pleases and celebrates the beloved.

God's name is God himself. He cannot be "hallowed," really, for he is holiness itself. We want him to be *seen* as holy, *honored* as holy, *accepted* as holy, by every one of his children. We want him to be holy in all of them.

And we want his Kingdom to come—his love gently possessing the minds and hearts and bodies of all. We want his will done, that is, his endless attempt to heal and forgive, to liberate and re-create, to make happy.

Jesus said, "Whatever you ask in my name I will do, so as to glorify the Father in the Son" (Jn 15:13). But at the same time, "Ask and you shall receive, that *your* joy may be full" (Jn 16:24; emphasis added).

'Ask and You Shall Receive.' Should we feel ashamed to ask for such things as a job, a home, a cure, or a spouse? Not so. But the standard of our asking is always that which we use with our best friends, those we most deeply love. At least when we are unselfish (and how can we deeply love if we are selfish?), we want *their* good first.

Our prayers of petition are not attempts to persuade God to do what he really does not choose to do; still less to inform him of our need. They are our persistent attempt to be wholly aware of our dependence on him. The more we think we need something—health, reconciliation, employment, protection—the more we realize that we are ultimately helpless.

That is not a disgrace, just the fact of being a creature. We have a Father who wants to share infinite riches with us. Persistent humble prayer is the way God can give us the best he wants to give. Sincere open prayer gives us the mind and heart of Jesus. Our only concern then is to be perfectly attuned to our Father's way.

Prayer and Praying. Our prayer is our life. If our lives are faith-filled, they are prayer. If our prayer is genuine, our life is faith-filled. This communion is the way of life for all who love. Just to be working in the house together is a source of satisfaction and pleasure to many husbands and wives.

But this is not enough. Precisely because they love each other, friends and lovers want to reserve certain times when they do nothing *but* communicate with each other. They simply want to *be with* each other.

So with prayer. Much as we may do our work in the peaceful awareness of God's presence, we are easily absorbed by that work. We do not see God as we see our friends. Our love needs to be nourished and stimulated—kept alive, we might as well admit—by times when we do nothing *but* communicate with God.

Ann Morrow Lindbergh once wrote that if her friends called to invite her to a party and she told them that she had an appointment with the hairdresser, it would be a perfectly valid reason for not going. But if she said she needed time for prayer, people would be puzzled. Yet without that "reserved" 15 or 30 or 60 minutes a day, we can easily become undernourished, a little less convinced, a little less ardent.

The *way* we pray is much less important than the fact that we do it.

Kinds of Prayer

1) *Vocal prayer* is prayer which has a set form—the Our Father, the Hail Mary, etc. It may be said aloud or silently. It gives a concrete form to expressions of faith and love. We do not have to worry about "making up" what we want to say. Especially when we are in physical or emotional pain, or find it hard to concentrate, familiar set prayers are our guide and sustenance.

2) *Mental prayer*—not a very apt name—is simply prayer which has no set form. It is not exactly the opposite of vocal prayer, however. It does not necessarily consist of "making up" words; it may be nothing but silence in the presence of God. It is informal and spontaneous, though it may follow some pattern. It is as hard to systematize as a conversation between friends.

This prayer may need a focus, something to fasten our thoughts on. Hence prayerful reading, especially from the Scriptures, may be a good way to begin. Not reading for information, or because we find an interesting subject; this is not a time of study. This reading is listening to the voice of God telling us about himself, so that we can respond.

Prayer is the response—in adoration, praise, thanks. It may be sorrow for sin. It may be petition, hopefully for the highest good, for God himself first; it may be thanks or petition concerned with other people.

It may be anything, as long as it comes from the heart. A better name than mental prayer, indeed, would be "prayer of the heart."

3) *The Jesus Prayer.* In recent years one form of prayer has been re-emphasized (it used to be called "making aspirations") under the influence of Eastern spirituality: the so-called "Jesus prayer." One simply says, "Lord Jesus Christ, Son of God, have mercy on me." This prayer is repeated—without hurry, from the heart, often rhythmically.

Other short prayers of this kind, of course, are at everyone's disposal, especially in Scripture: "Lord, I believe, help my unbelief." "Come, Lord Jesus." "Be it done to me according to your word." Above all, the traditional "doxology," the liturgical hymn of praise: "Glory to the Father, and to the Son, and to the Holy Spirit, as it was in the beginning, is now, and ever shall be!"

'Wasting' Time. Anyone who has tried to pray knows that more often than not it is just plain hard work. Like the writer who must first sharpen the pencil, then empty the wastebasket, then rearrange the books on the shelf, then do anything but write—so we avoid prayer. We not only find a hundred things to do before beginning to pray, but we also seem to have a thousand things we would rather do when we finally begin. In this difficulty, we are at least in good company. Even great saints found it hard to pray—or rather, they did not find it easy to pray.

God is a silent and mysterious God. He wants us to be his closest friends, but that involves truth, and the truth is that we are totally *creatures*, totally dependent. It is only when we admit our nothingness that our real "something-ness" in grace comes into being. This means total trust in God—often in silence, in lack of the supposedly necessary "enjoyment" of prayer, in trust.

Our prayer may get down to this: simply being in the presence of God. There may be no satisfaction in it for us, but we may in this way be led by a surprising route to a sense of what it means to depend on God.

Prayer, says Thomas Merton, cannot be measured in terms of *usefulness.* That is, we may not "get something out of it," or manage a neatly arranged series of emotional spasms, or come to clear conclusions. Prayer, he says, can only be understood as a complete surrender, a "waste" of time.

By "waste" Merton means being willing to give the time to God absolutely, simply because he is our absolute Lord and we owe him everything. This is not self-hatred but a sincere statement of the deepest reality. God is all, I am nothing. He has made me precious in his sight—I know that deep down—but all honor and praise belongs to him.

Prayer, Merton continues, has fruitful effects, but usefulness is not its purpose. In this, prayer is like friendship, which offers many "useful" benefits. But if these are the sole purpose for cultivating a friendship, there is really no friendship at all, only a business relationship

Merton has some reassuring words for us when we find prayer very dry and tedious. Especially in meditation, he says, we have to learn patience in the weary path that takes us through the dry places in prayer. This dryness grows more and more frequent, more and more difficult as time goes on. In a certain sense, aridity can almost be taken as a sign of progress in prayer, provided it is accompanied by serious efforts and self-discipline.

So prayer may sometimes have to be—or finally attain the privilege of being—just "wasting" time before God; that is, remaining in God's presence without being concerned about any personal benefit, but simply saying, "You are God. You are all. I adore you. I love you."

25.

Jesus' Light on Commandments Four Through Ten

Commandments Four through Ten concern the way we treat other people. All but the Fourth are negatively stated, drawing lines over which we may not step. Considering them only as negative, we cannot say they represent the extreme boundary even of natural morality. A person is not good merely because he or she does *not* kill or commit adultery or steal.

As one missionary used to say to the children: "That's what you *don't do;* but what do you *do do?*"

But God did not leave the Jews with only a list of negatives. In two separate places in the Old Testament, he made clear the attitude with which they should keep all commandments: "You shall love the LORD your God with all your heart" (Dt 6:5) and "You shall love your neighbor as yourself" (Lv 19: 18). Bringing all commandments to unity, Jesus combined these two commandments with his own specific command:

"This is my commandment:
love one another

as I have loved you." (Jn 15:12)

Whatever may be said as to whether or not Jesus taught a "new morality," this simple sentence lifted Christian morality beyond the most idealistic dreams of all the Platos of the world. Christians may still find it very difficult to form their conscience about a particular situation, as we have seen. But Christians have absolutely no doubt about the spirit, the attitude, the disposition, the heart of whatever they decide.

The standard of Christian conduct is not a law, but a person. Not "What would Jesus do?" but "What would Jesus' feelings be in this kind of situation, and how would he handle them? What would be his reasons for acting, his manner?"

Can we know how Jesus felt? Certainly, because we know how we feel. He had the same basic human feelings that we have because he was a true and normal human being. Ours are mixed with sinfulness and bad memories, perhaps, but there is a basic similarity in all human emotion.

One of the results of prayer has to be a deeper appreciation of Jesus the man. He cannot be telling us merely to imitate him externally (like the brother who coughed whenever St. Francis coughed) but in our innermost decisions.

What Is Love? Love has had many definitions, most of them ending with words like *moon* and *June.* Jesus summed it up simply: "Treat others the way you would like to have them treat you" (Mt 7:12).

Jesus calls us to look into the depths of our hearts where we find great incompleteness, loneliness and insecurity. We need other human beings who take us seriously, respect us, give us their trust and their affirmation, their bread and their forgiveness when we need it, and their willing and glad acceptance always.

This very unromantic definition of love will never make the hit parade but will suffice for all seasons: To love others is to give them what they need insofar as we are able.

Need is a deceptively simple word. What do *you* need? That's what *others* need. How far can you fulfill that deep human need which splits into a thousand needs in the prism of everyday life? My human resources—physical, emotional, spiritual—are limited, but the limits do not have to be further narrowed by my selfishness. Without craftiness or evasion, I can conscientiously let the light of Jesus shine on every circumstance and decide with *his* spirit.

Sounds complicated? So is life. But would I want anyone to do less for me? Can I claim to have the spirit of Jesus and do less for others?

Passing On God's Love. St. John was still a "son of thunder" when he bluntly stated,

If anyone says, "My love is fixed on God,"
yet hates his brother,
he is a liar.

One who has no love for the brother he has seen
cannot love the God he has not seen. (1 Jn 4:20)

Love of God, as we have said, is the response of total trust and self-giving
to the utter generosity of God. It is unthinkable that I could experience God's
unfathomable love without feeling an urgent need to pass on his love to others.
And this means treating people not only as I would like to be treated but as
Jesus would treat them. I know what I hope for from God—and I am sure it
will be forthcoming. My neighbor must be as sure of me as I am of God.

A beautiful story in the Gospels reveals an unexpected depth in love extended to a neighbor in such a simple act as sharing food. Jesus says, "I was
hungry and you gave *me* food" (Mt 25:35; emphasis added). These words are
addressed to us individually as we struggle to love our neighbors just as surely
as "I am Jesus, the one you are persecuting" (Acts 9:5) was addressed to Paul.

The second half of the story (Mt 25:35-46) does indeed relate the condemnation of those who refused the neighbor—that is, Jesus—food and drink,
clothing and shelter, comfort and presence. But we should not let this obscure
the tremendous glory Jesus declares is ours, even when we act without awareness of what we do: "As often as you did it to one of my least brothers, you
did it for me" (Mt 25:40).

Loving our neighbor as Jesus did means *serving* our neighbor in all the
areas superficially defined in negative terms by the Fourth through Tenth
Commandments: marriage and family life, sexuality, physical and spiritual
goods, justice, truth, respect. At the Last Supper, to show the meaning of his
death and the purpose of the Eucharistic bread, Jesus washed the disciples' feet
in the manner and spirit of a faithful servant. Then he said,

"What I just did was to give you an example:
as I have done, so you must do." (Jn 13:15)

It is not enough to refrain from adultery with someone else's wife or husband; I must serve them as persons, as husbands and wives, as people called to
love. It is not enough to refrain from stealing: I must serve all people in their
right to be treated justly.

A Non-Exclusive Love. We simply cannot imagine Jesus saying, "You owe me
one." He had some uniquely intimate relationships with friends, as we all do,
but it is unthinkable that he measured his relationships with others according
to what they might do for him. He did what he asks us to do: "Whenever you
give a lunch or dinner, do not invite your friends or brothers or relatives or
wealthy neighbors. They might invite you in return and thus repay you. No,
when you have a reception, invite beggars and the crippled, the lame and the
blind. You should be pleased that they cannot repay you, for you will be repaid
in the resurrection of the just" (Lk 14:12-14). Obviously Jesus would not have
us exclude our friends; he just wants to be sure we don't exclude the others.

Love is concern for another's happiness. We want to please the people we love, to see the smile on their face, or their relief from pain or worry. To love as Jesus did is to let this instinct open us up to the needs and feelings of those who are not our intimates as much as we reasonably can. "Reasonably" here is not an avenue of escape, but a call to embrace the full truth of a situation.

As always, charity is its own reward. To break through our selfish shell is to enter upon maturity and full human life. Jean-Paul Sartre once said, "Hell is other people." The exact opposite is true. Hell is not-loving-others set like cement for eternity. I am essentially incomplete: I need God absolutely—but, just as absolutely, I need you to show me his care and concern.

All very beautiful. But what of the unfairness, the selfishness, the meanness and pettiness and just plain "orneriness" of these people whom God presumably sent to show me his love?

Do As Jesus Does. Jesus' commandments here are very specific. They identify several aspects of the problem, and may be summarized thus: Don't judge others in your mind. Don't take revenge in your anger. Forgive those who hurt you. Love your enemies. And always the presupposition: *as I have done.*

Do Not Judge. When Jesus says, "If you want to avoid judgment, stop passing judgment" (Mt 7:1), he means the judgment of *condemnation.* I simply cannot help making an intellectual judgment about what is obvious. Everybody in town knows that this man is ambitious; even little children notice that this woman is determined to get revenge on the husband who deserted her.

What I may not do—in fact, *cannot* do—is judge the internal morality of anyone's actions but my own. I simply do not know how much awareness of sin other persons have. I simply do not know how free they are, what pressures of emotion and passion are upon them. I don't know their full emotional history, the love or lack of love with which they were raised, the ignorance or emotional disorder that may plague them. I don't know. I cannot make a moral judgment. I can only deal with externals.

Do Not Take Revenge. "Everyone who grows angry with his brother shall be liable to judgment" (Mt 5:22).

Anger is what I feel—it's like hunger, sadness, joy. It's there as a fact before it becomes moral. So I can call the Better Business Bureau and lodge a complaint against the company that gypped me; I can scold the dog for not asking to go out. So far so good. Or I can go after the salesman with a gun and beat the dog to a bloody pulp. Not so good.

Jesus is addressing himself to my *response,* my choice as to how to use my anger. Will I be a crazy fireman and turn the hose on the crowd or the other firemen instead of on the fire? (The gushing water, like my anger, is neither good or bad.)

Jesus says I may not retaliate; I may not seek revenge. "Offer no resistance to injury. When a person strikes you on the right cheek, turn and offer him the other" (Mt 5:39). I may not inflict hurt just to be inflicting hurt—unlike a parent who *must,* in real love for a child, teach him that we must take the consequences of our actions and therefore "grounds" him for a week.

160

"Turning the other cheek" means, *at least*, no revenge. Then Jesus pushes us a little further: We have to seek reconciliation. With the dog it's easy; she is loving and lovable and will make the first move, putting her head in my lap and wagging her tail till I tell her she's forgiven. That crooked salesman will be a little harder. I'm really going to have to put a lot of effort into a friendly hello next time I pass him on the street. Which leads us to forgiveness.

Forgive. Peter once asked Jesus, " 'Lord, when my brother wrongs me, how often must I forgive him? Seven times?' 'No,' Jesus replied, 'not seven times; I say, seventy times seven times' " (Mt 18:21-22).

According to the Jewish system of numerical symbolism, "seven" means some *definite* number of times. There must be a limit, Peter reasoned. But Jesus uses the same symbolic system ("seventy times seven" means an infinite amount) to make it indefinite: No definite number of forgiving acts makes our forgiveness perfect. It must go on, endlessly, like God's.

To forgive is to deal with a person, not an offense. It means that I still accept you and love you; your past makes no difference in that. I will not make you pay, vindictively, for your sin (though I have every right to ask the return of my money). *You* are worthy of my love, in Christ. Your action does not alter that.

Love Your Enemies. "To you who hear me, I say: Love your enemies, do good to those who hate you; bless those who curse you and pray for those who maltreat you. . . .If you love those who love you, what credit is that to you? Even sinners love those who love them" (Lk 6:27-28, 32).

One can absorb such "hard sayings" only in the light of Jesus' example of perfect human maturity. Jesus simply turns the world's values and standards upside down (though psychiatrists are coming close to realizing that to be "normal" is ultimately to be the image of God).

Jesus gives only one reason for loving the hard to love: "This will prove you are sons of your heavenly Father, for his sun rises on the bad and the good, he rains on the just and the unjust" (Mt 5:45). To be like God—that is enough.

Applying Jesus' Commandments to Commandments Four Through Ten

The Fourth Commandment. *"Honor your father and your mother" (Ex 20:12).*

The more a child knows about Jesus in his full humanity—including therefore his normal childhood and youth—the more will he or she see the Fourth Commandment as a natural and welcome part of life. The Fourth Commandment involves four things: *reverence, obedience, love* and *gratitude.*

Reverence recognizes parents as representatives of God, and therefore possessed of a special dignity as co-creators with God. Beyond the dignity of every human being, a child senses that particular worth of the persons who are the living source of his or her human life. Since religion is "caught, not taught," parents, of course, must live their own lives in a spirit of reverence and humility before God. No fathers and mothers are without faults; still, there is a special sinfulness in the scorn or bitterness, ridicule or contempt which children may visit on their parents.

161

Obedience accepts the fact that there is order in creation. Ultimately it is the acceptance of the authority of God, who did not put all equally on the same level. There is equality in dignity, but also a necessary subordination.

God does not speak directly to us, but through persons and—unless we are willing to welcome chaos—through persons in authority. Conscience must ultimately be our guide, and all children must grow up to make their own moral decisions. But conscience is only gradually formed and informed through the guidance of others.

Children (young and old) want to know "Why?" And since they must come to the place where their adult decisions have a solid moral "why" basis, parents must gradually direct the normal questioning and critical spirit of children towards understanding the reasons for their commands and rules—and the reasons why, perhaps, a day may come when they will have to say, "We must obey God rather than men."

Children in their formative years can sin seriously by directly rejecting the just authority of parents, by insolence and refusal to cooperate in the home, by causing parents great sorrow or financial hardship.

Grown children can sin too, of course. Scholars speculate that the Fourth Commandment originally applied to *grown children* primarily. There was a temptation, evidently, to simply abandon parents when they became "unproductive" and a financial burden, feeble or senile—a temptation simply to leave them behind in the desert when the caravan moved on. The modern equivalent is the refusal of adult children to help their parents financially and humanly according to their means and ability. A nursing home may be a godsend and a pleasant haven for a mother's or father's latter years. It may also be a convenient desert in which to abandon them.

Love and gratitude bring us back to the fundamental commandments of Jesus discussed above. Outside of one's spouse and children, who is more worthy (and in need) than parents of being loved "as I have loved you"? More likely to be the Jesus who says, "As often as you do it to these, you do it to me"? More worthy of patience, forgiveness and the withholding of judgment? More deserving of being loved as we love ourselves?

The Fifth Commandment. *"You shall not kill" (Ex 20:13).*

Implicit in the love and forgiveness spoken of above is a basic reverence for life itself, human life above all.

A Christian sees the world, and especially all human beings, as made for Christ, the eternal God and our brother. Human life is God's greatest creation: the mysterious, graced body-spirit made to be a conscious and free manifestation of God's own life and love, made to be possessed by God himself in a face-to-face ecstasy forever.

Human beings are precious—just as they are. They are not valuable because of what they can do, or what they have; not because of talent, beauty, strength or money. Just as they are. Bodies may be crippled for this relatively brief lifetime and minds clouded by physical or emotional damage. Life may burn low in the sick and the old, or violently in the criminal, or exasperatingly in our "enemies." But every person is loved into existence by a kindly Father.

Abortion. If one believes in the dignity of the human person, indeed believes that all human beings *are* body-spirit persons in God's care; if one believes that only God can—and does—create the light of reason and the freedom of spirit that characterize each new human being; and if one observes, with the exactitude of science itself, that nothing is "added" to this newly conceived person except warmth and nourishment, then there is no possibility of treating a not-yet-born person as a piece of unwelcome tissue, to be extruded and destroyed like a tumor or foreign substance in the body. One must conclude that this is a human being from the beginning, and has a right to be treated as such. Catholics and many others simply *respect life* in this case.

What about the case in which a mother is certain to die, not because of the presence of an unborn baby, but because of reasons with which the baby is only indirectly connected: tubal pregnancy or uterine cancer?

To achieve a good result, one may do something (good or neutral in itself) which may also have a bad result, provided that the good intended outweighs the evil and there is no alternative. The evil is not intended, and it is not the means of achieving the good result. It is only permitted. (This is known as the principle of double effect.)

For instance, if the *only* way you can avoid an oncoming car and certain death is to jump off a bridge, it is obvious that breaking your legs by falling to the street below is not the *means* of saving your life. You jumped (a good thing, or at least neutral) to save your life (a very good reason). Indirectly, you caused damage to your body, but this was not your intention, it was an inevitable result which was obviously a lesser evil than losing your life.

So, in the case of a pregnant woman who has a cancerous uterus, removal of the damaged organ is necessary to save the mother's life. In neither case is the death of the baby the *means* of saving the mother's life. Cruel as this may sound, it is at least the lesser of two evils. At least two persons do not die. It is as much as truly loving and caring persons can do.

The principle of double effect has constant application in our lives.

Respecting the Life of Our Body. Those who oppose abortion are sometimes accused of one-sided worry about life before birth, but not after; that is, of not being actively concerned that so many people live without proper nourishment, subject to disease, deprived of decent living conditions.

But there are other people who are in trouble as far as nourishment, sickness and "fitting" living conditions are concerned: *ourselves.* Nutrition books are now coming out by the scores, as our affluent society realizes the toll that junk food and overeating are taking. Americans are said to average 10 pounds overweight. Alcohol and drugs have become symbols of a national tragedy. The Fifth Commandment, seen through the eyes of one who believes the body to be the Temple of the Holy Spirit, forbids not only the vivid violence of murder, but also the slow silent violence of self-indulgence.

Self-Defense. I may choose to lay down my life for my brother or sister, but I may also defend my life—and others'—from anyone who wishes to harm or destroy that life. Catholic tradition has evolved these principles (whether for individuals or nations):

1) One may do what is necessary—but *no more*—to stop an aggressor. (If calling the police suffices, I have no reason to inflict injury; if escape is possible, I have no reason to use a gun.)
2) All non-injurious means must first be tried, if possible.

May one ever shoot another in self-defense? It may be difficult, considering the idealism of Christian love, to imagine a Christian deliberately killing another human being. But, applying the principles just cited, one can imagine a situation in which nothing short of the aggressor's death will save the life of the innocent party.

Let us suppose, for instance, that a man has already killed three hostages and is certainly about to kill the rest. The only weapon you have is a gun. You shoot to stop him from killing others (the good effect referred to in the double-effect discussion above). If there were any other way, you would choose it. You do not will his death, though it is probably inevitable. Vindictiveness is not your motive. You simply have no other way to save the lives of the hostages.

'Just War' and 'The Challenge of Peace.' The Church has a long tradition of teaching about war, and Vatican II reiterated these principles. In May 1983, after thorough discussion and lengthy dialogue with civil leaders, the U.S. bishops published *The Challenge of Peace: God's Promise and Our Response.*

"How we treat our enemy is the test of whether we love our neighbor," the bishops write, "and the possibility of taking even one human life is a prospect we should consider in fear and trembling. How is it possible to move from these presumptions to the idea of a justifiable use of lethal force?"

The bishops list the traditionally taught conditions for a "just war":

1) *Just purpose.* "War is permissible only to confront a 'real and certain danger'; i.e., to protect innocent life, to preserve conditions necessary for decent human existence, and to secure basic human rights."
2) *Competent authority.* "War must be declared by those with responsibility for public order, not by private groups or individuals." And, "While the legitimacy of revolution in some circumstances cannot be denied," just-war teaching must be rigorously applied.
3) *Comparative justice.* Which side is sufficiently "right"? Are the values at stake critical enough to override the presumption against war?
4) *Right intention*, that is, for the reasons listed under "just purpose." Right intention means pursuing peace and reconciliation, avoiding unnecessarily destructive acts or unreasonable conditions (e.g., unconditional surrender).
5) *Probability of success*—to prevent irrational resort to force or hopeless resistance. But sometimes "defense of key issues, even against great odds, may be 'proportionate witness.' "
6) *Proportionality.* This is one of two extremely important principles (the other is discrimination) which must be applied both in deciding

to wage war and in conducting war. This principle demands that the damage to be inflicted and the costs (spiritual and human, not just material) incurred by war must not be out of proportion to the good expected by taking arms. This principle applies in all self-defense (see above). To take the obvious example: Wiping out a nation (or the world!) is out of proportion to anything a nation may have done.

7) *Discrimination*, by its very name, means that a nation may not attack without discriminating between innocent civilians and military personnel and targets. Vatican II said, "Any act of war aimed indiscriminately at destruction of entire cities, or of extensive areas along with their population is a crime against God and man" (*Pastoral Constitution on the Church in the Modern World*, #80).

Both the principle of proportionality and of discrimination apply to the condemnation of *total* war. To destroy civilization by total war as it *could* be waged today would be a monstrously disproportionate response to aggression. Also, "just response to aggression must be discriminate: It must be directed against unjust aggressors, not against innocent people caught up in a war not of their making."

These principles apply to *any* disproportionate or indiscriminate use of weapons, including non-nuclear—for example, the firebombing of entire cities to make the enemy surrender. One may not directly kill innocent people for any reason. One may not do evil to achieve good. (It might happen that a relatively small number of civilians may be killed, for instance, when an offensive is launched against a massed tank concentration. But their death is not the means of stopping the enemy, it is not directly intended, and a far greater evil is prevented.)

Nuclear War. Speaking from these principles, the U.S. bishops say, "Under no circumstances may nuclear weapons or other instruments of mass slaughter be used for the purpose of destroying population centers or other predominantly civilian targets." This repeats the condemnation issued by Vatican II (above). The bishops apply this principle "even to the retaliatory use of weapons striking enemy cities after our own have already been struck. No Christian can rightfully carry out orders or policies deliberately aimed at killing noncombatants."

The bishops carefully word their statement on the initiation of nuclear war: "We do not perceive any situation in which the deliberate initiation of nuclear war, on however restricted a scale, can be morally justified. Non-nuclear attacks by another state must be resisted by other than nuclear weapons."

What about "limited" nuclear war? The bishops admit the *theoretical* possibility of a limited nuclear exchange, but advance many reasons why they think it is not a *real* possibility.

The bishops define deterrence as "the dissuasion of a potential adversary from initiating an attack or conflict, often by the threat of unacceptable retaliatory damage." In his 1982 message to the United Nations, Pope John Paul II said, "In current conditions, 'deterrence' based on balance is certainly not an end in itself but, as a step on the way toward a progressive disarmament, may still be judged morally acceptable....Yet it is indispensable not to be satisfied with this minimum."

After wrestling with the problem of deterrence, the U.S. bishops made these statements: 1) If nuclear deterrence exists only to prevent the *use* of nuclear weapons, then it is not acceptable that we go *beyond* this (e.g., planning for repeated nuclear strikes, planning to "win" a nuclear war). 2) If nuclear deterrence is our goal, then "sufficiency" in arms is enough— we do not need "superiority." 3) Nuclear deterrence must be a step toward progressive disarmament. 4) Some weapons seem to be useful primarily for a first strike—and this goes beyond mere deterrence.

The bishops express the fear that even this conditional acceptance of nuclear deterrence (i.e., presuming steps are taken toward meaningful and continuing reductions in nuclear stockpiles and eventually the phasing-out of nuclear deterrence altogether) "might be inappropriately used by some to reinforce the policy of arms buildup."

Military Service and Conscientious Objection. The bishops recognize in principle the right of a government to require military service, provided the government shows it is necessary—"legitimate defense." They repeat their support for conscientious objection in general and for selective conscientious objection to a particular war, either because of the ends being pursued or the means being used.

The Sixth and Ninth Commandments. *"You shall not commit adultery. . . .You shall not covet your neighbor's wife" (Dt 5:18, 21).*

As in the other negative commandments, this represents an extreme boundary. Implied in "keeping" the commandments is human love and, for Christians, a love that mirrors that of Christ and his Church.

How far from merely avoiding sin is the free and joyful consecration of two Christians who are already totally committed to Christ! They see each other as complement one to the other.

Love is the glad fulfilling of another's needs, and sexuality is an obvious sign of human incompleteness. Human life does not begin or continue through one person. Life, and the beginning of life, demands comm-union.

We are always sexual, male or female. We live our sexuality all the time— not necessarily with genital activity but as beings whose very bodies are God's sign that all human beings need each other for life, for spirit, for faith, for survival. This plan of creation set forth in male and female bodies is the greatest argument against selfishness. No one can fulfill God's creation plan alone. And on the broad scale of life, the primary sin is *not needing* God; and the second is like it: *not needing* others, living in a self-oriented, self-sufficient life.

Sexuality, then, is not something that has to do merely with our bodies, but with our whole persons. A human being is not just a body or just a spirit, but a body-spirit. In loving others in Christ, Christians respect their own body-persons and the body-persons of others.

Chastity. Chastity may be called the virtue of using our sexuality within Christian love in a way that is appropriate to our state of life.

For the married, it means loving reverence for one's spouse both in the full-bodied exercise of genital sex and in all the other situations of life. It prompts the loving physical-spiritual expression of love, and is disciplined against all tendency to abuse and selfishness.

For the unmarried, chastity means reserving genital activity for the life-long covenant of marriage. In the face of a pagan culture, chastity says that total physical expression was intended by God to express the total commitment of a whole person to lifelong faithfulness, trust and service.

Chastity knows what even the pagans find out: Without the commitment of marriage, genital sexuality is ultimately empty and unsatisfying, prey to insecurity, immaturity and selfishness.

Abuse. Like all sin, failures in chastity are abuses of God's good gifts. Adultery is the abuse of a sacred covenant, an injustice. Like fornication (the intercourse of unmarried persons) adultery is stealing the physical and emotional pleasures of marriage without being willing to put lives on the line in a promise of faithfulness. Unchastity is the abuse of persons—even if both persons can rationalize the abuse.

The Sixth Commandment also precludes physical actions whose nature is such that they cannot but propel any normal human beings to intercourse. The expression of love between unmarried persons is just that—an expression of Christian love. It is not naive, but fully recognizes the accelerating nature of physical expression. Neither is it prudish, preoccupied only with danger. It begins and is able to end in a love grounded in love for Christ himself.

It is possible, especially if we consider the passionate nature of sexuality, that one's mind or freedom can be so greatly clouded by emotion or passion that full guilt, or even partial guilt, is not incurred for particular acts. All depends on what the fact of the matter is. On the other hand, it is possible to incur guilt by a conscious *permitting* of factors which gradually dull the conscience. Both holiness and sin (hence chastity and unchastity) are acquired by slow degrees, by accumulating decisions.

Statistics indicate a great loss of respect for chastity today. Modern pagans probably view virginity in the unmarried as unusual as did their Roman counterparts. Christians are called to stand before the world with a courage that simply takes for granted that virginity of heart and body is part of the normal preparation for marriage.

The Seventh and Tenth Commandments. These two laws command respect for the rights of all human beings to material goods. Taken literally, the Seventh Commandment refers to external actions. The Tenth probes our mind and heart, where all sin begins, and forbids injustice in willful desire and intention.

As with the other commandments, Jesus offered very little specific teaching on justice. His concern was the basic attitude that must precede and enliven

167

the observance of all commandments.

He was concerned with the total well-being of people—with their dignity, with mutual love and support, with total trust in God through all life's circumstances. He also turned his attention to food and to healing and to freeing the little people from the hypocrisy and injustice of their leaders.

He did not propose tax relief or food stamps or social security. He proposed no economic or political theories because there was—and still is—a terrible urgency to convert *hearts* to a spirit of concern for other human beings. Human structures built by loving hearts will consider others' needs in every age and system.

Justice or Charity? Justice is said to concern what people have a *right* to; charity is said to go *beyond* rights. The trouble with these definitions is that they seem to make charity *optional.*

Christians know that charity is the heartbeat of life. With Jesus they look at all human beings, but especially to those close at hand, and say to themselves, "What do they need? What can I reasonably do for them, in the spirit of Jesus?"

Who ever heard of people who love each other making up lists of each other's rights and ignoring what is optional?

A Fully Human Life. Vatican II is clear on what Catholics are called to do: "There must be made available to all people everything necessary for leading a life truly human, such as food, clothing and shelter; the right to choose a state of life freely and to found a family, the right to education, to employment, to a good reputation, to respect, to appropriate information, to activity in accord with the upright norm of one's own conscience, to protection of privacy, and to rightful freedom, even in matters religious" (*Constitution on the Church,* # 26).

Private Property. Every human being has a right to have a share of material goods sufficient for subsistence. This is *prior* to anyone's natural right to own private property. We are to regard our lawful possessions not merely as our own, but also as common property in the sense that they can be of benefit also to others. All the children of God are obliged to come to the relief of the poor "and to do so not merely out of their superfluous goods" (*The Church in the Modern World,* # 69).

I Am My Brother's Keeper. The Christian's maturely formed conscience looks with the eyes of Jesus on all fellow human beings. There must be a Christian prejudice in favor of the weak, the poor, the little people. It is more than a matter of strict justice that we *care for* (not merely *take care of*) the emotionally disturbed and the handicapped, especially those who must live in institutions.

Above all, a Christian feels pain at the specter of hunger in the world and anger at the political and economic systems which cause it. One of the most blasphemous ways to pervert the Bible is to use Jesus' words, "The poor you will always have with you" (Mt 26:11), as an excuse for writing off slums and all the human degradation they involve as "a normal function of society." Those who think Jesus scorned "welfare" would do well to read the parable of "The Rich Man and Lazarus" (Lk 16:19-31).

A Christian is on the side of those who have no power in society, or very little; those who suffer the inheritance of decades or centuries of subhuman experience, the lack of normal relationships, the erasure of human dignity. One thinks immediately, in our country, of blacks, Indians, Spanish-Americans, Appalachians—all "those people" about whom it is so easy to compose a sour gospel of food stamp abuses, shiftlessness and waste.

Catholic Social Teaching and the U.S. Economy. In November 1984, the U.S. bishops issued the first draft of a pastoral letter on Catholic social teaching as compared with the U.S. economy. The first half of the letter deals with general principles, the second half with particular opinions and suggestions.

Central emphasis is placed on the dignity of the human person. The bishops remind their people that every judgment about economic life must ask two questions: What does this do *for* people, and *to* people, especially the poor and deprived members of the community, who have a special claim to our concern?

Whether or not a community is just is measured by its treatment of those whose side Jesus took—the powerless and the poor. The teaching of the Bible is the basis for a "preferential option for the poor" which challenges the Church—Christians—to speak for those who are defenseless and poor. The Church is called to be the community of disciples of Jesus in solidarity with those who suffer, and in confrontation with the sinful structures that institutionalize injustice.

Human beings should be able to find self-realization in their work and to fulfill their material needs by a just wage. The United States has indeed made great strides, but we still need a new national consensus that all persons have economic rights, and that society has the moral obligation to ensure that no one is hungry, homeless, unemployed or otherwise denied what is needed to live with dignity. Unequal distribution of income, wealth, education or job opportunities on the basis of race, sex or any other arbitrary standards can never be justified.

There are three principles which should be given priority in our economy:
1) The fulfillment of the basic needs of the poor must have the highest priority.
2) Increased participation by the marginalized takes precedence over the preservation of privileged concentrations of power, wealth and income.
3) Meeting human needs and increasing participation must be priority targets in the investment of wealth, talent and human energy.

All people have a right to employment, to just wages, to collective bargaining. People also have the duty to work. Workers and unions have responsibilities to society as a whole. Managers, investors and business must remember that no one can ever own economic resources absolutely, or use them without regard for others. Catholic teaching defends the right to private property, but this is not an unconditional and absolute right. No one can keep for exclusive use what is not needed when others lack the necessities of life.

Government has a positive moral function—protecting basic rights, ensuring economic justice for all, enabling citizens to coordinate their actions toward these ends. As for the scope of government, the principle of "subsidiarity" is primary: What can be accomplished on a lower level should not be transferred to a higher.

The human race is one moral community. We must work for the good of the whole human race. Our Christian faith and the norms of human justice impose distinct limits on how we view material goods and what we consume. Such limits are needed if we are to avoid "the most evident form of moral underdevelopment, avarice and greed" (Pope Paul VI).

The Church itself is bound by all the moral principles that govern the just operation of any economic endeavor—and that includes all the schools, hospitals, retirement homes, social service agencies or other institutions under its auspices.

Sins? It would seem that the greatest sins are committed against the Seventh Commandment by omission. Everyone is convinced that outright stealing is wrong, and that one must pay back whatever was stolen. Nothing is so sacred to some people as property.

But what of the sinfulness of paying unjust (though legal) wages that do not permit a decent family life, or perhaps any at all? What of deception in merchandising, defective workmanship in cars or clothing? What of the cruelty of a society in which inflation must be fought by hurting the poor and the elderly more than anyone else?

Social Sin. A good sign of the times, though we haven't done much about it yet, is the awareness of *social* sin, sin built right into the culture and its political and social institutions.

In an apostolic exhortation, Pope John Paul II addressed this issue of social sin. To speak of social sin, he says, is to recognize that there is a mysterious human solidarity whereby each individual's sin affects others in some way. There is a solidarity on the religious level also—the deep and magnificent mystery of the communion of saints, whereby we can say that "every soul that rises above itself raises up the world." By the same token, anyone who lowers oneself through sin also drags down the whole Church and, in some way, the world.

Social sin is every sin against justice—whether by the individual against the community, or vice versa. It is every sin against the rights of the human person, beginning with the right to life, including the life of the unborn. It is every sin against others' freedom, especially the freedom to believe in God and adore him.

Social sin is every sin against the common good. The term can be applied to the sins of leaders (political, economic, union) who, though they have the power, do not work for the improvement of society.

Having said all this, however, the Pope is careful to point out that one meaning of "social sin" is not acceptable: that which contrasts social and personal sin that leads to the watering down—or abolishing—of personal sinfulness, as if one had only a social responsibility. In this case, blame is placed on some vague entity like "the situation," "society" or "structures." But real responsibility always lies with individuals. Society, or a situation, does not perform moral acts. A situation is not morally good or bad—only individuals are. Thus, social sin is the accumulation of many persons' sins.

The Eighth Commandment. *"You shall not bear dishonest witness against your neighbor" (Dt 5:20).*

In the narrowest sense, this commandment forbids perjured testimony. For Christians, it opens up the aspect of Jesus as the *Truth* to be followed.

Pilate asked cynically—or perhaps sadly—the meaning of *truth* as if it could not really be captured by the human mind and heart (see Jn 18:38).

What *is* truth?

To be true, a word or a symbol must correspond with reality, with the way things really are. Now, the Spirit of Truth leads us to make our hearts and our actions correspond to the deepest reality seen and experienced by faith: God's love surrounding the world, healing and transforming it. We must act in accordance with this fullest reality. Christians, following Jesus, do not wish to cloud or distort the truth of his saving presence in their lives.

Jesus is, as he said, the truth (see Jn 14:6). He is the perfect, accurate expression of God. He is "true God," the full reality of God. He is "true man," what humans were intended to be. The Father is the Truthful One who sent Jesus, assuring us we can trust him absolutely. The Spirit of Truth Jesus promised awakens us to the really real, the full view of life, the vision of faith.

Hence, truthfulness rests on love. It is not enough not to tell lies. Nor is it, on the other hand, always wise to tell everything.

Speech and symbol, silence and gesture, "body language"—all are to communicate with others in the expression of Christian love. The community gathered around the altar is nourished with the *true* bread that comes down from heaven, and sincerely tries to show this communion by speaking what others need to hear, be it sympathy or forgiveness, frankness or warning.

Loving communication considers not just whether or not words are literally true but the whole context: who hears them, what is implied, what will probably be understood. (Sometimes, of course, others do not have a right to know certain facts, or one has a professional obligation not to reveal them.)

Lying, therefore, is an *unjust* refusal to let reality be perceived by others.

It is not unjust to conceal the truth, or let others be deceived, when a higher good is thereby preserved. It is certainly *truth*—correspondence with the fullest reality—to say anything necessary to save the life of a hostage unjustly kept, or to conceal the identity of someone who is in imminent danger of being murdered. It is Christian charity to keep a secret whose revelation would unjustly damage the reputation or social status of a person.

The determining principle is love's *reality.* What, in the most sincere openness to God, is the true communication of his will here and now?

Specific Sins. To make false charges or misrepresentations which defame or damage someone's reputation is *slander. Calumny* stresses the malice of such spoken or written words. *Detraction* is hurting someone's reputation by revealing unknown faults or defects without sufficient reason. A broken promise is as serious as the intention with which it was made—sincere or light.

Secrets are of three kinds: (1) *natural* secrets (those in which the revealing of the facts would, by their very nature, cause pain or damage; (2) *promised* secrets (those where the obligation of secrecy comes from a definite promise, though the secret may already be a natural secret); (3) *committed* secrets (those about which an explicit or implicit agreement is made before the secret is entrusted to someone). Committed secrets include all knowledge to which one has access as a professional (e.g., doctor, lawyer, counselor).

The obligation to keep something secret depends on the understanding between the parties when the secret is entrusted, and on the damage that would result from its revelation. A secret may be revealed for loving reasons—when keeping it risks greater damage to the common good, to an innocent third party, to the one to whom the secret was committed, or to the owner of the secret.

These distinctions are cold and legal, however necessary. They are made warm and lifegiving by the spirit of genuine respect and love for all human beings and a real compassion for their sufferings, whether these sufferings stem from actual sin or the accidents of life.

Love and truth—the truth that sees *all* reality—rest on each other. Faith is grounded in the security that God's Word is absolutely dependable, his love absolutely faithful. All our secrets are absolutely safe with him.

26.

Jesus' Mother and Ours: Mary

After Jesus, there is no person so beloved by Catholics of all ages as Mary, the mother of Jesus, the mother of God. Without our knowledge of her, Jesus would not be understandable—a mythic figure coming from nowhere. The Gospel pictures of a real baby in her arms are an essential part of our faith. Calvary and Easter are the heart of our faith; but Christmas must first touch our human hearts.

Luke gives us the most detailed picture of the infancy of Jesus and Mary's role in the divine mystery there. Let us look at the highlights of Mary's story as Luke tells it in the first two chapters of his Gospel.

The Announcement to Mary. Luke introduces us to Mary as "a virgin betrothed to a man named Joseph, of the house of David"—already a hint of an heir to David's throne. The angel Gabriel greets Mary: "Rejoice, O highly favored daughter!" (or, as in the familiar prayer, "Hail, full of grace!"). Mary is the special object of God's favor.

"The Lord is with you. Blessed are you among women." Mary is the flowering of all the faith that waited through the centuries for the coming of the Messiah. She is the greatest and humblest of the *anawim,* the poor in spirit. She senses the magnitude of the moment and is "deeply troubled." The angel reassures her: "Do not fear, Mary. You have found favor with God. You shall conceive and bear a son and give him the name Jesus. Great will be his dignity and he will be called Son of the Most High. The Lord God will give him the throne of David his father. He will rule over the house of Jacob forever and his reign will be without end."

Mary's Virginal Conception. Mary makes a forthright statement: "How can this be, since I do not know man?" To "know man" refers to having sexual relations. She is betrothed, but not married. Then Luke delicately describes the act of God whereby the Son will become man: "The Holy Spirit will come upon you and the power of the Most High will overshadow you; hence the holy offspring to be born will be called Son of God." Then, with magnificent simplicity, Mary says, "I am the servant of the Lord. Let it be done to me as you say."

She hurries to visit her cousin Elizabeth, and the unborn Baptist leaps with joy in his mother's womb, as David danced before the Ark of the Covenant (see 2 Sm 6:14). "Blest is she who trusted," Elizabeth says, "that the Lord's words to her would be fulfilled."

Mary is, above all, the woman of faith. She trusted, even before Joseph was called to share her trust. Her perpetual virginity was her total openness and unreserved love of God. She had to suffer, for a time, the pain of Joseph's bewilderment, until he was told that "it is by the Holy Spirit that she has conceived this child" (Mt 1:20).

The Virgin Birth. Caesar must count his people, and Mary must leave her home to give birth to her son in a strange town, in poverty. But Bethlehem is the town of David, and her son is a king. The first subjects to pay him honor are simple shepherds who become the first bearers of the Good News.

Mary and Joseph take the child to be presented in the Temple and consecrated to God, according to Jewish custom. They make the offering of the poor—a pair of turtledoves or two young pigeons. A holy man assures Mary that this baby is "a revealing light to the Gentiles, the glory of your people Israel," but also that "you yourself will be pierced with a sword."

The Finding in the Temple. Mary's faith was challenged as no one else's: to know the divine origin of this child and at the same time to see him as a helpless baby needing her motherly care, then a child with exploring eyes and wild feet, with sudden fears and laughter, with skinned knees and mud-streaked tunic. She pondered and waited.

A milestone along the way occurred at the first separation of mother and child. Remaining behind in Jerusalem in total adolescent absorption in the Temple rabbis' wisdom, Jesus caused Mary and Joseph three days of anguished searching. When they found him, he revealed a depth they had not suspected: " 'Why did you search for me? Did you not know I had to be in my Father's house?' But they did not grasp what he said to them."

Mary did not grasp, but she trusted, and waited, and may have suspected what the sword thrust would be. Then 18 years of Gospel silence, of which all we know is that Jesus "progressed steadily in wisdom and age and grace before God and men"—and Mary with him. (See Lk 1:26—2:52.)

'Woman.' Like all mothers, Mary realized she would sooner or later suffer the pain and the pride of seeing her son take his place in the world. But, even when Jesus began his public life, their separation was not complete. John tells of them together at a wedding in Cana and of her implicit request that he relieve the host's embarrassment when the wine ran out. His reply sounds cold: "Woman, how does this concern of yours involve me? My hour has not come" (Jn 2:4). The "hour" of Jesus is that of his glorification—the passion, death and resurrection by which our salvation is achieved. Only in view of that can Mary's request, even though she is his own mother, have any force.

Mary's greatest dignity is that she is a believer, one graced by God (even though that was never separated from her willingness to be Jesus' mother). The Church has come to see her as the woman of Genesis, and to regard Genesis 3:15 as the "first Gospel":

"I will put enmity between you and the woman,
and between your offspring and hers;
He will strike at your head,
while you strike at his heel."

The first woman was called Eve, because she was "mother of all the living." Mary is the mother of him who is life itself and thus of all those who are reborn with his life. She is the mother of the Church, the Eucharistic community nourished by the Word made flesh in her. In Revelation, John is probably referring to God's people when he speaks of "a woman clothed with the sun" (12:1), but the application to Mary is instinctive for all who read the passage.

Finally, it should be noted, Jesus *did* do something about the wine at Cana. He made 120 gallons of it, and thus let a bit of his glory shine through. His disciples believed in him (Jn 2:11). Perhaps only later they saw this as a fulfillment of an ancient prophecy. Not only would the Messiah bring bread in abundance, but the mountains would flow with wine (Is 25:6).

The Woman at the Cross. The sword pierced Mary's heart when a Roman soldier's sword pierced the heart of her son, already stilled in death. She who had the greatest reason to expect a glorious messianic victory, was for that very reason most tortured emotionally by his death as a criminal dispatched in disgrace and abandonment outside the city walls.

Perhaps she understood, in her deepest heart of faith, that this was her share of the New Adam's victory over the serpent. This *was* the crushing of the serpent's power, but it was also the wounding of the savior's heel.

John's Gospel seems to present Mary as the woman of Genesis when Jesus said, from the cross, "Woman, there is your son," referring to John the beloved disciple—and, as Christian faith soon realized, to all the sons and daughters of God and of the "mother" Church. When Jesus added, speaking to John, "There is your mother," he spoke to all who would be born of his death and resurrection.

Pentecost. One of the seven mysteries of the Franciscan rosary is: The Risen Jesus Meets His Mother. The Gospel has no record of this, of course, but who would deny that it happened? Then there would be no more "pondering" necessary, no more difficulty in grasping. Her faith—though she still had years on earth—was close to vision.

If Mary Magdalen wanted to continue to cling to the risen Lord, imagine the tender and ecstatic joy that must have filled Mary as she held him finally in her arms and understood. She could then be the calm and prayerful mother of the little Church as it waited for the Spirit of Pentecost (Acts 1:14).

Her mind and heart had long since been the dwelling place of the Holy Spirit. Now she moved quietly closer to the face-to-face vision.

The Assumption. The faith of the Church believes that Mary has received this face-to-face vision. She has been taken body and soul—full humanity—to the eternal vision of God. She is "in" heaven already. It is not said that she did not die, only that she has already received, according to her faith and holiness, what we will receive in fitting degree when we are finally brought to the Father. We cannot "prove" this; we believe it.

The Immaculate Conception. Considering the dignity God gave Mary, it was fitting that God made her the holiest possible ground in which the Vine could grow. Therefore, Catholics believe, Mary was conceived without original sin. This means that, just as she has received her eternal happiness ahead of us, so she was redeemed by the blood of her son at the very moment of her conception in her mother's womb—as we are at the moment of Baptism. Again, this cannot be proved, and it is useless to argue about it. It is the happily held faith of the Church.

Catholics' conviction of the holiness of Mary is beautifully described by Pope Pius IX: God's grace was given her "in such a wonderful manner that she would always be free from absolutely every stain of sin, and that, all beautiful and perfect, she might display such fullness of innocence and holiness that under God none greater would be known" *(Ineffabilis Deus)*.

Mother of God. In the early centuries of Christian history, the Church responded to doctrinal problems with slow and painful deliberation. After the great Christological definitions, the Council of Ephesus (431) summed up the faith of the Church that Mary is truly the *Mother of God* because she is truly the mother of the one Jesus who is truly God and truly man in one person. This declaration of the Council was in response to the heresy that denied that there was a real union of the human and the divine in Jesus. Mary was not just the mother of a man morally united to God, but of the one Person who is God and man. She is the mother of *God.*

Honoring Mary. Catholics honor Mary because they love her. She is one of them, not a goddess or a superhuman being. She too had to be redeemed; she too had to make the decision to trust God absolutely and, in a fascinating mystery, to find that God in the fruit of her womb. She is the first of Christians, praying with the Church and for the Church.

The prayer that has come to be a natural accompaniment to the Our Father for Catholics is the Hail Mary, which combines the words of the angel and of Elizabeth with the prayer of the Church: "Hail Mary, full of grace, the Lord is with you; blessed are you among women, and blessed is the fruit of your womb, Jesus. Holy Mary, Mother of God, pray for us sinners now and at the hour of our death."

The rosary is a prayer of meditation on the great mysteries of the faith as experienced by Mary. A decade (one Our Father and 10 Hail Mary's) is recited during each meditation.

Devotion to Mary has received great inspiration from her appearance to children at Lourdes in France and at Fatima in Portugal. The message in each case was essentially the same: prayer and penance. Strictly speaking, these are "private" revelations made to individuals, unlike the public revelation of God in Jesus. A Catholic does not have to believe in these private revelations, though millions have happily chosen to do so.

Protestant Reaction. Some Protestants have found Catholic devotion to Mary excessive, overshadowing the place of Christ. No doubt there have been instances of well-meaning over-emphasis on Mary, and Vatican II warned against this. But it also gave Mary the honor of a special chapter in its greatest document, in which it said, "In the bodily and spiritual glory which she possesses in heaven, the Mother of Jesus continues in this present world as the image and first flowering of the Church as she is to be perfected in the world to come. Likewise, Mary shines forth on earth, until the day of the Lord shall come, as a sign of sure hope and solace for the pilgrim people of God" (*Constitution on the Church,* #68).

27.
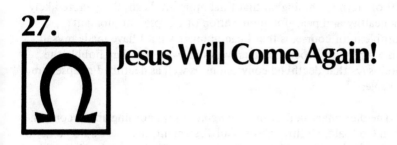
Jesus Will Come Again!

What theology books traditionally treated as the "Last Things" are death, judgment, purgatory, heaven and hell. At first glance, four of these five are painful prospects. Can the vision of faith brighten the negative image?

Death. If we could take a strictly objective view (which we can't), we would say that our last day, our death, is not the most important thing to consider. Rather, at the center of my life and all life, of time and eternity, is the death and resurrection of Jesus. That event makes sense of everything else. Jesus joins my death to his, and makes it beautiful. His resurrection prepares the way for mine.

Jesus shrank from death, at least from the horrible death that awaited him, so we need not feel guilty about our own fears. Death is not natural. It is a tragic tearing apart (no matter how slowly) of God's beautiful creation.

But suppose our death could be a gentle and instantaneous passage through the veil between time and eternity. Would that remove our fear? Probably not, but the fantasy at least brings us closer to the attitude faith produces in us, deep down, below our natural revulsion.

A fully Christian attitude looks first to the death and resurrection of Jesus for light and strength. It sees the possibility of suffering like Jesus did and shrinks away in human weakness. But it also sees Jesus, in his overall life-commitment, straining toward this "baptism" (see Lk 12:50) and longing to eat *the* Passover meal "before I suffer" (Lk 22:15). The shadow of Jesus' cross fell across his life from the beginning, and he fully and freely accepted it.

Jesus made a deliberate decision to die. Or, rather, his death was the final completely voluntary act of total self-giving to the Father. That attitude was there all the time, his "fundamental option" which was not swayed one inch by the terror that came upon him in Gethsemane.

So Christians, taking their life as a whole, place it in God's hands. "Into your hands I commend my spirit" (Lk 23:46) is the prayer of their life, not something tacked on at the end. Even in fear and trembling, Christians can be confident in their heart of hearts that death is the greatest moment of life, a summing up, a concrete act that says, "My whole life is yours, and I freely give it to you."

Obviously we are making this decision all our life. We leave it to a merciful God to give us strength at the actual moment of death to face courageously the natural fears of the moment. But *now,* in the calmness of prayer, we can see the light of eternity shining on that final moment. Is anything more likely to give us a healthy and peaceful appreciation of our present moment?

The problem, of course, is that I can unmake what I have made myself. Since this is a long slow process, human wisdom (we never dare hobble the grace of God) says that deathbed conversions as well as deathbed relapses are hardly probable.

Judgment. The dictionary definition of *judgment* says nothing about condemnation. When God said, all through the Old Testament, that he would come to bring *judgment* for his people, he promised precisely judgment *for* them—like a judge vindicating the rights of the innocent, restoring what had been taken and awarding recompense. It was only when his people deliberately refused to live by his covenant that God's judgment would turn against them.

In the New Testament the meaning of judgment is tempered by two emphases which run throughout like two vines intertwined: "already now" and "not yet." We are *now* saved, but we are *not yet* saved. We shall die, but we have already risen in Christ. Christ has come, Christ is with us all days, but Christ will come again. Christ is victorious, all things have been subjected to him; yet, as Hebrews sadly says, "But now we do not yet see all things thus subject" (Hb 2:8).

So there are two ways of looking at judgment: something that happens *already now* and something that has *not yet* happened.

Jesus situates judgment in the midst of daily life when he says that giving food to the hungry, welcoming strangers, clothing the naked, comforting the sick and visiting the imprisoned—a way of life—is the door to heaven. These things are done for him, even if one does not think of him explicitly (see Mt 25: 31-40).

The Particular Judgment. Judgment is *now.* My "particular judgment" at the moment of death will simply be the fact of what I have chosen to be, my "fundamental option" which we discussed above (Chapter 22). But *now* I am what I have made myself and *now* do deliberately affirm. It is like the image on film not yet developed.

True, God must "find guilty" all those who inflicted injustice and pain on the innocent. But, primarily, God *saves* his people—that is, his judgment is *for* his friends. Hence Jesus says:

> "I solemnly assure you,
> the man who hears my word
> and has faith in him who sent me
> possesses eternal life.
> He does not come under condemnation,
> but has passed from death to life." (Jn 5:24)

God's loving judgment is his endless attempt—his grace surrounding and filling us—to free us from all evil and possess us with his life and love. God is not a detective hoping to trap us in evil; even though he cannot but demand truth and love.

The General Judgment. "He will come to judge the living and the dead," we pray in the Apostles' Creed.

Formerly, in Masses for the dead, there was a long and chilling sequence called the *Dies Irae*–"Day of Wrath":

Day of Wrath! O day of mourning!
See fulfilled the prophets' warning,
Heav'n and earth in ashes burning!

A similar tone can be found in the "apocalyptic" passages of the Gospels–Mark 13, Matthew 24, Luke 21. How are we to understand these fearful passages?

First of all, scholars agree that two things are tangled together in these passages: the destruction of Jerusalem in 70 A.D. and the actual end of the world. It is impossible to sort out which verses refer to which event.

Second, we must remember that the biblical way of thinking is largely foreign to modern ways. The people of biblical faith saw concrete historical events as the judgment of God–for instance, the Jewish people being taken into exile.

It is the reality of the final judgment that Jesus emphasized, not its date. He gave clear warnings against trying to calculate the date. The human race, at any time in its history, lives under the reality of a final judgment. When particular things happen–for instance, the fall of Jerusalem–this final judgment seems to break into history–a sort of preview, as it were. When it does, it reminds us that the books will be closed, some day. This is a kindly warning to meet that judgment **every** day: "I am hungry *now,* and you give me to eat." The last judgment is always "near." Eternity is always hidden within time.

Christians, then, do not look forward to a final catastrophe, the *terrible* Day of the Lord described in parts of Scripture. Their "ministry of reconciliation" is to attempt to keep it from being a day of catastrophe for anyone.

For the Christian, the Last Judgment is the final and definitive establishment of the heavenly community, the Kingdom in its full eternal glory. Then God will bring all to completion. Then there will be perfect happiness, eternal joy and peace.

But the "General Judgment" cannot change the judgment with which we find we have judged ourselves when our lives end. And as we have seen, that judgment is made *now:* "Come! You have my Father's blessing! Inherit the kingdom prepared for you from the foundation of the world. For I was hungry and you gave me food. . ." (Mt 25:34-35).

Resurrection. We have already seen (Chapter 3) that Jesus' resurrection means our resurrection. Jesus said,

"I am the resurrection and the life:
whoever believes in me,

though he should die, will come to life." (Jn 11:25)

And Paul adds, "He who raised up the Lord Jesus will raise us up along with Jesus and place both us and you in his presence" (2 Cor 4:14). We will come to the full blossoming of human life, in face-to-face communion with God.

"The trumpet will sound and the dead will be raised incorruptible, and we shall be changed. This corruptible body must be clothed with incorruptibility, this mortal body with immortality" (1 Cor 15:52-53).

St. Paul anticipates our question: "Perhaps someone will say, 'How are the dead to be raised up? What kind of body will they have?' A nonsensical question! The seed you sow does not germinate unless it dies. When you sow, you do not sow the full-blown plant, but a kernel of wheat or some other grain. . . .What is sown in the earth is subject to decay, what rises is incorruptible. What is sown is ignoble, what rises is glorious. Weakness is sown, strength rises up. A natural body is put down and a spiritual body comes up" (1 Cor 15: 35-37, 42-44).

It is useless to speculate. More exciting is the realization that when God has finally worked his way through human freedom, and evil and darkness no longer hold us, he will "let himself go." And if human beings can give such happiness to each other, what will God give!

Heaven. We fear that heaven will get boring. We are prisoners of time, and one of our sad occupations is to "kill" it. We cannot imagine having enough to do to fill an infinite amount of time. But there will be no "time."

And that is our problem: trying to imagine what it means not to fear the loss of this present peace or pleasure or safety. Watch a wild bird or animal constantly alert, incessantly turning its head, on guard against danger.

We cannot imagine what the words mean: to be *possessed* eternally by fathomless happiness; to be *filled* with God's life, love, beauty, goodness. We can only try to hold these ideas in poor little boxes of human words, and the boxes collapse.

Best, again, to trust. What would *I* do for those I love without limit? Then, Jesus argues, "If you, with all your sins, know how to give your children what is good, how much more will your heavenly Father give good things to anyone who asks him!" (Mt 7:11).

John describes the impossibility of imagining perfect happiness as well as our trust that it will come:

> "Dearly beloved,
> we are God's children now;
> what we shall later be has not yet come to light.
> We know that when it comes to light,
> we shall be like him,
> for we shall see him as he is.
> Everyone who has this hope based on him
> keeps himself pure, as he is pure." (1 Jn 3:2-3)

The Communion of Saints. In the Apostles' Creed we state one of the fundamental beliefs of the Church: "I believe in the communion of saints."

Communion here means a sharing of the blessings of salvation, especially that of personal communion with all the "saints." And *saints* here means not just those who have been canonized by the Church, but *all God's holy people.* All who are in Christ have been made holy with the holiness of God. Thus Paul writes to the "saints" of Ephesus, Corinth, Achaia, Philippi, Colossus. Today he would write to the "holy ones" of Chicago or Brownsville or Ottawa–the ones gathered around the altar.

This communion-community has its basis in the community of God, the Holy Trinity. God gave us his Son to be our companion. He sits at our table, and he gives us the bread that fills us with the life of God. His Spirit is in us, and our communion with the Holy Spirit is communion with Christ and with the Father, because the Holy Spirit *is* that communion. All the members of Christ who share this life of God also share it with each other.

So, when the Church as such prays for its members, or when one individual member prays for the whole Church, or when one individual prays for another, this prayer takes place in the one Spirit. The Spirit takes the cry of the Bride of Christ and makes it resound before the Father along with the voice of Christ. The prayer may be expressed in active service, in Christlike suffering or the relief of suffering in others. In any case, "if one member suffers, all the members suffer with it; if one member is honored, all the members share its joy" (1 Cor 12:26). If our network of good friends on earth is so powerful a support, what must the support of all God's friends be!

This intercommunion of love extends throughout the whole Church–the members of Christ who are with him in heaven, his members in the purification of purgatory, and the faithful on earth. One for all, and all for one.

The Saving of God's Beautiful Creation. St. Paul says that "the whole created world eagerly awaits the revelation of the sons of God." Material creation, he says, was frustrated in achieving the end for which it was made because human sin disrupted the order in the world. But, Paul continues, "the world itself will be freed from its slavery to corruption and share in the glorious freedom of the children of God." Meanwhile, "all creation groans and is in agony" as it strains toward its fulfillment (see Rom 8:18-22).

What will happen to our world?

"What we await are new heavens and a new earth," says the author of the 2 Peter 3:13. St. Jerome comments: "He did not say that we will see different heavens and a different earth, but the old and ancient ones transformed into something better." And St. Thomas Aquinas adds, "God has formed all things that they might have being, and not that they might revert to nothingness."

We are realizing these days that we have abused God's beautiful creation instead of using it as God instructed Adam (see Gn 1:28-31). Energy, sky and water, forests and fields, city and country are gifts of God to be treasured and cared for. Our world is being saved along with us; it deserves our reverent care.

Hell. In the end, there can be only two groups of people (and let us hope one

181

group is very small, or perhaps non-existent): those who have accepted the responsibility of living according to truth and love as they experienced it, and those who have with full consciousness and full freedom rejected truth and love in their lives. The latter at death are *frozen* (an odd word to use in connection with hell) in their own *life choice.*

Hell is the state of being turned away from God by one's own free and deliberate option—a life-option shaped by many decisions freely made.

Even God cannot *force* love. Love must be freely given, or it is not love. God can surround us with his sacramental creation, send messengers of forgiveness, come in human flesh to die on a cross—but we must respond. Trust and love is the normal response; our whole being moves us to it. We are made for truth and love.

But it is possible to reject the light, to still the normal impulses of the heart, to *become* a life-decision of selfishness.

There must come an end, after a million moments of offered mercy. Death is meant to be the fullest moment of decision for God. For one who has died in spirit long before, it is the summing up of the fundamental decision. Hell is living with that decision forever.

God does not "send" people to hell. God did not create hell. Hell, along with sin, suffering and death, is *our* idea. The "hell" of hell is being unable to blame anyone, especially God, who did everything but take away freedom to save everyone from eternal misery.

Purgatory. The word *purgatory* is not found in the Bible. The doctrine has been one of the sore points of disagreement between Catholics and Protestants, so it behooves us to know exactly what the Catholic Church teaches.

The only *defined*—that is, officially declared—teaching of the Church is that there *is* a purgatory, and that the souls detained therein are aided by the prayers of the faithful, and chiefly by the Eucharist. There is nothing about fire, or length of time, or agony.

We must not make purgatory into a flaming concentration camp on the brink of hell—or even a "hell for a short time." It is blasphemous to think of it as a place where a petty God exacts the last pound—or ounce—of flesh.

Purgatory was originally a Latin adjective meaning cleansing, purgative. The doctrine of the Church does not depend on the word, but on the reality (or rather the probability) that almost all persons have some last, lingering reluctance in their service of God. We grow in the holiness God offers us through many developing stages, painfully, slowly. It is another instance of the patience of God that he loves us gently even though we shrink back in partial mistrust or selfishness.

Purgatory simply means this: If my death does not indeed represent a total giving of myself to God's love in full faith, hope and charity; if, that is, there is any sinfulness in me, no matter how slight, that must be removed before I come face to face with God. God must purify me not only from gross sin in life, but from all defilement. This is not some arbitrary arrangement, but the nature of God.

How does God do this? We don't know. His love brings me to full response. How long does it take? We don't know. How do the prayers of my friends on earth help me? The same way they helped me on earth.

The suffering of purgatory is not vindictive punishment. St. Catherine of Genoa, a mystic of the 15th century, wrote that the "fire" of purgatory is God's love "burning" the soul so that, at last, the soul is wholly aflame. It is the pain of wanting to be made totally worthy of One who is seen as infinitely lovable, the pain of desire for union that is now absolutely assured, but not yet fully tasted.

Postscript

A discussion of Purgatory may seem a wry way to end a book on life in Christ. But, as we saw, purgatory rests on a big *if.* There must be a period or process of purification *if* we need to be purified. It is possible that some persons are completely purified in this life.

So the present is purgatory too—adjective and noun. Being saved is being cleansed, liberated, raised up to the life of Jesus daily. Purification is the daily dying to whatever is selfish, untrue, unChristlike, and daily being raised by him to a deeper sharing in his own life.

We are called to be like persons in purgatory in one crucial way: We are trying to learn to say the last words of the Bible as they say them, with bursting desire. To say them with no lingering strains of selfishness, with no lack of trust, with our whole heart and soul, mind and strength:

Come, Lord Jesus! (Rev 22:20)

Appendices

A.
Believing in Jesus
and the RCIA

"The only possible way of approaching the Christian life: total, lifelong, deepening 'conversion.'" Those words from Chapter 16 of this book provide both a key to the book and a guide to its use for the Rite of Christian Initiation of Adults (RCIA).

It is appropriate that author Leonard Foley, O.F.M., uses these words to speak of the restored catechumenate itself. For "lifelong conversion" is the quite overwhelming truth about Christianity which the RCIA has rediscovered for us.

Acknowledging the dynamic of God at work in the life of the catechumen, the RCIA moves through a process of search and growth, through encounters with Jesus, his death and resurrection, and the Spirit—all within the faith community. The RCIA reverberates with the experience of early Christians coming to the life-changing realization that Jesus is Lord.

No book can bring about that realization for us. Words—someone else's faith experience—cannot substitute for one's own. Even Scripture can serve only as an opening to the divine mystery, not a replacement for personal belief.

Given that limitation, what place does *Believing in Jesus* have in the RCIA process?

Clearly, this is not a book of lesson plans for each session. It is not structured around an already existing RCIA schedule of topics. It has none of the actual rites that mark the stages of the catechumenate. It contains no descriptions of what the author calls the "countless details of Catholic life," the externals of the Catholic tradition.

What the book offers instead are a foundation, a focus and an attitude.

A Foundation, a Focus, an Attitude

Knowledge of Scripture, doctrine, the sacraments, morality establishes a *foundation* for Christianity and Catholicism. Thus, the information this book provides is quite rightly an indispensable element in the catechumen's journey toward membership in the community.

But this knowledge is not equivalent to the spiritual journey. One cannot reach mystery by piling fact upon fact and standing upon the stockpile.

Believing in Jesus therefore goes beyond a fact-oriented, question-and-answer approach. Its *focus* is clearly and strongly on Jesus, as the title implies. There is a natural flow to its structure, moving from a grounding in the religious heritage that was Jesus' own, to his life, death and rising, to the Spirit and the Church, to the sacraments and Christian morality.

And the *attitude* touching every aspect of the book is that of "lifelong conversion."

That conversion is personal. It must arise from our hearts and souls, the centers of our being. It does not come about by studying a list of doctrines put before us and intellectually affirming them. It originates not in the mind but in the Spirit.

That conversion is also endless. Each Christian is engaged in an ongoing formation process that continues beyond childhood religion classes, beyond adult Baptism. Ours is a lifetime journey, always a "becoming," as we reflect, pray, learn, search and grow, ever recognizing Jesus anew, ever deepening our insights. These are, after all, the "eternal questions."

Integrating This Book Into the RCIA Program

Believing in Jesus has been successfully used in the RCIA process by many parishes and in different ways: as the only text central to a program of study, as a supplement to class presentations, as one of a number of resource books. Some RCIA teams use it regularly, some suggest individual chapters, some simply make it available to those who choose to use it on their own.

The chapter-by-chapter study guide which begins on page 191 is designed to help RCIA teams easily and effectively integrate the book into their established programs. It presumes that session formats already exist, with time allotted for prayer, presentations, discussion, and perhaps readings, singing, breaks.

Most RCIA teams likely have a schedule of topics with which they are comfortable. A look through the table of contents of *Believing in Jesus* indicates that the chapters cover commonly used subject areas. Several possibilities for structuring a program or supplementing one already in use suggest themselves.

A Nonsequential Approach. Chapters *can* be treated out of sequence; some may not be discussed at all. One possible approach is:

Pre-Catechumenate

Scripture	Chapters 1, 2
Trinity	Chapter 11
Church	Chapter 12
Liturgy/Eucharist	Chapter 14
Sacraments	Chapter 15
Prayer	Chapter 24

Catechumenate

Jesus' Life and Teachings	Chapters 3, 4, 5
Jesus' Death and Rising	Chapters 6, 7
Jesus: God and Man	Chapter 8
Visible Church/Orders	Chapters 13, 21

Period of Enlightenment

Mystagogia

A Sequential Approach. There is also something to be said for following the sequence of chapters in the book. The structure has a certain integrity, with one chapter building upon another. A suggested division is:

Of course, no one chapter-by-chapter schedule will correspond to the interior process experienced by each person. But having the text offers the catechumen the chance to move freely about the book—referring back to certain sections, reflecting, being provoked and inspired, moving on through the deep, rich spiritual complexity of believing in Jesus.

Using the Study Guide With Catechumens

Reflection/Discussion Starters. It is recommended that participants read the appropriate chapters and reflect on the questions before they meet together. Catechists should avoid lecturing from the book and let the significant points of each chapter emerge in a natural and unforced way from discussion.

This a time for sharing one's insights and unique perspective, one's own faith experience and encounters with God. An atmosphere of encouragement and respectful openness is vital, for the exchange of what is deepest in us is taking place.

The reflection/discussion starters are meant to move back and forth between factual orientation and personal reflection; both are important. Some will demand intense personal questioning and cannot be answered quickly. Some may take an entire lifetime of experiencing and reflection, for they are eternal questions, open-ended in the ultimate sense.

Catechists should be wary of conveying an attitude that these questions have certain "right" responses or can be closed off in any way. And catechumens should know that their own questions are an integral part of the process. The goal is an easy and comfortable give-and-take between catechumens and sponsors and catechists, moving from experience to fact and back to experience.

Scripture Readings. The readings suggested for the chapters are primarily those scriptural passages mentioned but not quoted in the text. Note that the readings suggested are not the only biblical passages of importance for that chapter, nor are they always even the most important. Catechists can guide catechumens in exploring other relevant Scripture passages. The New Testament is, after all, not just *a* basis for our belief in Jesus, but *the* basis. And the Old Testament provides the origins, the tradition out of which Jesus taught.

In the RCIA process, catechumens, with the entire Church community, move through the celebrations of the liturgical year. Fittingly, many programs use the Lectionary as a guideline for session topics. Every program should strive to deepen participation in the liturgical year with the Liturgy of the Word.

Whether found in the weekly readings or in the chapter contents, Scripture is a rich source to be plumbed and very much a part of ongoing conversion.

Supplementary Material. Supplementary materials are of five types. "*Updates*" are issues of *Catholic Update* published by St. Anthony Messenger Press. A 1984 survey showed that *Catholic Update*s are the second most used teaching aid among 410 U.S. and Canadian parishes. Their four-page length and their adult-education approach make them particularly suited for use in RCIA programs. (They are also available at group rates.)

The *tapes* listed are also produced by St. Anthony Messenger Press. Where only one tape or talk in a series is appropriate, that one is indicated; it can be purchased separately. The audio version of *Believing in Jesus* is available as a set of 11 tapes, titled '*That You May Believe*,' also by Leonard Foley, O.F.M..

Again, St. Anthony Messenger Press is responsible for many of the *books* suggested for further reading. Those titles preceded by an asterisk are available from other publishers. Several *documents* from Vatican II and *encyclicals* are also included. Unlike the *Catholic Update*s or tapes, the books, documents and encyclicals are truly supplemental to the program, probably not usable within the group process. They can, however, provide beneficial resources for an individual to pursue.

Additional Activities

The exchange of individual faith expressions is essential to the RCIA and can be prompted and enhanced in ways other than reflection/discussion starters and supplementary material. For instance, methods like these can serve as the core of some presentations:

- Chapter 1 (Old Testament) and 14 (Eucharist): a Passover meal;
- Chapter 4 (Parables): writing one's own parable based on one's life and experience of God;
- Chapter 10 (Spirit) and 17 (Confirmation): inviting charismatics to speak;
- Chapter 11 (Trinity): exploring personal concepts of God and their evolution;
- Chapter 11 (Trinity) and 27 (Death, Judgment, Heaven): examining the question of suffering and death with someone ministering to the dying or the bereaved;
- Chapter 13 (Visible Church) and 20 (Marriage): discussing contraception, *Humanae Vitae* and dissent;
- Chapter 13 (Visible Church) and 21 (Orders): a panel presentation on roles of the laity, priests, religious, and ways to serve in the Church;
- Chapter 13 (Visible Church) and 21 (Orders): examining the place of women in the Church and the question of women's ordination with speakers active in furthering women's role;
- Chapter 15 (Sacraments): creating individual time lines of one's life, indicating significant moments of change and growth;
- Chapter 14 (Eucharist), 16 (Baptism), 17 (Confirmation), 18 (Reconciliation), 19 (Anointing), 20 (Marriage) and 21 (Orders): examining the rites of the sacraments, using role-playing when appropriate (especially helpful for Reconciliation);
- Chapter 20 (Marriage) and 21 (Orders): a panel presentation with married, single, religious and ordained persons speaking on different vocations or states of life;
- Chapter 24 (Prayer): demonstrating methods of prayer and prayer experiences. (This can actually be an ongoing process if session agendas regularly expose the catechumens to different prayer forms using Scripture, group prayer, silent prayer, meditation, song, etc. Common Catholic prayers and practices—e.g., the rosary, the Stations of the Cross—can also be used.)

For Individual Catechumens and 'Born' Catholics

So far our focus has been on using *Believing in Jesus* in a group situation. But individual catechumens may also find the study guide helpful for highlighting significant points and for triggering personal reflection.

Many "born" Catholics will want to use the study guide for the same purpose. As the restored catechumenate has reminded us, we are called to continually deepen our love of God, to repeatedly say yes to Jesus, to encounter the Spirit over and over in every aspect of our lives. We members of the Christian community are called to accompany the catechumens on their journey because it is our journey too.

Indeed, for some—perhaps many—of us that journey may scarcely have begun. *Believing in Jesus* cannot "make" one believe in Jesus. But if readers—

whether catechumens or "born" Catholics—let themselves be challenged by its words and shared faith experience, they may find it a genuine opening to God through Jesus in the Spirit, an opening they never quite knew before.

B.
Chapter-by-Chapter
Study Guide

Part I: Getting to Know the Bible

Chapter 1. Jesus' Bible: The Old Testament

Reflection/Discussion Starters

1) What does it mean to say the Bible is not just a record of events, but an interpretation of these events?

2) Reflect on the way the God of the Chosen People is described by Old Testament writers. How is this God similar to or different from the God of your experience?

3) The Exodus—Israel's liberation from physical and spiritual slavery in Egypt—is a model for our ultimate liberation in Jesus. Discuss how the Passover-Exodus parallels and foreshadows the death-resurrection of Jesus.

4) What is the covenant relationship God makes with the Israelites? Discuss the love God offers in this relationship and the response of the people. Do you see your own relationship to God as one of covenant?

5) What, in general, was the role of the prophets for the Chosen People? Does any one prophet speak particularly to you?

6) What are the concerns of the wisdom books? (You may wish to briefly examine the specific character of each of the seven wisdom books.)

7) Discuss the recurring theme of oppression and exile in the life of the Chosen People. Have you ever felt oppressed or in exile in your own life? What freed you?

Scripture Readings

In covering the entire Old Testament, this chapter can provide only a brief view of its contents. You may wish to examine more closely some of the books discussed. Four short passages that are significant as both a reference to a faithful remnant of the people and a foreshadowing of a savior are the "Songs of the Suffering Servant": Is 42:1-4; 49:1-7; 50:4-11; 52:13—53:12.

Supplementary Material†

Updates: "A Popular Introduction to Reading the Bible," by Macrina Scott, O.S.F.; "How to Understand the Bible: Examining the Tools of Today's Scripture

Scholars," by Norman Langenbrunner; "Seven Most-Asked Questions About the Bible," by Norman Perry, O.F.M.; "Passover: Jewish Feast, Christian Feast," by Leonard Foley, O.F.M.

Tapes: *Through the Old Testament With Father Stephen Doyle, O.F.M.; The Great Themes of Scripture*, by Richard Rohr, O.F.M.

Books: *The People of the Book*, by Anthony E. Gilles; *From Eden to Nazareth*, by Leonard Foley, O.F.M.; *God Calls a People: A Journey Through the Old Testament*, by Sister Blanche Twigg, M.H.S.H.; *The Major Old Testament Themes*, by William Heidt, O.S.B.

Chapter 2. Jesus in Inspired Human Words: The New Testament

Reflection/Discussion Starters

1) The New Testament writers were writing for believers and not simply to offer historical facts. Discuss how this approach colored their writing.

2) What distinguishes each of the four Gospels? Examine their major themes and individual approaches.

3) The letters were written out of different situations and for different purposes. What are some of the themes with which they deal?

4) Discuss the formation of the New Testament—how scholars believe it developed out of Jesus' life and teachings into the form we know it today.

5) Reflect on what it means to say the Bible is "inspired."

6) Discuss how the interpretation of Scripture must be guided by considering the style, form and purpose used by the individual writers.

7) The author speaks of two kinds of tradition. Discuss these two types and the role tradition plays in the beliefs of the Church.

Scripture Readings

It would be helpful to read at least one of the Gospels all the way through. In addition, you may wish to sample other books of the New Testament. Specific passages to examine include examples of the apostolic proclamation: Acts 2:22-24, 32-33; 3:12-26; 10:36-43.

Supplementary Material

Updates: "How the Gospels Were Written," by Leonard Foley, O.F.M.; "Matthew's Gospel: Jesus Ushers in God's Kingdom," by Hilarion Kistner,

---

†Throughout this guide:
Updates refer to issues of *Catholic Update*, published by St. Anthony Messenger Press.

Books and tapes not preceded by an asterisk are available from St. Anthony Messenger Press. Those titles preceded by an asterisk are available from other publishers.

The audio version of *Believing in Jesus* is available as a set of 11 tapes, titled 'That You May Believe,' by Leonard Foley, O.F.M., from St. Anthony Messenger Press.

O.F.M.; "Mark's Gospel: Messiah With a Cross," by Stephen Doyle, O.F.M.; "Luke's Gospel: God Cares for the Poor and Lowly," by Robert J. Karris, O.F.M.; "John's Gospel: The Light Is Among Us Now," by Stephen Doyle, O.F.M.; "The Infancy Narratives: How to Read the Nativity Stories of Jesus," by Macrina Scott, O.S.F.; "Understanding the Book of Revelation," by Macrina Scott, O.S.F.

Tapes: *Getting Acquainted With the New Testament*, by Anthony E. Gilles; *Through the New Testament With Father Stephen Doyle, O.F.M.; The Great Themes of Scripture*, by Richard Rohr, O.F.M.; *The Apocalypse: Biblical Revelation Explained*, by Patrick Sena, C.PP.S.

Books: *The People of the Way*, by Anthony E. Gilles; *God Speaks in Jesus: A Journey Through the New Testament*, by Sister Blanche Twigg, M.H.S.H.; *The Four Gospels: An Introduction*, by Bruce Vawter.

Part II: Jesus' Journey to Death and Life

Chapter 3. The Missionary Jesus: 'He Went About Doing Good'

Reflection/Discussion Starters

1) Mark writes that Jesus proclaimed "the good news of God." Discuss what the "Good News" might have meant for those hearing it at the time. What does the Good News mean to you today?

2) What is your concept of the Devil? Discuss the ways the Gospels treat the Devil or Satanic forces.

3) Discuss some of the "signs" Jesus worked. What was the mindset of the people toward "miracles"? Do you believe miracles take place today?

4) Reflect on the author's statement that Jesus' signs—both "extraordinary" and "ordinary"—"are the openings through which human love sees God and receives his life." What signs in your life have become openings to God for you?

Scripture Readings

Is 63:19—64:3; the Gospel of Mark.

Supplementary Material

Update: "Mark's Gospel: Messiah With a Cross," by Stephen Doyle, O.F.M.
Tape: *Understanding the Faith* (tape #3), by Rev. James J. Bacik.
Book: *Jesus' Saving Questions*, by Gloria Hutchinson.

Chapter 4. Jesus' Teaching-Stories: The Parables

Reflection/Discussion Starters

1) What are some common characteristics and themes of the parables Jesus told?

2) What is meant by the Kingdom of God? Discuss what the parables say about the Kingdom.

3) Which parable speaks the most to you? Why?

4) How do you experience the Kingdom in your life? Could you create your own parable that conveys your experience of the Kingdom?

Scripture Readings

(In a group, the parable readings given below can be divided up among individuals or smaller groups, with each person or small group discussing the specific passages assigned to them.)

In Matthew: 5:25-26; 12:43-45; 13:1-9, 24-30, 33, 47-50; 18:23-35; 20:1-16; 21:28-32, 33-46; 22:1-14; 24:32-35, 45-51; 25:1-13, 14-30, 31-46.

In Mark: 4:26-29, 30-32; 13:32-37.

In Luke: 7:29-35, 36-50; 10:25-37; 11:5-8; 12:13-21, 35-40; 13:6-9, 22-30; 14:15-24, 25-35; 15:3-7, 8-10, 11-32; 16:1-12, 19-31; 17:7-10; 18:1-8, 9-14.

Supplementary Material

Update: "What Is the Kingdom of God?" by Richard McBrien.

Book: *The Parables of Jesus*, edited by Joachim Jeremias.

Chapter 5. Jesus, a Danger to Church and State

Reflection/Discussion Starters

1) There were several points of contention between Jesus and the Pharisees. Which practices of the Pharisees did Jesus speak against? Do you see the qualities that Jesus criticized in the Pharisees present in people today? In society? In your own life?

2) Which of Jesus' actions and teachings disturbed the Pharisees? If Jesus were acting and teaching among us today, do you think some people would see him as the "scandal" that the Pharisees did?

Scripture Readings

Mt 23; 6:1-18.

Chapter 6. The Dying and Rising of Jesus: The Heart of Christian Life

Reflection/Discussion Starters

1) What does it mean to you to say that Jesus is the Messiah? How did this claim lead to Jesus' death?

2) Reflect on Jesus' last words and the ways they express themes within his life and message. Which speak to you most strongly for your own life?

3) For the three last statements that reflect back to the psalms, read the corresponding psalm (Psalms 22, 69, 31) and discuss the way its words are fulfilled

in Jesus.

4) Reflect on the reasons why Jesus died. Why was his life and death, as the author says, not simply "some 'nice' gesture, but a reflection of reality"? What does Jesus' death mean to you?

5) The mystery of the cross is that "one must die to live, one must lose in order to win." Do you see that mystery present in your life? Have you or have others you know ever had to lose in order to win, to die in small ways in order to live?

Scripture Readings

Mk 8:27-33, 34-38. The Passion Narratives: Mt 26—27; Mk 14—15; Lk 22—23; Jn 18—19.

Supplementary Material

Updates: "How to Read the Passion Narratives of Jesus," by Raymond Brown; "Who Is Jesus?" by Leonard Foley, O.F.M.

Tape: *Jesus' Passion and Resurrection*, by Hilarion Kistner, O.F.M.

Book: **The Lord*, by Romano Guardini.

Part III: The World Starts Over

Chapter 7. The Rising of Jesus From the Dead

Reflection/Discussion Starters

1) Why do we speak of Jesus' "death-resurrection" as a combined event? In what way is Jesus' death-resurrection the world starting over? Have you ever known a starting over in your life? Does your experience of Jesus' death-resurrection provide a starting over for you?

2) What does Jesus' resurrection say about the relationship between God and human beings?

3) Reflect on the ways you experience dying and rising as a part of your daily life.

4) After the resurrection, Jesus had to give the disciples the power to recognize him, to know him again. Does this process of recognizing Jesus go on today? Has this happened in your own life?

Scripture Readings

The Resurrection Accounts: Mt 28; Mk 16; Lk 24; Jn 20—21. 1 Cor 15:35-38, 42-44.

Supplementary Material

Updates: "The Resurrection: Its Meaning for Our Day," by William Marrin; "Who Is Jesus?" by Leonard Foley, O.F.M.

Chapter 8. Jesus, the Son of God: This Man

Reflection/Discussion Starters

1) What does it mean to say that Jesus is one Person with two natures?
2) Reflect on the humanity of Jesus. Think of ways his humanity is made evident in the Gospels.
3) Discuss how Jesus can be said to be a sacrament or sign. Consider the author's words that Jesus is "the self-revealing of God through the sign of the human body," and "the love of God made visible." What does this mean to you?
4) Who is Jesus for you? Do you experience Jesus as God? As man? What difference does Jesus make in your life?

Supplementary Material

Tapes: *Jesus and Our Daily Life*, by Paul Desch, O.F.M.; *Jesus, Perfectly Human!* by John Quigley, O.F.M.; *Jesus and His Church*, by Richard Rohr, O.F.M.; *Four Journeys* (talk #2), by Joseph W. Goetz.

Books: *'Christ Lives in Me': A Pastoral Reflection on Jesus and His Meaning for Christian Life*, by Joseph Cardinal Bernardin; **Jesus, God and Man*, by Raymond Brown.

Chapter 9. Jesus Is Lord: A Short Course in St. Paul

Reflection/Discussion Starters

1) Reflect on the different messages of Paul. Which seem particularly meaningful to you? Why?
2) What does Paul's declaration that Jesus Christ is Lord (Phil 2:11) mean to you? Do you experience Jesus as Lord?

Scripture Readings

The chapter includes many passages from Paul's letters. In addition, you may wish to read about Paul's life in Acts: 9; 12:25—13:14; 15:36-41; 16—28.

Supplementary Material

Update: "St. Paul: The Man Behind the Letters," by Macrina Scott, O.S.F.
Books: *Life and Holiness*, by Thomas Merton.

Chapter 10. The Spirit Given Through Jesus

Reflection/Discussion Starters

1) Discuss the ways the Spirit is described in Scripture.
2) What is the Spirit for you? How do you experience the Spirit in your life?
3) Reflect on the statement, "The Spirit is given to us for the same reason it

was given to Jesus: to make us holy." What does this mean to you? In the old Anglo-Saxon meaning of the word, *holy* meant whole, complete. Have you sensed in your life a need for wholeness? How have you tried to meet this need?

Scripture Readings

Acts 2; 1 Cor 12:1-11; 13; Is 11:2-3; Gal 5:19-23.

Supplementary Material

Update: "The Holy Spirit—Yesterday and Today," by Jack Wintz, O.F.M.

Tape: *Four Journeys* (talk #3), by Joseph W. Goetz.

Book: **Conspiracy of God: The Spirit in Men*, by John C. Haughey, S.J.

Chapter 11. To Know Jesus Is to Know the Father, Son and Spirit: The Trinity

Reflection/Discussion Starters

1) God as Father and God as Mother are similes that can help us understand God's relationship to us. Do you experience God as Father? As Mother? As Parent? In what ways?

2) What are some ways we explain suffering? Why can we say that God's explanation is the cross?

3) To what communities do you belong? Are there some to which you belong by choice rather than by circumstance? Do you have a need to belong to a community? Reflect on the concept of God as "community," the idea that "the very nature of God is to be 'with.'" What does it mean to you to say that we are called to "join the community"?

Supplementary Material

Tapes: *Understanding the Faith* (tape #2), by Rev. James J. Bacik; *Four Journeys* (talk #1), by Joseph W. Goetz.

Books: *God Never Says, 'Yes, But...,'* by Leonard Foley, O.F.M. (on the question of suffering, pain, God's will); **We Dare to Say Our Father*, by Louis Evely; **Your God Is Too Small*, by J. B. Phillips.

Part IV: The Saving Work of Jesus in the World Today

Chapter 12. Jesus Living in His Members: The Church

Reflection/Discussion Starters

1) Reflect on the statement, "The Church is the sacrament of Jesus just as

Jesus was the sacrament of God." Has the Church been a sign of Jesus for you? In what ways?

2) Discuss the different ways to speak about the Church: as the Mystical Body of Christ, the Vine and the Branches, God's Family, God's Building, Jesus' Little Flock, the People of God. Which is/are most meaningful to you? Why?

3) Is the Church identical to the Kingdom of God? What is the relationship between the two?

4) Interior conversion is essential for membership in the Kingdom. For each of us, life is an endless conversion, but, as the author says, "We must sooner or later...come to the mind-shattering realization that Jesus is *the* Lord." What has your own interior conversion experience involved? At what point on your journey of "endless conversion" do you find yourself right now?

Scripture Readings

Acts 1—4; Eph 5:25-27; 1 Cor 12; Jn 15; Ps 118:22; Mt 16:18; 1 Cor 3:11; 15:24; Mt 18:3.

Supplementary Material

Update: "Acts of the Apostles: The Church After the Resurrection," by Hilarion Kistner, O.F.M.

Tapes: *Understanding the Faith* (tape #4), by Rev. James J. Bacik; *Four Journeys* (talk #4), by Joseph W. Goetz.

Books: *The Story of the Church*, by Alfred McBride, O.Praem; *Christ, Sacrament of the Encounter With God*, by Edward Schillebeeckx.

Document: *Dogmatic Constitution on the Church* (chapters I, II).

Chapter 13. Trying to Make Jesus Visible: The 'Outside' of the Church

Reflection/Discussion Starters

1) What do you see the role of lay people to be in the Church? What is their role in the wider society?

2) Describe the kind of authority Jesus conferred on the Church. How do you see authority being exercised in the Church today?

3) How can the position of pope be traced back to Jesus' words?

4) Discuss the concept of infallibility. How has it been defined? When has it been invoked? Does it mean that Church leaders can never err in any position or statement?

5) Can a person dissent in clear conscience from the magisterium or "ordinary teaching" of the Church? Discuss some instances of dissent of which you are aware.

6) In what way are all Christians joined to the Catholic Church and non-Christians, even nonbelievers, related to the People of God?

Updates: "Tradition in the Catholic Church—Why It's Still Important," by Monika Hellwig; "The Papacy in a World of Change," by J. Michael Miller, C.S.B.; "Lay Ministry: An Idea Whose Time Has Come," by Ellen Frankenberg; "Birth Control and the Conscientious Catholic," by Kenneth Overberg, S.J.

Tape: *Understanding the Faith* (tape #7), by Rev. James J. Bacik.

Books: *Shaping Tomorrow's Church*, by Dennis G. Sullivan; *Crises Facing the Church*, by Raymond Brown; *A Concise History of the Catholic Church*, by Thomas Bokenkotter.

Document: *Dogmatic Constitution on the Church* (chapters II, IV).

Encyclical: *Humanae Vitae*.

Chapter 14. Jesus in His Church: Eucharist, the Radiating Center

Reflection/Discussion Starters

1) The Eucharist can be described in these ways: making present the fact and meaning of Jesus' death and resurrection; a new Passover meal; the transformation of the community; the one perfect sacrifice. Which of these ways of speaking of the Eucharist is/are most meaningful to you? Why?

2) Reflect on the "marvelous and extraordinary change" of the bread and wine into Christ's body and blood. What does this change mean to you?

Scripture Readings

Lk 22:19-20; Mt 26:26-28; Mk 14:22-24; 1 Cor 11:23-26; Acts 5:1-11.

Supplementary Material

Updates: "How to Participate More Actively in the Mass," by Thomas Richstatter, O.F.M.; "Is the Mass a Meal?" by Charles Gusmer; "Is the Mass Still a Sacrifice?" by Patrick McCloskey, O.F.M.; "A Priest Answers 10 Gripes about the Mass," by Jack Wintz, O.F.M.; "Why the Lay Ministers at Sunday Mass?" by Thomas Richstatter, O.F.M.; "Holy Communion From the Cup," by Leonard Foley, O.F.M.; "Communion in the Hand: Understanding the New Option," by Leonard Foley, O.F.M.; "Passover: Jewish Feast, Christian Feast," by Leonard Foley, O.F.M.; "First Communion: A Parish Event," by Sandra DeGidio, O.S.M.

Books: *Why Sunday Mass?* edited by Karen Hurley; *The Mass: Finding Its Meaning for You—And Getting More Out of It*, by Gerard P. Weber.

Document: *Constitution on the Sacred Liturgy* (chapters I, II).

Encyclical: *Mystery of Faith*.

Chapter 15. The One Jesus in All the Sacramental Actions

Reflection/Discussion Starters

1) Name some signs or symbols in daily life that are especially meaningful to you.

2) What are some of the signs used in the sacraments?

3) Reflect on the most significant or crucial moments of your life. In what ways do the sacraments mark significant moments in a person's spiritual life?

4) How do you understand grace? How have you experienced grace in your life?

5) Reflect on the statement that "every moment, every person, every situation is a kind of sacrament." How is that true? Is it true for you?

Supplementary Material

Updates: "The Seven Sacraments: Symbols of God's Care," by Sandra DeGidio, O.S.M.; "Grace: Our Love Relationship With God," by Leonard Foley, O.F.M.

Tapes: *The Sacraments: The Church at Prayer*, by Thomas Richstatter, O.F.M.; *Understanding the Faith* (tape #5), by Rev. James J. Bacik.

Books: *Signs of Love*, by Leonard Foley, O.F.M.; **The Meaning of the Sacraments*, by Monika Hellwig.

Chapter 16. Jesus Welcomes Strangers Into His Community: Baptism

Reflection/Discussion Starters

1) What does it mean to see the Christian life as one of "total, lifelong, deepening 'conversion'"? Do you experience your spiritual life in that way?

2) How does the restored catechumenate demonstrate that view of Christianity?

3) What does water represent to you? How does it symbolize death and rising?

4) How does the view of conversion as a lifelong process support the argument for baptizing infants?

5) If God's grace has entered your life already, why is the Sacrament of Baptism needed?

Supplementary Material

Updates: "Adult Baptism: The New Rite of Christian Initiation of Adults," by Mary Bohlen; "Infant Baptism: A Community Event," by Leonard Foley, O.F.M.

Books: *What Do You Ask for Your Child?* by Carol Luebering; *Our Journey in Faith: From Baptism to Christian Maturity*, edited by Jack Wintz, O.F.M.

Chapter 17. The Spirit of Jesus Sends Forth Witnesses: Confirmation

Reflection/Discussion Starters

1) Discuss the relationship between Baptism and Confirmation in terms of their meanings and purposes.

2) Why is anointing used in Confirmation? What does it signify?

3) What does it mean to you to say we are called to Christian witness in the world? How do you see this happening in your life? Have you experienced the Christian witness of others?

4) How would you explain the "Baptism of the Spirit" of which charismatics speak?

Scripture Readings

1 Cor 12:4-11; 13.

Supplementary Material

*Update*s: "Confirmation: Anointed for Fuller Witness," by Sandra DeGidio, O.S.M.; "How to Share Your Faith Today: A Short Course for Modern Evangelizers," by Jack Wintz, O.F.M.

Document: *Pastoral Constitution on the Church in the Modern World.*

Chapter 18. Jesus Brings Sinners Back to the Father: Reconciliation

Reflection/Discussion Starters

1) Discuss the concept of sin as a way of life, an attitude that grows, a gradual slipping from life to death.

2) Reflect on times when you wanted someone to forgive you. Did you receive that forgiveness? If not, how did you feel?

3) Reflect on times when you forgave someone. Was it difficult? Did you feel better afterward?

4) Why should reconciliation be part of the Church's ministry?

5) If God forgives us, what are the reasons for confessing to a priest?

6) What is the purpose of a "penance" to be done by a person after celebrating the sacrament?

Supplementary Material

*Update*s: "Why Confess My Sins?" by Leonard Foley, O.F.M.; "Confessing Face to Face: The New Option in Pictures," by Leonard Foley, O.F.M.; "How to Go to Confession—Using the New Ritual," by Leonard Foley, O.F.M.

Books: *Confession Can Change Your Life*, by David Knight; *Your Confession: Using the New Ritual*, by Leonard Foley, O.F.M.

Chapter 19. Jesus Heals the Whole Person: Anointing of the Sick

Reflection/Discussion Starters

1) "The whole person is brought to health" through the Sacrament of Anointing, says the author. Discuss the kind of healing, the strength that the sacrament offers. Have you known anyone who has received the sacrament? What effect did it appear to have on the person?

2) How can you explain the fact that, though physical healing is prayed for, it does not always occur?

3) Why is the presence of the Church community important for the celebration of the Sacrament of Anointing?

Scripture Reading

Mt 13:54-58.

Supplementary Material

Update: "The New Rite for Anointing of the Sick," by Thomas Richstatter, O.F.M.

Chapter 20. Jesus at the Heart of Married Love: Marriage

Reflection/Discussion Starters

1) Discuss the role of the Church community in Christian marriage. Why does the community care about the marital union of two people?

2) Why is marriage a sacrament? Why is it considered "a sacrament of daily life"?

3) Not every marriage is a Christian marriage. What distinguishes a Christian marriage from one that is not?

4) Discuss why *covenant* may be a better word to use than *contract* to describe Christian marriage. If you are married, do you think your relationship is more like a covenant or a contract?

5) Discuss the reasons for annulments, or declarations of nullity. Explain how the Church might judge that no marriage existed from the beginning.

6) Of the marriages you know, does there appear to be an equality or inequality between husband and wife? Which seem to be happiest? Do you believe there are certain roles in a marriage that a husband should fulfill? That a wife should fulfill?

Supplementary Material

*Update*s: "The Sacrament of Marriage," by Mary and James Kenny; "Why the Church Is Granting More Annulments," by Jeffrey Keefe, O.F.M. Conv.; "Ministry to the Divorced," by James Young; "Six Skills for a Happier Marriage," by Michael Cavanagh; "Mixed Marriages: Helping Interfaith Couples Grow," by Theresa Rebeck.

Tape: *The Spiritual Family and the Natural Family*, by Richard Rohr, O.F.M.
Books: *Marriage: Sacrament of Hope and Challenge*, by William P. Roberts; *Marriage Is for Grownups*, by Joseph W. and Lois Bird; *Beginning Your Marriage*, edited by John L. Thomas; *Lovers in Marriage*, by Louis Evely.

Chapter 21. Jesus Continues His Priesthood: Orders

Reflection/Discussion Starters

1) Consider the times when it has been necessary for you or a group of which you are a part to elect someone to represent you.

2) Why does the Christian community need priests? What are the functions of a priest?

3) Lay ministry is a growing phenomenon in the Church today. What functions or jobs do you see lay ministers performing that in the past were usually done by priests? Does this mean the role of the priest has changed?

4) Discuss celibacy for priests. What are its practical and sign values? Are there disadvantages? Should it be optional?

5) Should ordination be open to women? What are the reasons given both for and against the ordination of women?

6) What do you see as the role of religious communities in the Church?

Supplementary Material

Update: "Holy Orders: What Is the Priest's Role Today?" by Thomas Richstatter, O.F.M.

Book: *Priest and Bishop*, by Raymond Brown.

Document: *Decree on the Ministry and Life of Priests*.

Part V: Our Grace-full Response to the Commandments of Jesus

Chapter 22. 'With All Your Heart': Morality and Conscience

Reflection/Discussion Starters

1) What does the concept of fundamental option as applied to sin and morality mean to you? What is mortal sinfulness?

2) Think of times when you have attempted to judge someone else's morality—the moral goodness or evil of their actions. Consider times when others have attempted to judge you. Why is it impossible to judge someone else's moral goodness?

3) The author suggests there are four "D's" that make up the act of conscience. Consider a moral decision you have had to make. Did you carefully work through the "D's": dig for facts, deliberate between alternatives, decide, do?

4) Limited freedom or awareness can affect a person's moral choice. Give some examples of moral situations where that would be so.

5) Think of a moral situation in which a higher good, God's love, might conflict with a human law.

Supplementary Material

*Update*s: "Your Conscience and Church Teaching: How Do They Fit Together?" by Nicholas Lohkamp, O.F.M.; "Examining Your Conscience Today: A Guide," by George Alliger and Jack Wintz, O.F.M.

Tape: *Understanding the Faith* (tape #6), by Rev. James J. Bacik.

Book: *Living the Good News: An Introduction to Moral Theology for Today's Catholic*, by Nicholas Lohkamp, O.F.M.

Chapter 23. Jesus' Light on the First Three Commandments

Reflection/Discussion Starters

1) Reflect on the statement: "Jesus is our Law. And following that law will take us miles beyond the Ten Commandments, which are only the minimum, the guard rails of morality." What does Jesus' directive "Follow me" mean to you?

2) Consider the first three commandments in light of Jesus. How does he transform and fulfill them, bring them to perfection?

3) Give some examples of how faith, hope and love mark a true friendship. How do these virtues exist in our total commitment of friendship with God?

4) Jesus' call to us to "repent" can be said to mean: "Change your outlook, change your way of life." What kind of change does this mean, especially if a person's whole life has not been turned away from God? Have you experienced such a change?

5) What is mistaken about the attitude that I can do good, I can be holy with my own efforts?

Scripture Readings

Ex 20:2-11; Dt 5:6-15.

Supplementary Material

Update: "The Covenant and the Ten Commandments," by Norman Langenbrunner.

Books: *Why Sunday Mass?* edited by Karen Hurley; *The Mass: Finding Its Meaning for You—And Getting More Out of It*, by Gerard P. Weber.

Chapter 24. Jesus' Spirit in Us Responds to the Father: Prayer

Reflection/Discussion Starters

1) Do you experience prayer as a one- or two-way communication? Who initiates the communication—you or God?

2) Reflect on the ways Jesus prayed. What are the glimpses we have from

Scripture of Jesus at prayer?

    3) Do you find that words are necessary in your prayer? Or are they a hindrance?

    4) How much of your prayer involves petitions? What did Jesus say about petitionary prayer?

    5) Reflect on the statement that "our prayer is our life." If this is so, is it still necessary to take particular moments to pray?

    6) Which different ways of praying do you use? Do you use different ways at different times or for different reasons?

    7) How is prayer, in Merton's words, a "waste" of time, not to be measured in terms of usefulness?

Supplementary Material

    Updates: "Pathways of Prayer," by Jack Wintz, O.F.M.; "In Search of a Simple Way to Pray," by Rev. David Knight.

    Tape: *Relax and Pray*, by Virginia Ann Froehle, R.S.M.

    Books: *Touchstones for Prayer*, by William P. Roberts; *Family Prayer*, by Dolores Curran; *Six Ways to Pray From Six Great Saints*, by Gloria Hutchinson; *It Begins With Friendship: A Fresh Approach to Prayer*, by Greg Friedman, O.F.M.; *Thomas Merton on Prayer*, by John J. Higgins; *Opening to God*, by Thomas H. Green, S.J.; *When the Well Runs Dry: Prayer Beyond the Beginnings*, by Thomas H. Green, S.J.

Chapter 25. Jesus' Light on Commandments Four Through Ten

Reflection/Discussion Starters

    1) What does it mean to you that the standard of Christian conduct is not a law, but a person—the person of Jesus? Is it easier or more difficult to follow a person rather than a law or set of laws?

    2) Consider Jesus' commandment of love. What kind of love are we to give to one another? How are we called to pass on to others our love of God?

    3) Reflect on Jesus' commands: Do not judge; do not take revenge; forgive; love your enemies. In what situations did he issue these directives? Do these seem to be difficult commands to you? Why?

    4) Discuss the Fourth through Tenth Commandments in light of Jesus' commandment to love as he loved. You may wish to consider these points:

    a) Fourth—the reverence, obedience, love, gratitude we owe our parents;

    b) Fifth—abortion, the principle of double effect, self-defense, just war and the use of nuclear weapons, respecting the body;

    c) Sixth and Ninth—sexuality as marking the whole person, chastity in different states of life, the need for others;

    d) Seventh and Tenth—justice vs. charity, private property vs. the right to subsistence, social sin.

    e) Eighth—acting in accordance with truth, our hearts and actions corresponding to the deepest reality.

Scripture Readings

Ex 20:12-17; Dt 5:16-21; Mt 25:35-46.

Supplementary Material

Updates: "The Covenant and the Ten Commandments," by Norman Langenbrunner; "Abortion: Why It Can't Be Left to 'Personal Choice,'" by James Burtchaell, C.S.C.; "A New View of Sin: Our Growing Awareness of Social Evil," by Daniel C. Maguire; "The Challenge of Peace" (the U.S. bishops' pastoral in condensed format); "Making Peace in a Nuclear Age," by Archbishop John R. Quinn; "Sexuality—God's Gift: A Contemporary Guide to Sexual Morality," by Bishop Francis J. Mugavero; "Racism—and How to Fight It" (a shortened form of the U.S. bishops' pastoral on racism); "Facing Medical-Moral Questions," by Lisa Engelhardt.

Document: *Pastoral Constitution on the Church in the Modern World* (chapter III).

Encyclicals: *The Progress of Peoples; Mother and Teacher; Justice in the World.*

Chapter 26. Jesus' Mother and Ours: Mary

Reflection/Discussion Starters

1) Discuss the role of Mary in the Church. What does recognition of Mary bring to the Church community?

2) Reflect on the accounts of Mary in Scripture. What picture do they give to you of the woman she was?

3) Has your religious background included recognition of or devotion to Mary? What has Mary meant for you?

Scripture Reading

Lk 1:26—2:52.

Supplementary Material

Update: "Mary's Faith: A Model for Our Own," by Mary Ann Deak.
Book: *What Are They Saying About Mary?* by Anthony J. Tambasco.
Document: *Dogmatic Constitution on the Church* (chapter VIII).

Chapter 27. Jesus Will Come Again!

Reflection/Discussion Starters

1) Reflect on your feelings about death. How did you feel when someone close to you died? How does being a Christian affect your view of death?

2) Though we speak of a particular and a general judgment, in what sense can we say that judgment is happening now?

3) Discuss the ideas of heaven, hell and purgatory. How do you understand them?

4) In the Creed, we state our belief in the communion of saints. Whom do we mean by the "saints"? Of what does that "communion" consist?

5) Reflect on the idea that the present is, in a sense, a purgatory for us, a purification. What does this mean to you? Have you experienced that process of purification taking place in your life?

Scripture Readings

Mt 25:31-40; Mk 13; Mt 24; Lk 21· Rom 8:18-22.

Supplementary Material

Updates: "How to Help the Dying and Grieving," by Rev. Ken Czillinger; "Comforting the Bereaved: What the Parish Community Can Do," by Carol Luebering; "Overcoming Grief: Ten Suggestions," by Arnaldo Pangrazzi.

Books: *'To Comfort All Who Mourn': A Parish Handbook for Ministry to the Grieving*, by Carol Luebering; *What Are They Saying About Death and Christian Hope?* by Monika Hellwig; *Death and Eternal Life*, by Michael Simpson, S.J.

C.
Table of
Scripture Abbreviations

Acts—Acts of the Apostles
Am—Amos
Bar—Baruch
1 Chr—1 Chronicles
2 Chr—2 Chronicles
Col—Colossians
1 Cor—1 Corinthians
2 Cor—2 Corinthians
Dn—Daniel
Dt—Deuteronomy
Eccl—Ecclesiastes
Eph—Ephesians
Est—Esther
Ex—Exodus
Ez—Ezekiel
Ezr—Ezra
Gal—Galatians
Gn—Genesis
Hb—Habakkuk
Heb—Hebrews
Hg—Haggai
Hos—Hosea
Is—Isaiah
Jas—James
Jb—Job
Jdt—Judith
Jer—Jeremiah
Jl—Joel
Jgs—Judges
Jn—John
1 Jn—1 John
2 Jn—2 John
3 Jn—3 John
Jon—Jonah
Jos—Joshua
Jude—Jude
1 Kgs—1 Kings

2 Kgs—2 Kings
Lam—Lamentations
Lk—Luke
Lv—Leviticus
Mal—Malachi
1 Mc—1 Maccabees
2 Mc—2 Maccabees
Mi—Micah
Mk—Mark
Mt—Matthew
Na—Nahum
Neh—Nehemiah
Nm—Numbers
Ob—Obadiah
1 Pt—1 Peter
2 Pt—2 Peter
Phil—Philippians
Phlm—Philemon
Prv—Proverbs
Ps—Psalms
Rom—Romans
Ru—Ruth
Rv—Revelation
Song—Song of Songs
Sir—Ecclesiasticus (Sirach)
1 Sm—1 Samuel
2 Sm—2 Samuel
Tb—Tobit
1 Thes—1 Thessalonians
2 Thes—2 Thessalonians
Ti—Titus
1 Tm—1 Timothy
2 Tm—2 Timothy
Wis—Wisdom
Zec—Zechariah
Zep—Zephaniah

Index

Abba, 55, 63-64, 153
Abortion, 163
Abraham, 3-4, 21, 55
Absolution, 120
Acts of the Apostles, 16-18, 50, 69-70, 97, 114
Adam, 2-3, 48, 51, 55, 60, 70, 109, 175, 181
Adultery, 129-130, 141, 159, 166-167
Alcohol, 163
Amos, 9-10
Amos, 9
Ananias, 86, 97
Annulment, 130
Annunciation, the, 172-173
Anointing of the Sick, Sacrament of, 101-105, 122-126
Apocalypse, the. *See Revelation.*
Apocalyptic, 12, 19, 179
Apostles, 15-16, 20, 43, 49-50, 71-72, 81, 88-90, 112, 134, 153-154. *See also* the Twelve.
Apostles' Creed, 179, 181
Aquinas, Thomas, 100, 181
Ascension, 18, 20, 50
Assumption of Mary, 90-91, 175
Atonement, 51
Augustine, 100
Babylonian exile, 7-13
Baptism
of desire, 111
Sacrament of, 4, 58, 87, 101-103, 106-114, 119, 127, 135, 149, 151, 175
of the Spirit, 116
Bishop, 92, 107, 113, 133-136
Blood, 5, 98, 100
Body and Blood of Jesus, 95. *See also* Eucharist.
Body of Christ, 70, 72, 82, 87, 92, 97, 109, 118-119, 121, 124, 127, 133, 150
Body, respect for, 163
Bread and wine, 99
Cain, 110
Calumny, 171
Calvary, 34, 96-97, 99
Canon Law, 92

Canon (of the Bible), 21
Catechism, 107
Catechumen, 107-108, 111
Catechumenate, 107-108
Catholic Letters, the, 16, 19. *See also John* (Letters of), *Peter* (Letters of), *James, Jude.*
Celibacy, 136
Challenge of Peace: God's Promise and Our Response, 164
Charismatic movement, 72, 116
Charity, 168
Chastity, 167
Children, 132
Chosen People, 2-4, 6, 9, 34, 45
Chrism, 113
Christian life, 67-68, 148
Christmas, 172
Chronicles, 8
Church, the, 22, 51, 72, 80-93
as the Body of Christ, 99, 101. *See also* Body of Christ.
as the Bride of Christ, 81, 181
community, 84
early, 18, 39-40, 58 113
and ecumenism, 93-94
as God's building, 83
as God's family, 83
Holy Spirit in, 63-64
human, 86
as Jesus' Little Flock, 83
and the Kingdom of God, 84
laws of, 92
and marriage, 128
Mary as the mother of the, 42
as the Mystical Body of Christ, 82-84
as the People of God, 83-84
reconciling community, 118-119
as the sacrament of Christ, 80-81, 117
as sign, 102
as the Vine and Branches, 83
visible, 86-93
worship in, 94-100
Circumcision, 90
Clare, 86
Colossians, 18
Commandments, the, 2, 5-6, 146-152, 157-172
Eighth, 171-172
Fifth, 162-166

211

Fruits of the Holy Spirit, 116
Fundamental option, 141, 177-178
Gabriel, 173, 176
Genesis, 3-4, 42
Genesis, 75, 174-175
Gentiles, 17, 19, 39, 48, 84, 90, 109, 111,
   173
Gifts of the Holy Spirit, 115-116
Good News, the, 25, 84
Good Shepherd, the, 83
Gospels, 16, 19-20, 28, 40-41, 48, 53, 58,
   149, 154, 159. *See also Matthew,*
   Mark, Luke, John.
Government, 169-170
Grace, 94, 104, 119, 121, 123, 141
Great Commandment, the, 140
Guilt, 142
Hail Mary, the, 155, 176
Healing, 102, 123, 126
Health, 123
Heaven, 177, 180-181
Hebrews, 16, 19, 55, 178
Hell, 177, 181-182
Heresy, 53. *See also* Docetism,
   Nestorianism.
Herod Antipas, 13, 25, 34
Herod the Great, 13
Hesed, 5
Hezekiah, 7
Historical books (of the Old Testament), 3-8
Holiness, 72-73, 84-87, 167
Holiness of God, 77
Holy Communion, 82. *See also* Eucharist.
Holy Spirit, 18, 21-22, 50-51, 57-58, 62-64,
   67-69, 74-75, 77-78, 82-84, 88-91,
   101, 106, 111, 113-116, 143, 147-
   149, 153, 163, 171, 173, 175, 181
   fruits of, 73-74
   gifts of, 72-74
Holy Week, 39
Hope, 68, 147, 150, 182
Hosea, 9, 75
Hosea, 9
Humanae Vitae, 91-92
Ignatius of Loyola, 137
Immaculate Conception, the, 90, 175
Incarnation, the, 70, 87, 136
Ineffabilis Deus, 175
Infancy narratives, 172-174
Infant Baptism, 112

Inspiration, 21
Interpretation, 72
Irenaeus, 72
Isaiah, 9-11, 14, 24-25, 73, 144
Isaiah, 9-11, 24, 45
Israel, 2, 4-5, 8-10, 14-15, 24-25, 37, 40, 44,
   84, 88, 173
Israelites, 4, 6, 8, 33
Jacob, 173
James, 16, 19, 123
Jeremiah, 11, 41
Jeremiah, 11
Jerome, 181
Jerusalem, 7-8, 11, 16, 34, 39, 41, 90, 98,
   114, 174, 179
Jesuits, 137
Jesus,
   baptism of, 28, 73
   brother, 83
   commandments of, 147-149, 151, 157-162
   divinity and humanity, 52-58
   finding of in the Temple, 173-174
   head of the Body of Christ, 82
   human knowledge, 54
   infancy, 172-174
   last words of, 42-43
   missionary, 24-29
   New Adam, 175
   New Moses, 6, 17
   in the New Testament, 15-22
   oneness with the Father, 56-58
   parables of, 29-33
   Passion, 39-43
   post-resurrection appearances of, 48-50
   Priest, 19, 101, 114
   Priest, Prophet, King, 87, 92, 108, 134
   religious opponents of, 34-35
   resurrection of, 48-51
   risen body of, 50-51
   sacrament of God, 81-82
   and sacraments, 101-136
   Second Coming of, 177-183
   sign of God, 26-27
   Truth, 171
   virgin birth of, 173
Jesus Prayer, the, 156
Jews, 7, 11, 13-14, 17, 19, 35, 39, 41, 84,
   86, 93, 129, 157
Job, 14
Joel, 71

213

Mortal sin, 96, 117. *See also* Sin.
Mortal sinfulness, 141-142
Moses, 2, 4, 6, 8-9, 35, 40, 98-99
Mother Teresa, 86, 124
Mount Sinai, 4-7, 14, 17, 45, 72, 98, 114
Mystagogia, 108
Mystical Body of Christ, 82-83
Mysticism, 21
Nathan, 9, 30
Nehemiah, 12
Nehemiah, 12
Nestorianism, 54
New Moses, 17
New Rite of Penance, the, 119-120
New Testament, 13, 15-22, 25, 27, 48, 50,
    58, 69, 77, 88-89, 115, 147, 178
    formation of, 19-20
Non-Christians, 93
Nuclear war, 165
Numbers, 6
Oil, 102, 108, 113, 123
Old Testament, 2-16, 33, 40, 73, 114, 123,
    157, 178
    historical books, 3-8
    prophetic books, 3, 8-13
    wisdom books, 3, 13-14, 19
Order. *See* Religious communities.
Orders, Sacrament of, 92, 101-103, 114,
    133-137
Ordination of women, 136
Original sin, 69-70, 110, 175
Our Father, the, 154-155, 176. *See also* the
    Lord's Prayer.
Paganism, 35
Palm Sunday, 39
Papal infallibility, 90-91, 131
Parables, the, 20, 29-33
Paraclete, 57, 70-71. *See also* Holy Spirit.
Passion and death of Jesus, 19, 39-43, 58
Passover, 2, 5-7, 14, 34, 39-40, 98-99, 177
Pastorals, the, 18
Paul, 16-20, 27, 38, 44-45, 48, 50, 52, 72-73,
    78, 100, 105, 109-112, 114, 116, 118,
    125, 128, 130-131, 153, 159, 180-
    181. *See also* Saul of Tarsus.
Paul VI, 90-91, 92
Pauline privilege, 130
Penance, 102-104, 121-122, 127. *See also*
    Reconciliation, Confession.
Pentateuch, 2

Pentecost, 18, 50, 71-72, 80, 97, 111, 113-
    114, 175
People of God, 22, 83-84, 93, 125, 134
Peter, 17-18, 25, 45, 49, 56, 58, 71, 86, 90,
    111
Peter (Letters of) 16, 19, 26
Pharisees, 28, 30-32, 35-37, 39, 58, 141, 146
Philip, 81
Philemon, 20
Pilate, 39, 41, 151, 171
Pius IX, 90, 175
Pius XII, 20, 90-91
Poor, the, 169
Pope, 22, 88-91, 93, 115, 135-136
Prayer, 152-157
    Church's, 136-137
    kinds of, 155-156
    mental, 155-156
    of petition, 154-155
    vocal, 155
Pre-catechumenate, 107-108
Presbyter, 135
Presbyterians, 135
Priest, 92, 107, 134
Prodigal Son, parable of the, 30, 119
Progress of Peoples, 91
Promised Land, 6
Property, private, 168
Prophesy, 72
Prophesying, 116
Prophetic books (of the Old Testament), 3,
    8-13
Prophets, 8, 21, 37, 41, 75, 112
Proportionality (in just war), 164
Protestants, 22, 119, 135, 176, 182
Proverbs, 13
Psalms, 13, 42-43
Purgatory, 177, 181-183
Re-concile, 97
Real Presence, 96
Reconciliation, Sacrament of, 101, 104, 117-
    122. *See also* Confession, Penance.
    the new rite, 120-121
Redemption, 70
Reformation, 22, 90
Religious communities, 137
Remarriage, 129-130
Repentance, 24, 151
Rerum Novarum, 91
Restoration, the, 12

Resurrection, the, 15, 19-22, 28-29, 38, 40
48-51, 57-58, 60-61, 70-71, 84, 89,
96, 98-99, 101, 124-125, 147, 152,
174-175, 177, 179-180
Revelation, 13, 21
Revelation (Apocalypse), 13, 16, 19-20, 174
Revenge, 160
Rite of Christian Initiation of Adults, 107-108
Romans, 13, 37, 39, 41
Rosary, the, 176
Sabbath, 25, 34, 36, 43-44, 143, 150
Sacraments, 22, 51, 80-82, 94, 101-136
definition of, 102
of Initiation. *See* Baptism, Confirmation,
Eucharist.
as worship, 105
Sacrifice, 51, 98-100
Sadducees, 35
Saints, 21, 38, 82, 106, 112, 116, 156, 181
Salvation, 46, 48, 57-58, 64-65, 102, 111-
112, 123, 144, 151, 174, 181
Samuel, 7
Samuel, 7
Satan, 39
Saul of Tarsus, 7, 37. *See also* Paul.
Scribes, 35-37, 39, 141, 146
Secrets, 172
Self-defense, 163-164
Separation in marriage, 130
Sermon on the Mount, 33
Seven (the number), 73, 115, 161
Sexuality, 166-167
Sign of the Cross, 108
Sin, 110-111, 117-119, 121, 141, 144, 151-
152, 160, 162, 166-167, 170, 182.
See also Mortal sin, Sinfulness, Social
sin, Venial sin.
Sinfulness, 118-119, 141, 161, 170
Sirach, 14
Slander, 171
Social sin, 170-171
Social teaching, Catholic, 169-170
Solomon, 14
Son, the, 57-58, 75, 77-78, 83, 88, 149,
154, 181
Song of Songs, the, 14
Songs of the Suffering Servant, 10
Speaking in tongues, 72, 116
Spirit. *See* Holy Spirit.
Sponsor, 108, 112

Suffering, 76, 123-124, 181-182
Suffering Servant, 33
Symbols, 102
Synoptic Gospels, 20. *See also Matthew,
Mark, Luke.*
Synoptics, 28. *See also* Matthew, Mark,
Luke.
Temple, the, 8, 11-12, 14, 24, 40-41
Teresa of Avila, 137
Thomas, 49
Torah, 3, 6, 12, 34
Tradition, 21-22
Transfiguration, 153
Trinity, the, 56-57, 74-78, 83, 109, 113,
148-149, 181
Truth, 171
Twelve, the, 28, 30, 39, 89, 92. *See also*
Apostles.
Unions, 169
Vatican I, 90
Vatican II, 22, 66, 80, 82-88, 92-93, 107,
115-116, 120, 125, 134, 164-165, 168
Venial sin, 118, 121. *See also* Sin.
Virtues, 150
Vows of poverty, chastity, obedience, 137
Water, 102, 110
Wedding at Cana, the, 174
Wisdom books (of the Old Testament), 3,
13-14, 19
Wisdom, 14
Women in *Luke*, 17
Word, the, 51-52, 56, 78, 150-151
Jesus, 174
Scripture, 88, 104, 120, 134
World hunger, 168
Zacchaeus, 26
Zachary, 70

Also by Leonard Foley

Books

A Story of Jesus—For Those Who Have Only Heard Rumors.
SBN 078 $2.95

Slowing Down the Our Father. SBN 756 $4.95

Saint of the Day. Vol I: January—June. SBN 164 $3.50
            Vol II: July—December. SBN 202 $3.50

Audiocassettes

The Communion of Saints: 'People Who Need People.'
AC 1187 $5.95

*'That You May Believe': A Popular Overview of Christ's
Teachings.* CAS 012 $79.95

Available from Saint Anthony Messenger Press
1615 Republic Street, Cincinnati, Ohio 45210